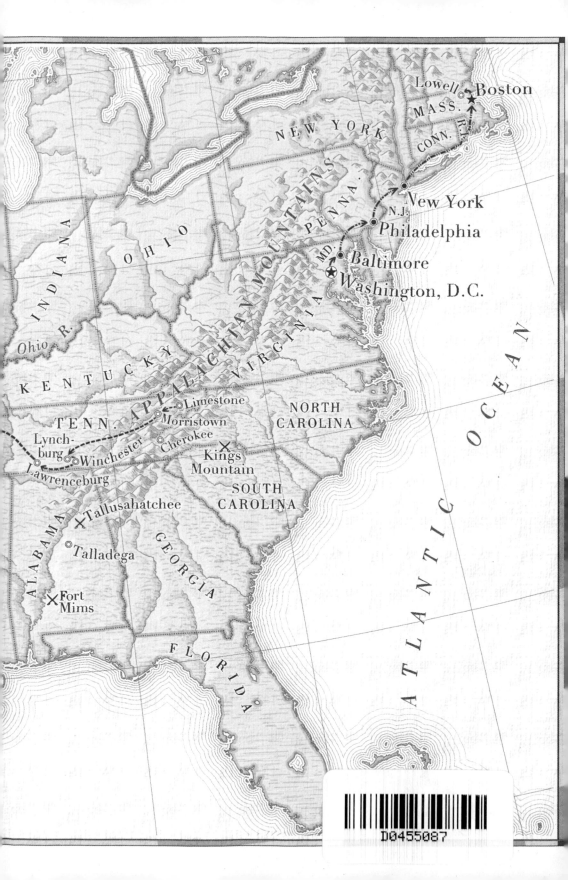

Born on a
Mountaintop

Born on a Mountaintop

ON THE ROAD WITH DAVY CROCKETT AND
THE GHOSTS OF THE WILD FRONTIER

Bob Thompson

Crown Trade Group

New York

Published in the United States by Crown Publishers,
an imprint of the Crown Publishing Group,
a division of Random House, Inc., New York.

www.crownpublishing.com

CROWN and the Crown colophon are registered trademarks
of Random House, Inc.

Library of Congress Cataloging-in-Publication Data is available upon request

ISBN 978-0-307-72089-4
eISBN 978-0-307-72091-7

PRINTED IN THE UNITED STATES OF AMERICA

Jacket design by Christopher Brand
Map illustrations by David Lindroth

1 3 5 7 9 10 8 6 4 2

First Edition

For Deborah, Lizzie, and Mona

CONTENTS

⊰ 1 ⊱

"Play That Song Again"

Minutes after I walked into Alamo Plaza, I saw my first Davy Crockett ghost. He took the form of a solidly built man in an outsized coonskin cap—the kind with a cute little raccoon face as well as a bushy tail—who handed me a business card.

"He's my great-great-great-grandfather," David Preston Crockett said. "Yeah, I'm a grandson of the famous Davy Crockett."

David had put on his Crockett finery for the occasion, which was the 175th anniversary of his ancestor's death at the Alamo, most likely within a few yards of where we stood. In addition to the cap, he wore a long fringed jacket and matching pants that looked as if they were made of buckskin but weren't.

"Would you believe this stuff came from Walmart?" he asked. Then he told me how he'd bought some chamois cloth, maybe ten years before, and learned to sew.

San Antonio, Texas, was my last stop on a search for traces of the historical and mythical Crockett—for the "ghosts," as I'd come to think of them, of an extraordinary American life. Colorful threads of Davy's story had been spun into legend while the man himself was still alive, and that story's epic ending on the morning of March 6, 1836, had rendered him immortal. If you were hunting Crockett ghosts, on this anniversary weekend, the Alamo was the place to be.

For starters, there were all the *other* guys decked out in raccoon caps and brown fringed garments.

At one point, I saw two Davys in full regalia—both associated with a production company that specialized in historical films—shake each other's hands in front of the Alamo church. Up walked a tourist who'd heard that the real Crockett might have carved his name on the church's iconic facade. One of the Davys set her straight.

"Mr. Crockett was a gentleman. Mr. Crockett would not do that," he said. "I'll take that to the bank."

A few hours later, waiting for a reenactment of the siege and battle to begin, I found myself standing next to two more Davys. Mike and Mark Chenault of Dallas were identical sixtyish twins wearing identical Crockett outfits. I asked one of them—I'm pretty sure it was Mark—what made them fans.

"Just Crockett's devotion, his patriotism to America," he told me. "He came all the way from Tennessee, you know, and the timing was just so *perfect.*"

I don't think Davy would have agreed about the timing. The former congressman hadn't planned on coming to Texas just to die. Still, dying was what the Crockett we'd all come to see was about to do.

Doug Davenport was a craggy-faced reenactor from the San Antonio Living History Association; he wore the usual cap and fringed coat, but his legwear set him apart. I had no idea whether the real Crockett ever wore white pants, but the unusual look, oddly enough, made Davenport seem more authentic, less like a Hollywood clone. This was a good thing, because the thirteen-day siege and battle about to be re-created were desperately serious. General Antonio López de Santa Anna had just marched into town to quash the Texas Revolution, taking Crockett and the rest of the vastly outnumbered garrison by surprise.

"Get everyone into the Alamo!" someone yelled.

"Give us a position, and me and the Tennessee boys will protect it for you," Davy told his commanding officer, William Barret Travis, who assigned him to defend a wooden palisade that filled a gap in the south wall.

Then it was hurry up and wait.

It is not easy to evoke twelve tense days in which little actual fighting occurred, but in the short time allotted to them, Davenport and his colleagues did their best. Defiant cannon shots were fired. Messengers rode out and back. Longed-for help failed to arrive. "I would just as soon march out there and die in the open," Crockett confessed at one point, just as the real Crockett is said to have done.

He didn't get his wish. On the thirteenth day, shortly before dawn, Santa Anna finally ordered his men to storm the walls.

I lost track of Davenport during the booming, smoky chaos of the assault, then spotted him slumped against the palisade. There he stayed, cap twitching occasionally, until the words "Remember the Alamo!" came over the loudspeaker and the defenders sprang back to life. All available Davys were soon posing for photographs. Adults and children crowded around, and as I watched, I heard a young ponytailed mom try to convey to her son the seriousness of the moment he was experiencing.

"You are walking where *Davy Crockett* walked around," she told him. "That is really cool!"

Decades before that mom was born, Walt Disney made Davy Crockett the coolest guy in American history—and walking where he walked can still give people chills.

Davy's 1950s apotheosis came about through a wildly unpredictable combination of circumstances. Among them were the emergence of television as an irresistible cultural force; Disney's drive to fund his innovative new Anaheim theme park; Fess Parker's bit part in a film about giant mutant ants; and possibly the stickiest song ever written, with lyrics thrown together by a man who had never tried writing a song before. (All together now: "Davy, DAY-VEE Crockett, King of the Wild Frontier!") Disney hadn't planned to spark a Crockett craze any more than Crockett had planned to get killed at the Alamo—Walt just thought he was making a three-part TV series—which goes to show that even a marketing genius needs a helping hand from fate now and then.

Americans' obsession with Davy Crockett also showed—and not for the first time—how powerfully his story resonated with that of the nation itself.

For anyone who loves U.S. history, Crockett is a wonderful point of entry, because he intersects with so much of it. You'll find him in the middle of the bitter struggle between settlers and Indians, for example, taking different sides at different times. He personifies the radical expansion of democracy in the age of Andrew Jackson—far better, in fact, than the patrician, plantation-owning Old Hickory himself—as well as the unstoppable migration westward that drew ambitious, adventurous men and women to places such as San Antonio. Crockett was constantly pulling up stakes. He spent a lifetime striving to escape the "have-not" side of a class divide that Americans like to pretend doesn't exist. A fierce resentment of the "haves" sparked his political career; getting too cozy with them helped end it.

There is far more to the Crockett story, however, than a fascinating man's real life.

To start with, there's Legendary Davy, a character who took shape long before the real David—the version of his name he preferred—

left Tennessee for Texas. Created by the image-conscious politician himself, Crockett's exaggerated backwoods persona was magnified and distorted, especially after he arrived in Washington, by the political and media culture of his time. The rapid spread of Crockett's fame may come as a revelation to those who think of celebrity politics as a recent phenomenon. Here was a nineteenth-century John F. Kennedy whose PT-109 equivalent, fighting Indians, became grist for a campaign biography. Here was a Ronald Reagan–Sarah Palin blend whose common touch and theatrical persona inspired a play called *The Lion of the West*, with an unmistakably Crockettesque figure playing the title role.

David Crockett went to check out his alter ego at a Washington theater in December 1833. Congressman and actor exchanged bows.

Twenty-seven months later, the real man would be dead and Mythic Davy would take his place. Over the next 175 years, this Crockett would shift his shape from Texas martyr to tall-tale superhero, from silent-movie star to icon of the TV generation—and, more recently, to symbolic flash point of the culture wars. Elusive and immortal, an Everyman who is also larger than life, Mythic Davy has always reflected Americans' evolving sense of who we are.

Why did fate cast David Crockett in this role? Crockett himself is said to have offered the beginning of an explanation. "Fame is like a shaved pig with a greased tail," he has been quoted as explaining, "and it is only after it has slipped through the hand of some thousands that some fellow, by mere chance, holds onto it!" As with many sayings attributed to Crockett, unfortunately, this one has been disputed, but it has a nice, self-deprecating ring and it suggests part of the answer.

Not all of it, though.

Something besides luck drew people to David when he was alive, and something besides commercial mythmaking—though there was plenty of that—drew them to his story after he was dead. Understanding his attraction and its staying power was one of my chief goals when I set out in pursuit of Crockett ghosts.

I had a more personal reason, too.

It's not what you're thinking. Unlike so many members of my generation, I had no fond childhood memories of Disney Davy, mostly because I never saw those Crockett shows. My father didn't want a TV in the house, and as a New England kid, growing up just a few miles from Lexington and Concord, I was more attached to Paul Revere and Johnny Tremain anyway.

All of which meant that I was hopelessly unprepared when—forty years after his Disney debut—history's most charismatic frontiersman took over my family's life.

The car music was doing what car music is supposed to do. It was an old Burl Ives collection, folksy and melodic, and it was keeping the girls quiet while their mother drove. Burl sang "Shoo Fly," Mona's favorite, his opulent voice caressing each line ("I *feel* . . . I *feel* . . . I *feel* like a morning star . . ."). He sang "Big Rock Candy Mountain," "What Kind of Animal Are You?," and "Polly Wolly Doodle," then broke into a bouncy number that Mona and her older sister, Lizzie, had never heard before.

"Born on a mountaintop in Tennessee," Burl Ives sang. "Greenest state in the land of the free . . ."

When the music stopped, there was a moment of silence from the back seat. Lizzie broke it.

"Play that song again," she said.

She'd hit her fourth birthday not long before, and her sister was two and a half. There's no way she could have known what she was getting us into. Deborah and I didn't know either. We were new parents, just beginning to understand that children rarely learn anything in exactly the way, or at precisely the time, adults expect them to. Kids see the universe as an endless web available for browsing. Click on Burl Ives. Click on Davy Crockett. Hmm, that's interesting: let's go to the next level, and the next, and now let's follow that line over there. Before you can say "Remember the Alamo," your firstborn is trying to make sense of the brutality of nineteenth-century Indian wars, the gender gap in frontier legends, and the complex relationship between heroic narratives and historical truth.

All before you've had time to research essential facts, such as: Where *was* Davy Crockett born, anyway?

Not on any mountaintop, it turns out.

After that first replay request, Lizzie began to ask for "The Ballad of Davy Crockett" again and again, and her mother started having flashbacks. Deborah, unlike me, could summon fond images of the little yellow record with the song in its grooves and of the hunky, buckskinned Parker playing Crockett on TV. So she fielded the girls' initial questions as best she could, and we set out to supplement our knowledge.

One part of the task was to separate fact from fiction. Another was to explain the difference.

As it happens, there was quite a lot on Davy in the children's section of our local library, most of it divisible into two categories. There were works of the *Davy Crocket: Young Rifleman* variety, which were either fact-based junior biographies or fictionalized versions of the historical Davy's life. And there were tall tales, books with titles such as *The Narrow Escapes of Davy Crockett,* in which Davy appeared as a wholly legendary, Paul Bunyan–like figure who hitched rides on lighting bolts, climbed Niagara Falls on the backs of alligators, and walked across the Mississippi on stilts. One of the most helpful books—Robert Quackenbush's *Quit Pulling My Leg!*—

bridged the genres; the main text narrated the real history, while in the margins, a skeptical cartoon raccoon debunked assorted Crockett myths.

For weeks, Lizzie's bedtime reading was all Crockett, all the time. When we hit the library, she'd head straight for the Crockett bios and start pulling them off the shelf. By now both she and Mona had memorized the Davy song. Was it true, they asked, that he "kilt him a b'ar when he was only three"? Probably not, we explained; that was a "tall tale." Was it real that, as the Burl Ives version has it, he "fought and died at the Alamo"? Yes. Was he, in fact, born on that Tennessee mountaintop? Well, no, he was born on a riverbank near where Big Limestone Creek flows into the Nolichucky River, but yes, it was in what we now call Tennessee, except that Tennessee wasn't quite a state yet, and . . .

There are a number of concepts in that Crockett ballad that require explanation when you're talking to a preschooler. There's statehood, for example, which gets you into the federal system, and there's Congress, as in "He went off to Congress an' served a spell," which gets you into the whole notion of politics and representative government. Still, I'd never have predicted that we'd get so far into Davy's historical context that we'd end up reading Lizzie, at her insistence, a 150-page American Heritage Junior Library biography of Andrew Jackson.

The real Crockett's career was closely linked to Jackson's. Davy did not fight "single-handed" in the Indian wars, as the song has it, but as a volunteer under General Jackson. After Jackson became president, Representative Crockett's outspoken opposition to his fellow Tennessean became an irritant. Tennessee's Jackson-dominated Democratic machine turned Crockett out of office and sent him on his fateful way to Texas.

But those are facts, and we weren't confining ourselves to facts. To the girls, at that stage, "Andy" was essentially a mythic figure, just like "Davy." What's more—according to one of our favorite tall-tale books, Irwin Shapiro's *Yankee Thunder*—they formed a two-person mutual admiration society.

"You're the best man I ever clapped eyes on," Shapiro's Davy tells Andy, "and o' course I'm Davy Crockett."

"Then by the great horn spoon," Andy roars in reply, "let's find out which one o' us is the best o' the two! And that man will run for president!"

Bragging, roaring, battling: alert readers will have noticed that, while our children are both girls, Davy is as stereotypically guylike as they come. We noticed, too, and were glad to see that Crockett never got rejected as a "boy thing." At the same time, we found it impossible to view him as anything other than what he was: the exceptionally likable hero of an exceptionally male narrative.

Neither of Davy's real-life wives, we learned, gets much play in the biographies, although their stories, if they were better known, would shed light on both Crockett's character and the American frontier experience. The legendary Davy comes with a legendary wife named Sally Ann Thunder Ann Whirlwind, a rough-and-ready charmer who grins the skins off bears and wins Davy's heart by knotting six rattlesnakes together to form a rope. Lizzie and Mona liked Sally Ann Thunder Ann well enough, but there was never any question of divided loyalty. There is, after all, no Queen of the Wild Frontier.

We worried about this some, but not too much. That's because we had a far more troubling part of the Crockett saga to deal with.

More than a year after Lizzie discovered Davy, we got her a plastic Alamo set, complete with bayonet-wielding blue plastic Mexicans and rifle-toting brown plastic Texans. She and her sister took to it immediately, arranging Crockett, Travis, Santa Anna, and the rest in a variety of warlike configurations. Yet Deborah and I couldn't help but notice, at least until a neighbor boy joined the game, that their favorite activity was tucking in the troops for the night.

This was fine by us. Serendipity had blessed us with the Davy

Crockett story, which had opened some wonderful historical windows. Precisely what happened at the end of the Alamo fight was one window we didn't mind keeping shut for a while.

When Lizzie was first memorizing the Crockett ballad, she asked to hear the penultimate verse, the one with Burl Ives's "fought and died at the Alamo" line, a few extra times. Beyond that, the girls didn't actively pursue the idea of Davy's death. They didn't ignore it but seemed to be giving it time to sink in. The children's books and audio tales we got them handled it gently. "We lost the battle, but we won the war" is how the CD from the Rabbit Ears *Treasury of Tall Tales* wraps things up, with narrator Nicolas Cage evoking Davy-the-Legend's continued blissful existence in "the celestial vapors from where I speak."

We did learn, well into our Crockett phase, that a historical death scene *could* produce obsessive interest. Looking for a "favorite president" to complement her sister's beloved Andy, Mona settled on Abraham Lincoln. When we checked out picture books about Abe, she would stare at the inevitable assassination illustrations and ask us to read the relevant text over and over. A bit later, she asked her mother, "Is dying real?"

None of this, however, prepared us for what happened when we got to the end of that American Heritage biography of Jackson. Lizzie was curled up in bed, with Deborah reading. Davy's sparring partner had retired to his Tennessee home, where "as spring drifted into summer along the Cumberland," he wrote a last letter to President James K. Polk, advising him on some incomprehensible financial matter. Deborah read on as the old man bade farewell to servants and friends and expired quietly on June 8, 1845, "long before the late-setting June sun had sunk behind the western hills." Then she turned to Lizzie, and saw that tears were flooding down her face.

Lizzie loved Andy Jackson. His location in time was confusing. And it had never once occurred to her that he was dead.

I have to admit that I got choked up, too.

Not by Jackson's death, though I was moved—as any parent would be—by my daughter's grief. The more I had read about the real Andy, the less lovable he had seemed. And not by any Disney-implanted worship of his coonskin-capped adversary. By now, researching Davy's story during our family recapitulation of the Crockett craze, I was fully aware that there was a flawed human being behind the irresistible Fess Parker reinvention.

And yet . . .

There's a great scene in that Rabbit Ears narration in which Davy, to raise the spirits of the embattled Alamo defenders, climbs up on the ramparts one night, flaps his arms, crows like a rooster, and hurls "a good round of brag" into the menacing darkness. "I am half alligator, half horse and half snapping turtle with a touch of earthquake thrown in!" he roars as David Bromberg's fiddle picks up the tempo in the background. "I can grin a hurricane out o' countenance, recite the Bible from Genosee to Christmas, blow the wind of liberty through squash vine, tote a steamboat on my back, frighten the old folks, suck forty rattlesnake eggs at one sittin' and swallow General Santy Anna whole without chokin' *if* you butter his head and pin his ears back. . . . I shall *never* surrender or retreat."

Listening to this for the first time, I was astonished to find that my eyes were moist.

Why had I found that fictionalized brag so moving?

I didn't know.

The question would become one I set out to answer—years later, long after Lizzie and Mona had moved on from Davy, Andy, and Abe—as I marched deeper and deeper into Crockett territory.

The alchemization of history into myth has always fascinated me, and I wanted to explore the way the transformation got made in Davy's case. Yet at the same time, no matter how many legends and myths I encountered, the real David's story continued to move me.

Here was a man who started life as anonymous as you could get and almost as poor. He struggled, failed, pulled himself together, and struggled some more. He turned out to be better at politics than anything else, bear hunting excepted, and his feel for his frontier audience, along with a gift for humorous gab, earned him a high-profile job in Washington. There, like a lot of other politicians, he got in over his head. His "friends" built him up, then let him down when he stopped being useful. The road to Texas looked like the road to redemption, and when he got there, he thought he'd found the Promised Land.

"I am in hopes of making a fortune yet for myself and family bad as my prospect has been," he wrote in his last letter home.

That letter was written in San Augustine, in east Texas, not far from where Crockett volunteered to fight for Texas independence. I wanted to go there. I wanted to check out the landscape farther north, near present-day Honey Grove, that Crockett called "the richest country in the world." I wanted to visit Crockett's birthplace on that east Tennessee riverbank, from which I was hoping you could at least see a mountaintop, and to look for traces of him in nearby Morristown, where he grew up in conflict with his father, a debt-ridden tavern keeper who liked to drink. I wanted to go to Alabama, where he and Jackson fought the Creeks; to the site of Mrs. Ball's Boarding House, a few blocks from the White House, where Congressman Crockett bedded down; to Lowell, Massachusetts, one of the most revealing stops on his epic political book tour; and to more Crockett sites in middle and west Tennessee than I could keep track of, among them Lynchburg, Bean's Creek, Lawrenceburg, Rutherford, and Memphis. I wanted to dig up rare Crockett almanacs, poke around the Disney location where Fess

Parker thought he might get fired before his Davy could even get to the Alamo, and, of course, make a pilgrimage to the Shrine of Texas Liberty itself. Along the way, I figured, I would seek out historians, museum curators, park rangers, fellow pilgrims, and Crockett obsessives of all stripes—anyone who might help me get a feel for the real, legendary, and mythical character I was pursuing.

At some point, before my travel plans were complete, Deborah introduced me to a familiar-sounding children's song by family favorites They Might Be Giants. It seemed, in its own weird way, to sum things up:

> *Davy, Davy Crockett*
> *The buckskin astronaut*
> *Davy, Davy Crockett*
> *There's more than we were taught*

Yes, there is. The ghosts of David Crockett haunt the American psychic landscape. I couldn't wait to start tracking them down.

⊰ 2 ⊱

Remember King's Mountain!

Not long after hitting the Crockett trail, I found myself on Interstate 85 near Durham, North Carolina, trying to identify a tough-looking frontiersman whose giant statue advertised a shopping mall.

"Davy?" I thought. "Is that you?"

Nope. The thick beard was one giveaway. Paintings of Crockett (there are no photographs) all show him clean-shaven. The sign underneath the statue—barely glimpsed as I zoomed by—was another.

THE SHOPS AT DANIEL BOONE, it read.

It seemed appropriate, somehow. The fabled pioneer of the Cumberland Gap and Kentucky, Boone was the original King of the Wild Frontier—though no one actually called him that—and he held the title for close to five decades before anyone outside of Tennessee had heard of Crockett. Then Alamo Davy knocked poor Dan'l out of first place. A martyr's death will trump a peaceful old age every time.

But I'm getting ahead of myself.

The Boone sighting came five hours south of my starting point in Washington, D.C. I had spent most of those hours fighting highway traffic that sometimes, especially around Richmond, Virginia, slowed to the pace of an ox-drawn Conestoga. Still, I would end up 420 miles from home that night, a distance that would have taken a traveler several weary weeks in 1786, the year David Crockett was born. I would bed down in a bug-free motel room with a TV, an Internet connection, a flush toilet, a shower, and enough surplus bed space, by David's standards, to share with most of his eight siblings.

At one point en route, seeking distraction, I turned on a classical radio station and was startled to realize that the symphony it was playing was composed by a contemporary of Crockett's. You don't usually think of Ludwig van Beethoven in the same breath with David, despite the 1955 "Peanuts" cartoon in which Schroeder and Charlie Brown angrily debate their merits.

A bit later, trying to get into the spirit of things, I imagined Crockett hunkered down in the shotgun seat of my rented subcompact, entertaining me with stories from his life. How cramped would he have been? I didn't know. (In the reading I'd done, people couldn't seem to agree on David's height; sometimes he's five-eight and sometimes he's over six feet, though no one disputes that he had a muscular build.) What yarns would he have been spinning? Well, maybe the one about how he almost drowned in a flatboat on the Mississippi, emerging naked and "literally skin'd like a rabbit." Or the one about how he followed a bear into an earthquake crack, "made a lunge with my long knife, and fortunately stuck him right through the heart." Or any of a number of tales in which he outsmarts snooty political foes with the aid of a quick wit and free drinks all around.

They're all true, according to *A Narrative of the Life of David Crockett, of the State of Tennessee*, the autobiography Crockett published in 1834. He claimed it was "written by himself"—though he had considerable help from a friend and fellow congressman—and he hoped it would do three things: debunk some "false notions" being spread about him, produce enough cash to get him out of debt, and help him win his next election.

Alas, it failed on all three counts.

Like most political self-presentations, it is marred by occasional fabrications and frequent distortions. The Crockett scholar Joseph Arpad, in an introduction to the version he edited in 1972, called it "an imaginative story told by Crockett to satisfy America's desire for a romantic frontier hero," adding that it "exaggerates, understates, dissembles, or omits other facts of his life that would give an accurate indication of his character and behavior." Nonetheless, the *Narrative* has been widely praised as a literary gem (a "classic in the native tradition of American humor," as the back cover of Arpad's edition has it), and it remains the best guide we have to Crockett's early years.

It's also what made me want to start my tour at Kings Mountain National Military Park, the relatively obscure South Carolina battlefield to which I was now headed.

The Battle of Kings Mountain is one of the great stories of the Revolutionary War. It took place on October 7, 1780, nearly six years before Crockett was born, but he tells us a few pages into the *Narrative* that his father, John Crockett, fought there. David seems proud of this; indeed, it's one of the rare positive things he says about the old man. And why not? The more I learned about Kings Mountain, the more it looked like a perfect distillation of the frontier ethos in which David Crockett grew up.

Short version: The voice of authority—in this case, a cocksure British major named Patrick Ferguson with a thousand or so loyalists under his command—warns the American settlers west of the Appalachians that he'll destroy their homes and hang their leaders if they don't support the Crown. For good measure, he calls them "the dregs of mankind."

Not smart. The dregs of mankind schlep their hunting rifles across the mountains and wipe him out.

Kings Mountain is really a modest-sized hill in the far northwest corner of South Carolina. A park brochure describes it as "a rocky spur of the Blue Ridge that rises 150 feet above the surrounding area," but as I approached the visitor center on Battlefield Drive, I couldn't see the rocks for the trees. Pulling into the parking lot, I saw the flash of a red coat in the morning sunlight and a cluster of white tents. I headed over to investigate.

"We're the Backcountry Militia," the red-coated man informed me when I caught up with him. "We do an event here once a month." Rick Stuck turned out to be a local history teacher decked out as a loyalist physician, but his costume was a bit of an anomaly: all but about 120 loyalists at Kings Mountain wore everyday clothes, Stuck said, as did their rebel counterparts. All around me, mingling with park visitors, I saw men in fringed cloth shirts and wide-brimmed hats or head scarves. Long-skirted women discussed midwifery and prepared to cook. Pretty soon it was time for the main event.

"Come on—follow those guys with guns!" I heard a twenty-first-century dad urge his son.

In an open area near the tents, seven militiamen lined up for a shooting demonstration. But first two of the guys with guns talked about the very different weapons used here by the loyalists and rebels in 1780—because without knowing that, you can't begin to understand the battle.

"This is a Brown Bess musket," said John Soule as he stepped forward, .75-caliber smoothbore in hand. The standard weapon of a British or loyalist infantryman wasn't very accurate—"I could pick you out of a crowd and probably hit you at sixty yards," Soule said, "but beyond that I could not"—yet the Brown Bess could be loaded and fired "conservatively speaking, three times a minute, so it was the rapid-fire weapon of the age." A multifaceted people killer, it was sturdy enough to be used as a club if necessary. More important, it came with a seventeen-inch steel bayonet, the triangular blade of which made gruesome wounds no eighteenth-century surgeon could heal.

"This was not made for hunting," Soule said. "It's purely a weapon of war."

Now it was Paul Desrosiers's turn. "This is the other alternative for a weapon at the time," Desrosiers said, showing off a sleeker, lighter gun he identified as an American long rifle. Unlike the smoothbore musket's, the rifle's barrel was grooved, putting a spiral on the bullet and making the gun far more accurate: "It's like a football. You throw a football, if you get a good spiral on it, it goes and goes and goes." At just .45 caliber, the long rifle also used "a lot less powder. That's what I want out here in the backcountry, because I'm a hunter, I'm a farmer—I'm not trying to kill people, I'm trying to kill animals. And if I can do it with a smaller caliber and less powder, that's more money in my pocket. Because I don't *have* a lot of money. Okay?"

He also doesn't have a bayonet. Why would a hunter need one? "But I've got sights. That means I hit what I'm aiming at"—maybe even from two hundred yards away.

It was long rifles that John Crockett and his fellow volunteers brought to the mustering grounds at places such as Sycamore Shoals, near what is now Elizabethton, Tennessee, after getting word of Patrick Ferguson's threats. (Rick Stuck summed up the frontiersmen's reaction in five words: "*Who* are you talkin' to?") It was long rifles that those "over-mountain men" carried as they rode through the snowy, 4,682-foot Yellow Mountain Gap and down the eastern slope of the Appalachians, looking to confront Ferguson before he could attack them. And it was long rifles they used to utterly destroy the loyalist army on the slopes of Kings Mountain.

The victory was as lopsided as Santa Anna's at the Alamo, but way more impressive, not just because at Kings Mountain the opposing forces were roughly even in number, but because the victors there lost fewer men than the Mexicans (only around thirty rebels died). There was some less-than-heroic unpleasantness at the end, part of the brutality of what was, to both sides, more a bitter civil war than a "civilized" military campaign. It took the over-mountain men quite a while to stop shooting after Ferguson's troops surrendered. A few days after the battle, they strung up nine captured loyalists before their leaders could calm them down. Then they rode back over the mountains and went home.

They had no way of knowing how significant their effort would prove. Ferguson's command had been the left wing of a major offensive by Lord Cornwallis, a British general who'd been waging a successful campaign in the Carolinas as part of the new British "southern strategy." Kings Mountain stopped Cornwallis in his tracks and made it a lot harder to recruit loyalist troops. Thomas Jefferson, perhaps exaggerating just a bit, called the battle "the turn of the tide of success" in the Revolution, and on its 150th anniversary, President Herbert Hoover came to South Carolina to help commemorate it. "History has done scant justice to its significance," Hoover told tens of thousands of people assembled on the hillside, "which rightly should place it beside Lexington and Bunker Hill, Trenton and Yorktown."

Walking up the park's Battlefield Trail, I stopped to read the numerous historical markers. By the time I got to the spot where John Sevier, an over-mountain leader from Crockett's neck of the woods, most likely launched his attack, I had begun to understand that the battle could have gone either way.

CHARGING COLD STEEL—THREE TIMES read the title on the Sevier marker. As I gazed uphill at Ferguson's position, the principal disadvantage of the long rifle—the fact that it took at least a minute to load—became frighteningly clear. "Just think about *this*," Paul Desrosiers had said, describing a line of loyalists with bayonets charging down the slope. "A minute to load, right? Well, my good-ness. If they get within fifty yards of me and I shoot at them and take one out, what do you think's going to happen to me?"

"You're going to get killed!" came the response.

Yes, indeed. So what Sevier's men had to do, once they'd crept up the slope, stepped from behind the shelter of the trees and fired their highly accurate but cursedly slow-loading rifles, was turn tail and run downhill again. They were good at loading on the move, but still, it would have been awfully easy to keep on running.

They didn't, though. Three times they turned and headed back up. It was those men—hot-tempered individualists, crack shots, veterans of a brutal battle they had won by refusing to give in—among whom David Crockett would be raised.

Including his own father. Except . . . there's a complicating foot-note here.

Beyond what David asserted in his autobiography, I had not found hard evidence that John Crockett was actually at Kings Mountain. The most authoritative source I would come across later, when I tried to pin this down, put him on a list of men who "pos-sibly" participated—and it seemed likely he was on that list because of what David wrote.

Still, in the relevant passage of his *Narrative,* David described his information as coming not just from his father but from "many others" with memories of the Revolutionary War.

And think about it: If you had neighbors like John Crockett's neighbors, wouldn't you expect them to call you out, pretty damn fast, if you lied about being at a fight like Kings Mountain when you'd really stayed home?

"The past is a foreign country," as the novelist L. P. Hartley wrote, but I think Hartley badly understated the problem. The past is a foreign country that's *impossible to visit*. You can't just skip across the border, hire yourself a translator, and ask old John Crockett where he was on the afternoon of October 7, 1780—let alone get up close and personal with his celebrity son.

When I think about the frustration this causes historians and biographers—not to mention Davy Crockett tourists—I'm reminded of a passage in *Footsteps*, a wonderful meditation on the art of biography by Richard Holmes. In 1964, when he was eighteen, Holmes set out to trace the route through south-central France that Robert Louis Stevenson had followed in *Travels with a Donkey in the Cevennes*. Reaching the town of Langogne, Holmes crossed a bridge over the Allier River, just as Stevenson had done, and suddenly, strangely, began to sense the presence of the man he was shadowing.

"The feeling that Stevenson was actually waiting for me, in person, grew overwhelmingly strong," Holmes wrote.

> I began to look for him in the crowds, in the faces at the cafe doors, at hotel windows. I went back to the bridge, took off my hat rather formally as if to meet a friend, and paced up and down, waiting for some sort of sign. People glanced at me: I felt an oddity, not knowing quite what I was doing, or looking for. The twilight thickened; bats began to dart over the river. I watched their flickering flight over the gleaming surface, from one bank to the other.
>
> And then I saw it, quite clearly against the western sky, the old bridge of Langogne. It was about fifty yards downstream, and it was broken, crumbling, and covered with ivy. So Stevenson had crossed *there*, not on this modern bridge. There was no way of following him, no way of

meeting him. His bridge was down. It was beyond my reach over time, and this was the true sad sign.

But Holmes went on to become a biographer anyway, writing the lives of Samuel Taylor Coleridge and Percy Bysshe Shelley, among others, and he developed a biographical method based on the literal pursuit of his subjects. He described it as "a tracking of the physical trail of someone's path through the past, a following of footsteps. You would never catch them; no, you would never quite catch them. But maybe, if you were lucky, you might write about the pursuit of that fleeting figure in such a way as to bring it alive in the present."

Davy—is that you?

I was thinking about Holmes's unbridgeable chasm as I wound north and west up U.S. 441 on my way from Kings Mountain to David Crockett's Tennessee birthplace. Pulling into the Newfound Gap overlook at the crest of the Smokies, I gazed down at valleys that can't have looked too different from the ones the over-mountain men saw, a hundred miles or so farther north, on their trek home. "Great Smoky Mountain National Park is a sanctuary," a marker informed me. "This is one of the few places in the Eastern United States where animal populations can live, propagate and die with relatively little influence from humans." And a good thing, too, I thought, considering the camera-wielding hordes clogging the parking lot and the clueless folks herding a terrified small boy up the rocky slope behind the CLIMBING PROHIBITED sign.

I didn't try to gaze into the eighteenth century for too long, though. It was late in the afternoon, and I wanted to get in a round at Ripley's Davy Crockett Mini-Golf.

Gatlinburg, Tennessee, comes as a shock when you descend from the Smokies on 441. One minute you're surrounded by greenery;

the next you're running the gauntlet of the Hollywood Wax Museum, the Bubba Gump Shrimp Co., Ranger Bob's Trading Post, and the Hard Rock Cafe—and yes, right next to the Marriott Fairfield Inn & Suites, a goofy-looking, rifle-waving Crockett astride a grinning brown bear. Mini-Golf Davy has a bag of clubs strapped to his back; an unskinned raccoon perches on his head.

I played eighteen holes. My score was better than it should have been, given that I was putting with one hand. I had a camera and a notebook in the other, which must have made me look plenty ridiculous as I scrambled to keep ahead of the nine-year-olds behind me. Cutesy statues of possums, coons, turtles, bears, and beavers jabbered loudly at us from all sides. There was a stockade called Fort Crockett that came with a sound track of Indian war chants, and at one point I heard a talking crow say, "Wasn't it nice of Davy to give us our own course?" But there were no bridges to the past, even broken ones, unless you count the cheerful rendition of "I've Been Working on the Railroad" by what sounded like Alvin and the Chipmunks.

⭐

The Davy Crockett Birthplace State Park turned out to be a beautiful spot—far more so than I had imagined.

Perhaps I'd been swayed by the bad press about the absent mountaintop, though as I approached the park, I could see a hazy line of Appalachians behind some newly plowed red-dirt fields. Perhaps I was still hungover from Gatlinburg and its sister city in hideously unchecked commercialism, Pigeon Forge. In any case, I wasn't expecting the low-key loveliness that engulfed me as soon as I got out of the car: the family birthday celebration beside the Nolichucky, complete with pink tablecloth and blue balloon; the cows grazing

in the slanting sunlight across the river; the well-proportioned replica of the Crockett cabin blending naturally into the scene.

Nor was I expecting to meet a relative of one of Crockett's Alamo
comrades five minutes after I arrived.

David and Joyce Lindley were visiting from Virginia Beach. Dave,
who had spent much of his career doing quality control on defense
and aerospace work, said he had long been interested in history.
He hadn't known he had an Alamo connection, however, until a
friend had come back from San Antonio and said, "Hey, there's a
Lindley on the wall!" Jonathan Lindley turned out to be a cousin of
Dave's "third or fourth 'great' grandfather," Joyce said, a young man
from the midwestern branch of the family who'd gone to Texas in
search of the same things most Anglo immigrants sought: opportunity and land. He was manning a cannon in the back of the Alamo
church, the Lindleys believe, when the Mexicans broke through.

Dave said he'd done some reading on Crockett—"the real man
as opposed to the Disney character"—and he wasn't inclined to
overglorify him: "The real man made a lot of mistakes, like most
humans do, so putting him on a pedestal, to me, is not a proper
place." Yes, he did some extraordinary things. But if he'd died in
bed, instead of at the Alamo, "he would be a footnote."

We talked a bit more about the hazards of studying the past and
how the more you dig, the more uncertain a story you thought you
knew can become. History is messy, Dave said, "not pie in the sky
and cosmetically perfect. It's a mosaic—and the pieces don't always
fit."

There's a colorful information kiosk outside the cabin, near
where I'd run into the Lindleys, and there's a one-room park museum nearby. Both do a nice job of condensing an eventful life into
a small space. Still, after saying good-bye to Joyce and Dave, I found
myself noticing pieces of the Crockett mosaic that didn't fit.

Take the Davy versus David question, for example. The two

state parks in Tennessee named after Crockett—the other is David Crockett State Park in Lawrence County, where he began his political career—can't agree on which version of his name to use. Or take his reputation as a musician. "Crockett was a fiddler," a birthplace museum headline states unequivocally, but the word "allegedly" pops up right away in the smaller type, which goes on to credit only "tradition" for the story that he amused the men of the Alamo with his fiddle playing.

Did David really wear a coonskin cap? Some historians don't think so, but I wasn't prepared to pass judgment on that yet. Still, the museum's stash of coonskinned, buckskinned Disney Davy memorabilia reminded me what the Backcountry Militia guys had told me about frontier outerwear.

"You always think of Davy Crockett with the buckskins and all that," Paul Desrosiers had said. "Well, you try walking around out here with buckskins on and get 'em wet one time. It will freeze you to *death*. And they get slimy, and they're just—they're terrible."

"They wore linen. Or wool," John Soule had agreed.

Really? No buckskins?

"That's Hollywood."

"Yeah—a lot of Hollywood going on there."

Meanwhile, I kept adding to my list of uncertainties about Crockett. It's uncertain—in fact, it's highly unlikely—that the reconstructed cabin sits on the right spot. (David wrote only that it was "at the mouth of Lime Stone, on the Nola-chucky river.") It's uncertain when the Crocketts arrived in the vicinity or how old David was when they left. The fact is that we know very little about how the Crockett family came to be in the area commemorated by the Davy Crockett Birthplace State Park.

Crockett wrote that his father was "of Irish descent," though historians more often describe the family as Scots-Irish and at least one, William C. Davis, drops the Irish part entirely as misleading.

But never mind the ethnic technicalities: their story, as Davis puts it, "was the story of a whole population of the poor who started moving from the British Isles in the 1700s and simply never stopped."

The quotation is from *Three Roads to the Alamo,* Davis's 1998 book on Crockett, James Bowie, and William Barret Travis, the most illuminating recent study of Crockett's life. *Three Roads* described the likely path of Crockett's immigrant grandfather, for whom David was named. The first David Crockett "probably landed in Pennsylvania and migrated west to the Susquehanna," Davis wrote, "before turning southwest through the Cumberland Valley along with the rest of the tide of Scottish immigrants, reaching Virginia's lower Shenandoah Valley by 1755." A couple of decades later, he and his family had crossed the Appalachians and were settled in what is now Rogersville, Tennessee, thirty or so miles northwest of the birthplace park. Grandfather David and his wife were killed there by Indians in 1777, and you can visit the small, well-kept cemetery where they are buried.

"Happily for our story," as another biographer put it, John Crockett wasn't home at the time. Not long afterward, he married Rebecca Hawkins, with whom he would go on to have nine children: six boys and three girls.

David was the fifth son. He was too young to remember much that happened at or near his birthplace, but he retained a vivid memory of his older brothers taking a canoe out one day and nearly going over a waterfall that "went slap-right straight down." If a neighbor hadn't waded into the Nolichucky to rescue them, they might have drowned. I walked over to look at the falls, which are past the park's RV camping area, a couple hundred yards downstream from the cabin. They evoked David's presence—a small boy on the riverbank, blind with fury at having been left behind—as nothing else had. Still, they seemed at bit tame. They couldn't have been much more than two feet high.

Hey, he was a little kid, I thought.

Then I went back to the kiosk and learned that what I'd seen was "all that remains of the once impressive falls of the river," which had been "eroded by time."

A few days later, I stopped at the birthplace again to talk with park manager Mark Halback, who hadn't been around on my first visit. Halback's previous job had been at a park that was all about recreation, not history, and he had been delighted when the birthplace assignment came along. In his office he displays a photograph, framed for him by his aunt, of his barefoot, four-year-old self in Crockett attire: "Got the toy rifle and the suit with the fringes, the coonskin cap. Looking off to the distance into the setting sun."

His task now was to change that image. "What we're doing here is trying to separate Crockett the myth from Crockett the man," he said. "A lot of people think of Davy Crockett as being the great Indian fighter; they think of him as, you know, the *buckskins*; they think of him as the trailblazer going out and opening up the frontier. That was Daniel Boone." He then gestured at a museum wall filled with portraits of a rosy-cheeked gentleman dressed for nineteenth-century success.

"*This* is Davy Crockett," he said. "Davy Crockett was a *politician*."

There are no surviving images of the prepolitical David, unfortunately. You didn't get your portrait painted, in those days, unless you were famous or rich. But there *was* a modern attempt to reconstruct him, in the form of a framed poster near the museum entrance. It showed a ramrod-straight young man, in profile, wearing buckskins and gripping a rifle almost as tall as he was. Dark brown hair hung past his shoulders; a thick sideburn curved well past his ear. His face glowed as if catching the light of an unseen fire.

From the neck down, this handsome Davy was just an artist's rendering, Halback said. But the face was something else. "What they did was this computer generation thing," he explained, "where they can take the corner of the eyes, the nose, the mouth, the ears, and everything" from the existing Crockett portraits, average them out, and then—like policemen putting together the image of a crime suspect—ask the computer to approximate "what he looked like when he was a young man."

Later I would learn that the poster, titled "David Crockett 1810," was a relic from an unmade Hollywood film project. The Direct Descendants and Kin of David Crockett had donated it to the birthplace, which had hosted the 2008 family reunion. But I didn't ask more about its origins at this point. I was too distracted by a resemblance I couldn't place.

Halback nailed it. "Doesn't that look suspiciously like Elvis Presley?" he asked.

From the museum we walked down to the one-room cabin. It is the second reconstruction on the site; local enthusiasts built the first one in response to the 1950s Crockett craze, Halback said, and it wasn't quite as authentic in its period detail ("from what I've heard, there were some telephone poles in there"). He paused at a corner to point out the half-dovetail-notch construction, then took me through the back door—normally, visitors just peer through the metal grate on the front one. Pretty soon a few people followed us in and Halback launched into an impromptu frontier-living seminar.

Why was the cradle kept under the bed? So Frontier Mom could reach down easily and rock it when the baby cried in the middle of the night. Why were those baskets hanging from the ceiling? To hold needlework or gun parts or whatever the grown-ups were working on that they didn't want kids messing with. What did you do when your broom wore out? Well, you just replaced the corn husks.

"Huh. So they made brooms out of corn husks?" a woman said.

The boy with her, who looked to be about twelve, didn't miss a beat. "Now we just go to Walmart," he said.

When my elder daughter was twelve, she had barely begun riding the Washington subway by herself. When David Crockett was twelve, as he recalled in his autobiography, his father hired him out to go hundreds of miles "on foot with a perfect stranger." He helped that stranger, Jacob Siler, drive a herd of cattle from east Tennessee to near Natural Bridge, Virginia—a trip that, on today's maps, looks like 250 miles one way, much of it on what was then known as the Wilderness Road. When they arrived, Siler wanted David to keep working for him, and David, having been taught "many lessons of obedience by my father," at first thought he was obligated to do so. Then he changed his mind, got up three hours before dawn, and walked seven miles through deepening snow to join some wagoners who had promised to help him get home.

He encountered no Walmarts along the way.

What he almost certainly did encounter was a stream of ragged poor people bound for the frontier. Consider the observations of a journal-keeping traveler on the Wilderness Road in 1796, two years before David set out. "I cannot omitt Noticeing the many Distress.d families I pass.d in the Wilderness," Moses Austin wrote, "nor can any thing be more distressing to a man of feeling than to see woman and Children in the Month of Decemb' Travelling a Wilderness Through Ice and Snow passing large rivers and Creeks with out Shoe or Stocking, and barely as maney raggs as covers their Nakedness, with out money or provisions except what the Wilderness affords."

Austin—whose son Stephen would pioneer the American settlement of Texas—went on to record a back-and-forth between himself and the Kentucky-bound poor he called "these Pilgrims." What did they expect to find at the end of their journey? "Land." Did they have anything to buy it with? "No." Had they ever seen Kentucky? "No but Every Body says its good land." The pilgrims were right,

Austin conceded: Kentucky was "a goodly land." Yet when they reached it, they would find that it was "to them forbiden Land," beyond their economic reach. And in the end, "worn down with distress and disappointment," they would become mere "hewers of wood and Drawers of water."

The Crocketts were poor, but not quite *that* poor. By 1798, they were living in what is now Morristown, Tennessee. Since their days on the Nolichucky, they had moved at least twice: once within Greene County, where John Crockett and a partner started a grist-mill that was promptly wiped out by a flood, and then west to Jefferson County, where he went into the tavern business. The word "tavern" might convey a bit of a false impression. As David wrote, his father's enterprise "was on a small scale," and you'll have a better idea of it if you imagine a family-sized cabin on a muck-filled track with a sleeping loft upstairs and corrals outside for the cattle, sheep, and pigs being driven between Knoxville, Tennessee, and Abingdon, Virginia. Lodging cost pennies a night; travelers who stayed with the Crocketts couldn't afford the gentlemen's accommodations a few miles up the road.

"It was a third-rate tavern," Jim Claborn told me. "Like a third-rate truck stop today."

Claborn is the Morristown area's premier Crockettologist. A high school history teacher, newspaper columnist, and historical storyteller who has played Davy in area celebrations and made numerous TV appearances, he had agreed to meet me in front of the Crockett Tavern Museum on Morningside Drive.

This two-story 1950s replica, tucked into an otherwise unmemorable neighborhood, is considerably larger than the original. Its weather-beaten walls reminded me of the abandoned houses you see returning to nature all over rural America, though that was an illusion created by the absence of paint and the fact that, on this April evening, the place hadn't yet opened for the season. Claborn, meanwhile, reminded me of the history obsessives I've met on Civil War battlefield tours. He showed up wearing a camouflage hat and a PROUD TO BE AN AMERICAN T-shirt, and he immediately corrected another false impression the reconstructed tavern conveys: the Crockett place would have faced in the other direction, he said, fronting the road now known as Morris Boulevard. Years before, the man who had bought the road-front property had asked him to do a historical survey on it, "and so I did, and then he poured six or eight feet of red clay on it and built a gas station there. It's a real historical site, but now it's for all purposes been ruined."

"Jump in the car, and I'll show you some places," he said a minute later. So I folded myself into his Camry, and we set out to follow the route thirteen-year-old David Crockett took when he left home a second time.

This time, he stayed away for two and a half years.

In the fall of 1799, David's father scraped up enough money to send him to "a little country school" in the neighborhood. Four days into his education, as Crockett tells the tale, he had "an unfortunate falling out with one of the scholars" and—afraid the schoolmaster would whip him for the fight that ensued—stopped going to class. Inevitably, his father found out. John Crockett, who had been drinking, threatened David with a hickory branch, and father and son lit out running "at the top of our speed." Soon John was "puffing and blowing, as tho' his steam was high enough to burst his boilers," and David gave him the slip.

Where did he go next?

"This is the road," Claborn said.

We had pulled past the offending Shell station onto Morris Boulevard and were cruising east, past the Sagebrush Steakhouse, over the Davy Crockett Parkway, and past the Holiday Inn Express Hotel & Suites and the Davy Crockett Restaurant (EGGS WITH BACON OR SAUSAGE BISCUIT AND GRAVY 2.99). Angling off Morris, which has been straightened a bit since Crockett's time, we stopped in front of a lovely white house with a parklike lawn on Barton Springs Drive. "This house is a log cabin with white wood on it," Claborn said, explaining that, as with many such old houses, clapboards now covered the original logs. "The strong *tradition* is that Crockett stayed in that. That's called the Crockett Room, top left-hand corner right there."

Not when he was running away, surely?

No, the tradition says it was while he was going to that neighborhood school. But Claborn wasn't buying this: "He only went four *days*, you know." It seemed more likely that David sometimes "worked for old Preacher Barton and spent the night with him."

Tradition. Oy. There are endless local traditions about Crockett, as I would soon discover, especially in Tennessee and Texas. The trick is to be skeptical without dismissing them too quickly—because some of them might be true.

From Barton Springs we kept as close as we could to the eighteenth-century roadbed, which involved a jog back across Morris and onto U.S. Highway 11E. We were headed for the site of an old store at Cheek's Crossroads, four miles or so from the tavern, now occupied by a Mahle Industries plant ("German company. Makes pistons for bulldozers and stuff"). It was here, as Claborn reminded me, that the runaway David hired himself out to Jesse Cheek, who had some cattle to drive to northern Virginia.

Remember, he was only thirteen.

Off they went, through Abingdon and Charlottesville and on to Front Royal, roughly four hundred miles away. Cheek sold his cattle there and Crockett headed home—or at least started to. But he soon met a wagoner named Adam Myers, a "jolly good fellow," and decided to reverse course and tag along with him to Gerrardstown, West Virginia. He worked some months for a farmer there, then hooked up again with Myers, who was now heading for Baltimore, because he wanted to "see what sort of a place that was, and what sort of folks lived there." On the Baltimore wharves, he was "much delighted to see the big ships, and their sails all flying; for I had never seen any such things before, and, indeed, I didn't believe there were any such things in all nature." A captain told him he was looking for a boy willing to ship out to England. And David would have done just that—perhaps to make his fortune, more likely never to be heard from again—except that when he went back to get his clothes and the few dollars he'd given Myers for safekeeping, the wagoner refused to let him go.

It took him another couple of years to get home. Out of money, he apprenticed himself to a hatter, who went bust after eighteen months and didn't pay him a dime. Needing to cross the New River near present-day Radford, Virginia, he found that "the white caps were flying so" that no one would ferry him across. He ended up in a borrowed canoe, half filled with water, two miles from where he'd intended to land. When he finally got back to the Crockett Tavern, his family didn't recognize him—he was almost sixteen now, after all—and it wasn't till he'd sat down to supper that one of his sisters took a longer look, "seized me around the neck, and exclaimed, 'Here is my lost brother.'"

Not your average teenage road trip, even then.

"I'd *love* to retrace that trip to Baltimore," Claborn said when I mentioned I was going to hit at least part of it on my way back to D.C.

We were in front of the tavern again, sitting in the car and talking. Before it had gotten dark, Claborn had taken me out to see "another one of those log houses that have been covered over with boards," the oldest in the area, which has "been in three different states." The Coffman house, he explained, was built when North Carolina still owned the over-mountain territory. It ended up in Tennessee. And for a few years in between—including the year

Crockett was born—it was part of an attempt by the east Tennessee settlers to secede from North Carolina. They named their isolated chunk of the frontier after Benjamin Franklin and tried to join the Union on their own.

You can't really blame the author of "The Ballad of Davy Crockett" for leaving that out, though. "Born on the banks of a river in the state of Franklin" doesn't quite scan.

By now Claborn was calling me "Bobby," in what I took to be a friendly southern way. Still, he was wary of my inner Yankee and wanted to steer me away from a clueless mistake about the rich local dialect I'd been hearing. "Here's something just for a piece of information," he said. "What we talk here is not southern. It's an *Appalachian* accent," and it comes from "the Scots-Irish who came and stayed in these mountains."

When it came to Crockett, meanwhile, there was a far more important misperception to clear up. "One year more than half his life, he lived here in east Tennessee," Claborn said—which is true, if you include the road trips—but biographers skim over those twenty-five years too quickly. "My theory is, this is where he developed his character and his soul."

He was talking about the David Crockett who would take "Be always sure you're right—then go ahead!" as his motto and about the congressman who would vote against Jackson's Indian Removal bill because he thought it "a wicked, unjust measure," and damn the political consequences. His mother, Claborn thinks, must have helped shape this David, though we know almost nothing about her except that she attended Bethel Church, a mile and a half or so west of the tavern. "John Crockett never went, Davy never joined up—but you see that influence from his mother, who was the only churchgoer in the family." Another who helped him build his inner strength was an old Quaker, John Canaday, on whose farm David went to work six months after returning from Baltimore. (He'd been working off his father's debts, and he worked off one owed to Canaday.) The Quaker, whose name is sometimes given as "Kennedy," was a different kind of father figure than John Crockett had been. "A big, big effect on his life was spending the time with Canaday," Claborn said.

I didn't know enough yet to judge this theory one way or another. I had a few theories myself, though I was trying to hold them in check. But one had to do with another aspect of David's east Tennessee life—the part where he declared undying love for three different young women before he was twenty years old—and I couldn't help throwing it out there.

"This is a boy who wants to get out of the house!" I said. "He wants to be on his own—not with his parents!"

Claborn was patient with me.

David had already proved his independence on that Baltimore trip, he said, and sure, it was time for him to be on his own. But who *wouldn't* want out of a place with "eight other children in there, besides him, in a tiny, tiny house—plus the visitors coming through."

He gestured toward one side of the dark tavern. "They'd put the kids in a little loft, right there, over that kitchen." On the other side, "the two closed windows up there are where the travelers would have stayed. They'd eat in the kitchen and they'd come in here"—the main downstairs room—"and sit around and chew tobacco and drink whiskey and stuff, and talk. Whenever they got ready to go to bed, John and Rebecca would sleep in that room, the big room right there, and the kids went up the stairs. There weren't *beds* for kids; they'd throw out pallets, you know, quilts and skins and stuff for them to sleep on. And nine kids in that little old area? Hello? *Yeah,* you'd want to be out of there."

He's right, I thought. Anyone would have wanted to be gone from such a place. But it was only later that I understood the strangest part of this conversation. Sitting in front of the Crockett

Tavern as Claborn sketched his portrait of the family's life inside, I had completely forgotten that I was looking at a replica—way too big and facing the wrong direction—of a building that had burned down nearly a century and a half before.

The past may be a foreign country—but for a few minutes, against all odds, Jim Claborn had taken me there.

⁘ 3 ⁘

The Ballad of Polly Finley

The first young woman who set David Crockett's heart to fluttering "like a duck in a puddle," as he put it, was the niece of his Quaker employer, John Canaday. When he got up the courage to tell her he would "pine down to nothing" if she refused him, she gently broke the news that she was engaged to her cousin, one of the Quaker's sons.

Rejection had a galvanizing effect on David: it made him think he'd be more attractive to women if he could read and write. He spent a few months working part-time for another Canaday son, a schoolteacher, in return for the only book learning he would ever get in his life.

But the next object of his affection rejected him, too—and far more harshly. There are competing versions of the story, sometimes conflated and frequently exaggerated.

In his autobiography, David wrote that he courted this second beauty relentlessly, giving her "mighty little peace, till she told me at last she would have me." They picked a wedding date. A few days before it came around, he went to a shooting match and won the prize, a whole beef, which he proceeded to sell for $5. Confidence boosted, he started toward the young woman's house, because "though the next Thursday was our wedding day, I had never said a word to her parents about it." Too late. On the way, he met her sister, who burst into tears and told him his sweetheart was about to marry another man.

A less flattering version comes from *The Life and Adventures of Colonel David Crockett, of West Tennessee*, an anonymous biography that appeared a year before David's book and was soon reprinted as *Sketches and Eccentricities of Col. David Crockett, of West Tennessee*. As we'll see later, *Sketches* played a major part in the growth of Crockett's legend in the 1830s. For now, what's important to know is that its authorship, sourcing, and reason for being have all been subjects of dispute among Crockettologists—though whoever wrote it appears to have gotten some of his material from Crockett himself. The *Sketches* account of the jilting story has David scheduled "to pay a visit and ask for his bride" but getting distracted by a "frolic." He parties into the night—no one "drank more whiskey, saw more fun, or sat up later than David Crockett," we're told—and fails to show up at his intended's house as promised.

The young woman's name was Margaret Elder. We know this because David visited the Jefferson County courthouse in Dandridge, Tennessee—twenty miles southwest of Morristown—on October 21, 1805, and acquired a marriage license on which her name appears.

All this was just prelude, however.

David was about to meet the woman who would marry him, bear his children, follow him west, die too young, and be immortalized as the love of his life. Her name was Mary "Polly" Finley (sometimes spelled Findley, Finlay, or Findlay), and, as is the case with most women on the early-nineteenth-century frontier, we have no direct knowledge of what she did, thought, or felt. All we know is what her husband told us—and his autobiography devoted more space to a single bear hunt than it did to the woman he called "an affectionate good mother" and "a tender and loving wife."

So there's no choice but to use our imaginations here. We can paint Polly and David's life together in lighter or darker shades, depending on whose point of view we take and what scenes we choose to portray.

Here's a happy one to start with, taking off from what David wrote. It's from *A Man Called Davy*, an ambitious outdoor drama by John Lee Welton, a longtime theater professor at Carson-Newman College in Jefferson City, Tennessee. Portions of the drama premiered behind the Dandridge town hall in the summer of 2006, two centuries after Polly and Davy took their real-life wedding vows a few miles away.

Davy has been out hunting and, uncharacteristically, has gotten lost. But wait—who's this he sees running through the woods? It's Polly, with whom he's recently become infatuated. She's been trying to catch a runaway horse, but now she's lost, too, and it's late, and a storm is coming.

Lightning. Thunder. Polly screams.

"Now, don't you be scared," Davy tells her, reaching out a protective arm. "My ma used to say thunder was jist angels dancin', and lightnin' was jist the good Lord clappin' his hands in joy."

Before long they're knocking on the door of a lonely cabin. The old man who answers tells them they're welcome to spend the night on his porch.

He brings them a quilt, and they huddle together under it, smiling, as the scene discreetly ends.

✬

I wasn't lucky enough to be in Dandridge the day the town brought Polly and Davy back to life. When I did get there, on a mild spring evening almost four years later, I wasn't planning to stay long. I knew the courthouse had a little museum with a few Crockett-related artifacts, and I figured to drop in for an hour or so when it opened the next morning, then be on my way.

Parking at dusk in front of Tinsley Bible Drugs, I peered through the window at a cigar-store Indian with a red-white-and-blue breechclout. Walking around the corner to Main Street, I passed a graveyard where at least one Kings Mountain veteran is buried. A sign there informed me that Dandridge, which was settled in 1783, is the "second oldest town in the state." Next to the graveyard sat the former Shepard's Inn, a boarded-over log structure (like the ones in Morristown) that had hosted presidents Jackson, Polk, and Andrew Johnson. Across the street stood the red-brick town hall, and behind it, a giant earthwork that holds back the waters of the Douglas Reservoir.

A historical marker titled THE DIKE THAT SAVED DANDRIDGE noted that more than sixty thousand acres of prime agricultural land had been lost when the Tennessee Valley Authority dammed the French Broad River in 1943. There had been no alternative, it claimed: the dam was "critical to providing the power needed for the Manhattan Project in Oak Ridge."

Andy Jackson, Davy Crockett, Kings Mountain, and the atomic bomb—Dandridge had me intrigued. That made the choice between having dinner at Smoky's Steak & BBQ or heading back to the Ruby Tuesday near my highway motel an easy one. The waitress at Smoky's introduced herself as Susan. I ordered grilled pork shanks and took her advice about the barbecue sauce. Then she saw my open notebook on the table.

"Are you writing a book?" she asked.

I explained.

Susan said she couldn't tell me much about Davy herself, but there was a man in town who knew absolutely everything about Dandridge history. She didn't know his name but didn't think he'd be hard to find. He wasn't. When I dropped in at the town's visitor center the next morning, volunteers Judy and Joe Moon identified him without hesitation.

"The county historian, Mr. Jarnagin. He's seventh generation," Judy said. "He knows everything there is to know since the Revolutionary War. Jarnagin insurance—two doors down."

"His truck is here, so he's here," Joe said. He offered to walk me over and introduce me, and I accepted. But first we spent some time on the subject of Davy, and the Moons filled me in on the hottest Crockett news in town.

"Now, what we're telling you is hearsay," Joe cautioned, before relaying the tale with appropriate relish. It seems that David's license to marry Margaret Elder had caught Jefferson County's attention a few years back when "a lady in Tampa brought it to the *Antiques Roadshow.*" Her story: The county court had thrown it out decades before, and a relative of hers who worked there had just happened to pick it up. Jefferson County's response: *No way.* The county sued and got the license back.

Speaking of Margaret:

After she jilted Davy, Joe said, "he met Polly Finley."

"*Pretty* Polly Finley," Judy corrected.

"Pretty Polly Finley, who was raised between here and Jefferson City. If you follow 92, it goes through a little cut in Bays Mountain and just off to the right there, as I understand it, is where she was raised."

I had no idea where Bays Mountain was. But it didn't matter. The Man Who Knows Everything was about to take me there.

Bob Jarnagin was a bit too young to have been caught up in the original Crockett craze. He was born in 1954, the year Disney Davy hit the small screen, but his childhood hero was Roy Rogers—"though

I did have my coonskin cap and all that good stuff." Trim and fit-looking, with silvering hair and the high-energy style of someone two decades younger, he greeted me enthusiastically at the offices of H. B. Jarnagin & Company (H.B. was his grandfather) and said he'd be happy to talk Crockett as soon as his secretary got back from an early lunch.

I walked up Main Street to look at the courthouse museum while I waited. One of the first things I noticed was that Hollywood poster of Elvis—sorry, I mean Davy—in 1810, a year when he and Polly were still living in Jefferson County. Around the corner hung an action-packed drawing featuring multiple, overlapping Davys in a single frame. In it, Crockett shoots a snarling bear in a tangled canebrake, swings a clubbed rifle at a crouching Indian, speechifies in front of an American flag, and poses, larger than life, near the replica tavern.

Down the hall and around another corner, past a wonderful hodgepodge of non-Crockett artifacts, I caught up with Davy again. A glass case held copies of the Margaret Elder marriage license as well as a marriage bond dated August 12, 1806, less than ten months after the Margaret fiasco. More terrifying than a mere license, it bound David Crockett and his cosigner, Thomas Doggett, to pay the unimaginable sum of $1,250 if anything should come to light that would "obstruct the marriage of the said David Crockett with Polly Findley."

Who were they kidding? I wondered. Crockett never saw that much money in one place in his whole life!

Ten minutes later, Jarnagin and I were ordering the catfish special at Smoky's and he was telling me how his ancestor Captain Thomas Jarnagin had helped pioneer "America's first Wild West." Captain J. had fought in the American Revolution, and that service had earned him—along with many others—a land grant in North Carolina's over-mountain territory. In 1783, he became one of the first settlers of the Dandridge area. Crockett was a latecomer by Jarnagin family standards: he didn't make his trips to the court-house until two decades later.

After lunch we got into the car and headed for Polly Finley territory.

We turned right off 92 near Bays Mountain—which turned out to be a long Appalachian ridge running southwest to northeast—and onto Dumplin Valley Road, cruising through farm country with just a few modern houses scattered here and there. "We've still got a lot of nice farmland back here," Jarnagin said, though "there's some roads like this in the county so developed now, it brings a tear to my eye when I drive down them."

He pointed out the passenger-side window.

"See the stone sticking up out there in the field? Just past that little row of trees? That's the William Finley gravesite." Billy Finley, as he is often called, was Polly's father. Most of his small farm was here in Dumplin Valley, Jarnagin said, but a finger of it extended up the ridge to the right. Before we headed that way, though, we pulled over by a historical marker at the intersection of Dumplin Valley Road and the Chucky Pike.

"Legendary frontiersman David Crockett and his first wife, Polly Finley, were married on August 14, 1806, at the home of Polly's parents, William and Jean Finley, one-fourth mile southeast of here," it began.

The marker went up in the winter of 2007, not long after the Davy/Polly two-hundredth-anniversary celebration, and I wasn't surprised to learn that Jarnagin had had supporting roles in both. In the drama, he played the old man in the lonely cabin: "I've got a nightshirt on, and a cap, and I answer the door." As for the marker, it was there in large part because of his friend Joe Swann, who has been researching Crockett in east Tennessee for decades.

Swann had figured out where the Finley homesite was, Jarnagin explained, by using Crockett's autobiography and "old documents that the Brooks family had, that own the farm now." Anna Brooks, the old woman living on the site at the time, "possessed the legend that Crockett had been married there." A log barn, no longer standing, had been "attributed to William Finley." And so on. Jarnagin's contribution involved what he called "my hobby": helping people interested in family history by plotting their ancestors' landholdings, overlaying them on topographical maps, "and going out there and finding them." He had helped Swann research not just the Finley property but also that of other local Crockett-related figures.

"Joe Swann I consider to be *the* authority around here on Crockett's life," Jarnagin said. I told him I knew Swann's name already, because he was the co-owner, with his brother Art, of one of the most coveted Crockett artifacts: an elegant long rifle that David owned when he lived in this vicinity.

We turned right at the marker and headed up the Chucky Pike toward Finley Gap. On the way, I recalled the tale of David and Polly's romance as told—from his point of view, of course—twenty-eight years after the fact.

Heartsick over Margaret Elder, he agreed to attend a neighborhood reaping because he'd been promised an introduction to "one of the prettiest little girls there I had ever seen." Polly didn't disappoint. Looking to continue his courtship, he "went home to the Quaker's and made a bargain to work with his son for a low-priced horse." Then came the stormy night in the lonely cabin. Impatient to be married, David sold or traded his rifle (the autobiography is unclear on this point) to shorten the amount of time he needed to work for that horse.

The modest one-story house on the Brooks/Finley property was empty, but Jarnagin had permission to walk around the yard anytime, and we did. He showed me a spring out back, complete with a few original casing stones, that was probably the reason the Finleys chose the spot. ("A good source of fresh water is where they built their cabins.") We peered into a weathered outbuilding to admire an old three-pronged plow, small enough that one person with a mule could handle it. Only the spring dated to Crockett's time, yet I could almost see him riding eagerly through the gap and into the clearing with his wedding-day entourage: two brothers, a sister, a sister-in-law and a couple of friends.

Polly's father approved of the match, but her mother did not. Perhaps she was angry about that night in the cabin. Perhaps she wanted something better for her girl than a young man who couldn't afford a horse and a rifle at the same time. In any case, David arrived in Finley Gap fully prepared to carry Polly back to the Crockett Tavern and marry her there. But Billy Finley persuaded his wife to make up with their future son-in-law so their daughter could be married at home.

✦

Less than twenty-four hours later, I was standing in pastureland that used to belong to neighbors of the Finleys, listening to Dr. Charles Faulkner talk about bricks.

Faulkner, an eminent retired University of Tennessee archaeologist, explained that the bricks fired here on the old McCuistion place didn't date back as far as Davy and Polly's time. "These come in about 1830 or 1840," he said, holding one that had just been dug out of the sinkhole he was standing in. He'd identified it without even having to knock the clay off. "They were real popular in the middle of the nineteenth century."

Once he got going, there was no stopping him—not that anyone had any interest in trying.

"These would be fired in what's called a stove kiln," he said.

"They took two or three days to burn, and you'd have to wait I don't know how long for them to cool out. The bricks closest to the fire are called maroon bricks. If you see handmade bricks that are kind of dark red—some even have melted surfaces—those bricks were used on the outside walls. The bricks furthest away from the fire were called soakers, because they absorb water. If you have a three-brick house, the inside bricks would be those soaker bricks. And you can tell a poor brick mason if you ever see an old house that has soaker bricks on the outside."

You never know what you'll learn when you start following Davy Crockett around.

My presence at Charlie Faulkner's brick seminar came thanks to Bob Jarnagin, and by now I was wishing I'd left Susan the waitress a much bigger tip. As Jarnagin and I had finished up the Finley Gap tour, the Man Who Knows Everything—who knew better than I did that I needed to meet Joe Swann—had mentioned that Faulkner and Swann were planning to check out a nearby site soon. Would I like to come along? A phone call that evening made the invitation more specific. Could I be at the Waffle House off I-40 at 11:00 A.M.?

Yes, I could.

There were four of us: Jim Claborn, who's a friend of Jarnagin and Swann, showed up, too. Swann had driven up from his home in Maryville. We left three cars in the Waffle House parking lot, and he piloted us past the Crockett wedding site toward a farm in the Long Creek neighborhood where the McCuistion family—who were ancestors of his—once lived.

A solidly built man of sixty who both spoke and moved at a measured pace, Swann was the president of Workshop Tools Inc., based in Pigeon Forge, and had recently completed a stint as Maryville's mayor. His professional and civic duties had a tendency—deeply regretted by his fellow Crockett obsessives—to interfere with his research on David. "I've got about two hundred pages written of a book on the early life of Crockett, with about three hundred footnotes," he said, adding matter-of-factly, "I don't think I'll be able to finish it."

His goal was to fill a gaping hole in the narrative.

To understand this, all you have to do is look at the work of James Atkins Shackford, Crockett's first serious biographer, whose 1956 book, *David Crockett: The Man and the Legend*, remains an essential Crockett source. "Shackford wrote twelve pages about the first half of his life," Swann said. "The quote from Shackford was 'What's known about Crockett's early life would be shorter than the epitaph on a poor man's tombstone.'" As a result, "there was just no recognition in this area that there was any Crockett connection."

One of the most famous Tennesseans in history got married in Finley Gap, lived in the neighborhood for six years, and fathered his first two children there—yet "nobody around here knew."

Swann first learned about Crockett at the age of six, when he stood in line in Knoxville with a bunch of other kids to shake hands with Fess Parker. Afterward, he started asking questions. His Dandridge grandmother and his dad explained that the real Crockett had been a neighbor of theirs: "Why, hell, he lived up there near your kinfolks."

Then his dad told him about the rifle.

"It was like pouring gas on a fire," Swann said.

The story, naturally, comes in more than one version. What Swann's dad told him "was that our McCuistion ancestors—these people that lived up here where we're going today—had a store of sorts." Crockett owed money there, so he gave James McCuistion, Jr., his rifle "in payment for what he owed him at the store." Passed down through another branch of the family, the gun traveled west to Oklahoma (where Joe's father saw it as a boy in 1916) and on to California. Joe and Art Swann bought it in 1978 and returned it to

Tennessee, where it's now on loan to the East Tennessee Historical Society's museum in Knoxville.

No one doubts that it's a genuine Crockett rifle, but Swann is forthright about the question marks that remain. His father's story, he said, "doesn't *exactly* jibe with what Crockett says. So there may have been two rifles. . . . It's uncertain as to whether this rifle was his very first one that he talks about in his autobiography." If it was, maybe McCuistion paid off what remained of Crockett's debt on the horse, taking the gun in exchange. Maybe there's some other explanation. "I'm trying," Swann said, "but there may be details we'll just never be able to figure out."

As the afternoon wore on—sunny, memorable, and unexpected— I learned more about bricks and the construction of frontier housing. The McCuistions may have sold some of their bricks for use in chimneys, Faulkner said, at a time when whole brick houses weren't yet being built in the Dandridge area. Earlier than that, cabins had stone chimneys or else "the firebox was made of stone and the chimney itself was built of logs." When settlers built a log chimney, "they plastered mud on the inside and laid the logs on that, and it stood away from the house." Sometimes ropes were attached, so if the chimney caught on fire, "they could run out and pull it off."

Moving on from chimneys, we talked about the Great Indian Warpath, a kind of Native American interstate that ran from Georgia to upstate New York and passed within a mile or so of where we were standing. Somebody picked up a few flakes of chipped flint, by-products of prehistoric arrowhead production. While discussing the authentication of historic sites, Faulkner mentioned that techniques such as tree-ring dating can make archaeologists plenty unpopular—for example, when they show that what's being marketed as the historic home of Kings Mountain hero and Tennessee governor John Sevier was built two decades after Sevier's death.

We talked more about David and Polly, too.

That reaping where the two met?

"There's a real good chance that these people would have been there," Swann said, meaning the McCuistions.

The old Jacobs place at the top of Finley Gap, which Swann pointed out as we went by?

"The guy that lived *there* as a little boy knew Crockett" and, as an old man, wrote down his memories.

"Crockett was a poor man when I first saw him," John Jacobs recalled in 1884. He was "making rails for my father" and "frequently called on me to hand him the wedge or glut, which ever he wanted."

And where were David and Polly living at the time?

Jacobs said it was three-quarters of a mile away, but the site has never been pinned down. "Bob and I have been trying to figure that out," Swann said. "We've got a lot of leads, but we're not exactly sure." All that's known for certain is that after the wedding, Crockett rented some land and a cabin not far from his in-laws.

Key word: "rented."

"There's no deed for me to put my hands on," Jarnagin said. "But if there's a little old log cabin on somebody's farm around here, there's a story out there somewhere that *that* was the Crockett honeymoon cabin."

✦

It's a lovely concept, that honeymoon cabin, and I can't help hoping that David and Polly found happiness inside. But we're back in use-your-imagination territory here. "I do reckon we love as hard in the backwood country, as any people in the whole creation," Crockett declared in his autobiography, but he offered no details.

What's really hard to imagine, though, is the rest of Polly Crockett's life.

This is partly because David, as we've seen, wrote little about her—but it's also because we don't know much about the lives of any poor women on the Appalachian frontier. When I went looking for economic and social context, I figured there'd be plenty of historians who could help. Silly me. Women's history is just like any other form of history, in that it's heavily biased toward people who leave paper trails. You have to be literate to do that, of course, and, as the expert I finally tracked down reminded me, there were no free public schools in Polly Crockett's Appalachia.

"Her chances of being literate are just about zero," Wilma Dunaway said.

Dunaway was a Virginia Tech sociologist and the author of an exhaustively researched book called *Women, Work, and Family in the Antebellum Mountain South*, published in 2008. "You have to dig in all kinds of places to find women's history," she said. She gleaned what she could from hundreds of letters, diaries, and other documents (mostly male-generated), but she also built a database of some twenty thousand Appalachian households using census data and tax lists. As a result, *Women, Work, and Family* corrects some of the widespread misperceptions created by historians who generalize from the better-documented lives of the upper class.

The biggest misperception? That someone like Polly would only do "women's work."

Upscale travelers through nineteenth-century Appalachia were shocked to find white women working the fields along with white men and slaves. But the notion of southern females as "loving nurturers" whose labor was "divided spatially" from that of men—as a 2006 *Encyclopedia of Appalachia* entry described the situation—is, in Dunaway's view, simply false. Wealthy women with access to slave labor might have lived that way, but in 1810, four years after David and Polly married, only one in ten Appalachian Tennessee households reported owning slaves. White households in southern

Appalachia were "nearly twice as likely to be poor as families in the country as a whole," and more than half of those households, like the Crocketts, owned no land.

Why should we be surprised that women did whatever it took to help their families survive?

I wanted to get Dunaway's take on Polly's world, so I summarized what I knew about her economic situation. I mentioned David's father's chronic indebtedness (no help to be had in that quarter); Polly's modest dowry (two cows and two calves); David's horse; a much-needed wedding gift from his old Quaker employer, John Canaday ($15 in credit at a local store); and Polly's skill with her spinning wheel. I talked about the farmland and cabin the couple rented—in his autobiography, David described the rent as "high," though he doesn't say if he paid in cash or with a share of his crops—and about his preference for hunting over farming when he had access to a gun.

"She would have worked the fields more than he did," Dunaway said promptly. Her spinning and weaving would have helped, producing cloth to be traded or sold, but "they would have been scrounging in the winter months."

Soon enough they were scrounging for four. John Wesley Crockett was born in 1807 and his brother William two years later. David says nothing about the joys of fatherhood, but he does make note of its burdens: "I found I was better at increasing my family than my fortune," he wrote—and nothing he could do in east Tennessee was likely to change that. In either the fall of 1811 or the spring of 1812, the Crocketts headed west, like so many others, in search of "some better place to get along."

Better place number one was near present-day Lynchburg, two hundred miles or so from Finley Gap, but they didn't stay there long. By 1813, they had moved to better place number two, a small community on Bean's Creek, ten miles southwest of Winchester. Here, as in east Tennessee, they settled on rented land. And whatever share of the farmwork Polly had done before was about to increase.

The United States had gone to war with Great Britain the year before, but aside from unfounded rumors about the British arming hostile Indians, the War of 1812 seemed far from the Tennessee frontier. Then, in September 1813, came news that hit closer to home: Creek Indians had massacred hundreds of settlers in southern Alabama, at a place called Fort Mims, and the state of Tennessee was calling for volunteers.

David decided to sign up.

His reasons appear both straightforward and complex. Looking back on his decision, two decades later, he would describe himself as not having a particularly warlike disposition. Though he "had often thought about war, and had often heard it described," he had persuaded himself that he "couldn't fight in that way at all." The news from Fort Mims changed that "instantly." His whole community was up in arms, and it was entirely natural that he would join in.

Crockett had additional reasons to fight that were unmentioned in the autobiography. Since marrying, he had moved twice and worked three different plots of land yet had gained no economic traction. Military volunteers would be paid, and history suggested that they might receive land grants as well. It's also likely—given that David had first left home at age twelve and would keep leaving it for the rest of his life—that sheer restlessness played a part.

He had one obstacle to overcome, however: Polly was begging him not to go.

"She said she was a stranger in the parts where we lived, had no connexions living near her, and that she and our little children would be left in a lonesome and unhappy situation if I went away," he wrote in his autobiography, adding that he found it "mighty hard to go against such arguments as these."

Still, he talked himself into it: "I knew that the next thing would be, that the Indians would be scalping the women and children all about there, if we didn't put a stop to it. I reasoned the case with her as well as I could, and told her, that if every man would wait till his wife got willing for him to go to war, there would be no fighting done, until we would all be killed in our own houses; that I was as able to go as any man in the world; and that I believed it was a duty I owed to my country."

His next sentence may be the most telling snapshot we have of Polly Crockett's world: "Whether she was satisfied with this reasoning or not, she did not tell me; but seeing I was bent on it, all she did was to cry a little, and turn about to her work."

David Crockett, Indian Fighter

I didn't have much luck getting people to talk about Davy Crockett in the first middle Tennessee place he tried to settle. It's not easy for a man who passed through Lynchburg two centuries ago, no matter how famous he became, to compete with the Jack Daniel's distillery. There is a Crockett marker a few miles out of town, which claims to be near where he built a cabin, but I had to find it on my own. The nice woman in the visitor center was better informed about a more recent local celebrity, Little Richard, and his habit of driving around in a black Cadillac Escalade.

The Crocketts' next home, the one near Winchester, lay in a broad, green valley a few miles north of present-day Alabama. David named it Kentuck, or so his biographers tell us, differing only in their speculations about the reason. (Did he think he might move north someday? Was he honoring Daniel Boone?) A Tennessee Historical Commission marker on U.S. 64 endorses the naming story as well. "The homestead which David Crockett occupied and named in 1812 is now marked by a well standing in a field 3½ miles south and to the east of this road" reads the text under the simple headline "Kentuck."

Jerry Limbaugh doesn't buy it.

I met Limbaugh in the history room of the Franklin County Library in Winchester, where I'd dropped in to go through the Crockett files. He's the county historian, and like his Jefferson County counterpart, Bob Jarnagin, he's good with old deeds. Limbaugh told me that Crockett had rented his farm from a woman named Fannie Gillespie, whose maiden name was Henderson and who was born in Boonesborough, Kentucky, in 1777. He showed me a family history that claimed that Fannie was "the first white child born in the state, of parents married in that now great commonwealth."

"So that's why it would be called Kentuck," Limbaugh said. "It had nothing to do with Davy Crockett. That's what *I* think."

Among many other things he showed me was a document involving the estate of one Jacob Vanzant, who owned a mill at which Crockett may have run up some debts. Limbaugh isn't sure he has it all figured out, he said, but there are several notations about money owed by Crockett, including one for the substantial sum of $516.25. It would remain uncollected: the document dates from 1837, a year after the Alamo.

As for that well at Kentuck: apparently two local wells have been claimed as Davy's, though "the general tradition" makes one site more likely. "If you want to go look at it, the fellow you need to get ahold of is Jim Hargrove," Limbaugh told me. "He's the tour guide down there."

Two hours later, I was riding shotgun in Hargrove's green Ford Sport, bouncing along a right of way through a plant nursery adjoining his own six acres. Commercial shrubbery had replaced the crops—corn surely among them—that David and Polly had planted when they got here in 1812. A big man on the far side of seventy, Hargrove said he'd begun his career as a construction ironworker, moved up "to foreman and general foreman and so on," and ended up on salary, traveling all over the world. He wore faded blue-jean overalls and had a black brace strapped to his right leg. "I stumbled into some vines up there in the woods. Fell for thirty minutes," he said, laughing.

He stopped the truck, pulled a walker out of the back, and led the way to a less-than-scenic square of concrete poking out of some tall grass.

The original Crockett well, he said, "was just level with the top of the ground. And the people who owned this farm in later years, they poured that concrete around the top of it." Peering down through the added-on concrete square, I could see a cylinder of old stones below it. Ferns and moss added green to the gray. I couldn't see the bottom. Hargrove said he'd let a rope down once to measure it. He thought it was maybe twenty-four feet deep "with six to eight feet of water in it."

That reminded him of a story.

"When I was just a boy, my daddy owned a farm right over there in the bend of the mountains"—he gestured to where the Cumberland Mountains rise east and south of the lush farmland—"and we had a hand-dug well." The well would go dry in the summer and need cleaning out. One year, being the youngest and smallest, Hargrove got the job. He was winched down into the well along with an empty nail keg, and he used a short-handled shovel to fill the keg with mud. Then he made the mistake of looking up from the bottom of the dark, narrow hole he was in. "And when that nail keg come up I was setting on top, and I said, 'Daddy, you whip me, do whatever you want to—I *ain't* going back down that well.'"

Over the next hour or so, I got an extended tour of the Bean's Creek neighborhood. As the late-afternoon sun bathed fields and ridges in a golden glow, I had no trouble imagining why Hargrove had come home to retire or why the Crocketts had chosen to settle here in the first place. I also got a lot more stories. Some were about things Hargrove had seen and done as a boy. Others involved legendary murders and out-of-control floods. One was about the brutal killing of two boys in 1812—the last recorded instance, he said, of "Indians creating a disturbance in Franklin County." That was a year before David Crockett signed up to fight the Creeks.

There was a story about David and Polly, too.

"My grandfather, he was a storyteller," Hargrove said, "and of course my great-great-great-grandfather *knew* David Crockett," because he'd settled here six years before Crockett arrived. After David went off to fight, the story goes, "Polly had nothing to eat. And there was an Indian, a Cherokee Indian lived in this vicinity here, name of Lightfoot," who felt sorry for her. Lightfoot would hunt and fish for his own family "and share anything he had left with Polly. And she would, in her turn, give it to her kids."

Truth? Myth? You be the judge. All I can say is that it's a great story—and that its irony is impossible to miss.

Here was David, marching off to protect his wife and kids from Indians. And here was an Indian trying to keep them alive.

James Shackford used the very first line of his Crockett biography to paint a big picture behind David's life story. "The frontiersman," Shackford wrote, "was history's agent for wresting land from the American Indian." Then he laid out the familiar cycle of westward expansion: Whites push "inexorably into Indian territory." Indians resist, often violently, always futilely. A treaty gives "legal sanction to the latest accommodation of lands illegally acquired by these frontiersmen." And the cycle starts over again.

Yet the more I learned about David Crockett, the more I began to think his biographer was really talking about Daniel Boone.

Boone, the prototype of the American pioneer and Indian fighter, was certainly "history's agent" in Shackford's metaphorical sense. More concretely, he served as an agent for the kind of large-scale land speculators whose unrestrained ambition—call it greed, if you prefer—fueled the westward push. In 1775, Boone helped the speculator Richard Henderson persuade the Cherokees to sell him most of Kentucky and a big hunk of middle Tennessee. "Even before the Treaty of Sycamore Shoals was signed," as the historian John Finger has observed, Henderson sent Boone to oversee the building of the Wilderness Road "through Cumberland Gap to Henderson's new empire."

A few years later another frontier hero, John Sevier, marched back from Kings Mountain and led a series of attacks on Cherokee towns south of the over-mountain settlements. The attacks served a dual purpose: they helped protect the settlements, and they opened more land to settlers and speculators.

As for Crockett, he certainly met the definition of the word "frontiersman." Yet, with the notable exception of his Creek War service, he was not directly engaged in pushing Indians off their land. The wild frontier moved faster than David did. Nine years before he was born, as the killing of his grandparents proved, east Tennessee was still contested ground. But by August 17, 1786, the Crocketts and their neighbors were no longer threatened, and by the time David and Polly headed west a quarter century later, there wasn't much Indian land left in middle Tennessee. Every time Crockett pulled up stakes, in fact, he resettled in territory whose native inhabitants had recently given it up.

Still, I could see Shackford's big picture all over the East Tennessee Historical Society's museum in Knoxville when I dropped in to look at the Crockett gun Joe Swann owns.

Near the museum entrance, I paused beside a big illustrated label titled "Longhunters: Freewheeling Competition." It showed a wary frontiersman toting a rifle through a snowy forest. Men like Boone, the text explained, had ventured "deep into the frontier" to compete with Indians for animal pelts—but the real threats to the Indian way of life were the "enticing descriptions of the land" that the hunters brought home.

Next I noticed a quote from the 1785 Treaty of Hopewell between the Cherokees and the U.S. government. Any non-Indian trying to settle on land allotted to the Indians as their hunting grounds, a reasonable-sounding clause proclaimed, would "forfeit the protection of the United States and the Indians might punish him or not as they please." Reasonable-sounding but dead on arrival: this deal had no more chance of being enforced than the British Proclamation of 1763, which had sought to keep settlers from crossing the Appalachians in the first place—and which Finger described as "a triumph of naivete, geographical ignorance, and wishful thinking."

Around the corner, an artist's take on Kings Mountain drew my eye. Redcoats charged down the slope, over-mountain men fired up at them, and, in the middle of it all, an outsized Crockett-like figure swung his rifle like a club. He looked as if he'd wandered off the set of a bad Alamo movie, and he distracted me enough that I didn't immediately notice David's actual rifle, beautifully displayed in a case in the center of the room.

The museum label seemed more certain of the gun's history than Swann is. It had Crockett trading his rifle to John Canaday for a "courting horse" and Canaday, in turn, selling it to James McCuistion. But never mind: here was an object that the real David Crockett had held in his hands! Built to be as light as possible, it had a soft barrel and a spare stock, though not so spare as to exclude some gorgeous decorative brass work featuring a tiny profile of an Indian's face. Here was a piece of the past I could reach out and touch—if it weren't for the display case, of course—and it gave me the shivers.

Then again, so did the mural on the wall behind it.

Headlined "A Land Too Small," it showed a wagon train filled with Cherokees, bundled against the cold and flanked by blue-coated soldiers, heading west on the Trail of Tears. The text quoted principal chief John Ross "and 19 others" as asking, "Is it true you will drive us from the land of our nativity and from the tombs of our Fathers and of our Mothers? We know you possess the power but, by the tie that binds us yonder, we implore you to forbear."

Many deaf ears were turned to that plea. The deafest belonged to Andrew Jackson, who, as president, possessed the power to push an Indian Removal bill through congress in 1830. Jackson's policy faced plenty of opposition even at the time, and most Americans today see his treatment of the peaceful and rapidly "civilizing" Cherokees as horrific and unjustifiable. Yet to comprehend the big picture of Indian-white relations in Jacksonian America, you have to consider a crucial point that hindsight tends to obscure: many white Americans opposed the president's methods—but far fewer opposed his goal.

Those Indians had to be moved off that land.

Some of Jackson's predecessors, including George Washington and Thomas Jefferson, had hoped to do so peacefully. Washington's secretary of war, Henry Knox, had served as point man for a policy under which the federal government would take over all negotiations with Indians, establishing lawful boundaries and ultimately buying their land. The Indians would have options—they could retreat as the frontier moved west or they could assimilate, as individuals, within the dominant culture—but hanging on to millions of acres of prime land was not one of them.

An 1803 exchange between Jackson and Jefferson is telling. As Gregory Waselkov pointed out in A Conquering Spirit: Fort Mims and the Redstick War of 1813–1814, President Jefferson was responding to criticism that the federal Indian agent Benjamin Hawkins "was too sympathetic toward the Creeks to effectively negotiate land away from them." Not to worry, the president reassured Jackson, who had recently become a major general in the Tennessee militia: the essential goals of federal Indian policy—"1. The preservation of peace" and "2. The obtaining [of their] lands"—had not changed.

Jackson didn't share that first goal. "The whole Creek nation shall be covered with blood," he wrote after a small party of Creeks killed some settlers on Tennessee's Duck River in 1812. The *Nashville Clarion* agreed with him, arguing bluntly that the murders offered a "pretext for the dismemberment of their country." Unfortunately for Jackson and his like-minded allies, Agent Hawkins undercut this pretext by pushing the Creek national council to punish the murderers themselves.

Fort Mims took care of that problem.

It was impossible not to be horrified by the accounts of the hellish massacre that spread across the frontier. Some reported that between four hundred and six hundred soldiers and civilians had been killed, and they featured gruesome descriptions of women scalped and children's brains bashed out against stockade walls. Jackson got the news as he was recovering from serious wounds received in a Wild West–style Nashville gunfight (calling it a duel, as some have, makes it sound much too formal and dignified). The general realized immediately, in the words of his biographer Robert Remini, "that his moment for military glory had arrived." A few weeks later, "still pale and weak, with his arm in a sling," he took command of an army of volunteers that included David Crockett.

Nearly seventeen years later, Representative Crockett would cast his vote against Jackson's Indian Removal bill. But when David signed up to fight the Creeks in the fall of 1813, he could scarcely have imagined that moment.

He couldn't even see six weeks ahead, to when he and his fellow Indian fighters would follow Fort Mims with a hellish massacre of their own.

✶

The town where it took place was called Tallusahatchee, or Tallas-seehatchee, or Tallasehatchee, or Tallasahatchie, or Talluschatches, and besides not knowing the best way to spell the place, I hadn't found anyone who could tell me precisely where it was. But I drove down to Alabama anyway. It was too big a part of Crockett's story to skip.

I'm using the word "down" literally. Never having been in north-eastern Alabama before, I didn't know it would take me most of an hour just to get off the Cumberland Plateau. Down, down, down I rolled on green, uncluttered Highway 79, passing tempting signs for the Walls of Jericho Hiking Trail and Mom's Family Restaurant (REDNECK MUSIC LIVE TUESDAY). The instant I clicked on the radio, I got a classic Hank Williams tune:

> I'll pretend I'm free from sorrow
> Make believe that wrong is right
> Your wedding day will be tomorrow
> But there'll be no teardrops tonight.

Ears popping, mind wandering, I wondered how David had spent the night before Margaret Elder got hitched.

Back on flat roads, I hugged the shore of gorgeous Lake Guntersville for a while, then, nearing Gadsden, hit one of those stretches of cookie-cutter America that could be anywhere. I counted two Walmarts, three Waffle Houses, and three Walgreens stores before the traffic thinned enough to let me get back up to speed—yet even those Waffle Houses managed to remind me of Crockett. Keeping the army fed during the Creek War was a largely unmet challenge for Tennessee's military brass. General Jackson's otherwise commendable refusal to sit still meant that he was always pushing ahead with insufficient supplies. And that meant that Crockett and the rest of Jackson's volunteers spent much of the war half starved.

An All-Star Special with waffles, toast, eggs, and bacon would have looked like manna from heaven to them.

Crockett's war had sent him into Alabama through Huntsville, a bit west of the route I'd chosen, and it began with him having authority issues. His skills as a woodsman got him selected for a scouting mission, and he picked a young man named George Russell to go with him. The mission's leader, a certain Major Gibson, disapproved of his choice: Russell "hadn't beard enough to please him," Gibson said, and "he wanted men, and not boys." David made a joke of it in his autobiography—"I didn't think that courage ought to be measured by the beard," he wrote, "for fear a goat would have the preference over a man"—but at the time he got "a little wrathy" and argued the point. He won, and Russell got to come along.

His next run-in with authority left him with a permanent dislike of the officer class. The scouting expedition had split up, with Major Gibson leading one group and Crockett the other. After several tense days in the wild, Crockett and his men hustled back to give their commanding officer, Colonel John Coffee, some scary information they'd obtained about a large party of warriors crossing the Coosa River. But Coffee paid the news no mind until Gibson showed up with a similar report. "This seemed to put our colonel all in a fidget," Crockett wrote, still angry two decades later, "and it convinced me, clearly, of one of the hateful ways of the world." An officer's word will be believed where that of "just a poor soldier" will not.

The alarm proved false, but Coffee's men found Indians to fight soon enough. They heard of a town filled with hostile Creeks and enlisted two friendly members of the tribe to guide them there. Some nine hundred troops surrounded it; then one company went forward as a decoy to lure the Indians out.

I'm going to let Crockett take over the Tallusahatchee story at this point—but first, some cautionary notes.

His autobiography, as discussed, was written two decades after the event and with a political purpose. The Creek War section is far longer than in the unauthorized *Sketches and Eccentricities,* which barely mentions Crockett's military exploits. A strong military record, then as now, was a plus for an ambitious politician, but in trying to bolster his standing vis-à-vis Jackson, "the Hero of New Orleans," David made a few things up. Crockett's narrative, Shackford wrote, has him fighting a couple of battles in January 1814 in which he did not actually participate. Worse, it places him in the midst of what he portrays as a successful mutiny against Jackson by hungry men whose enlistments were up and who wanted to go home. In truth, Jackson faced down the mutineers. Crockett's unit wasn't even on the scene, and his own enlistment wasn't up at the time.

Why, then, should we pay attention to what he says about Tallusahatchee?

Well, for one thing, this part of Crockett's account meshes with what we know from more obscure sources. It's more graphic than General Coffee's official report (the colonel had recently been promoted), but that's hardly surprising. For another, we *have* to pay attention if we're trying to understand David, because the passage is central to a long-standing argument over his attitude toward Indians. Those who admire his stand against Indian Removal tend to read it one way; those who think his pro-Indian record has been exaggerated read it differently.

So here's what he wrote, picking up at the point where the decoy company, led by a captain named Hammond, approached Tallusahatchee:

> He [Hammond] had advanced near the town, when the Indians saw him, and they raised the yell, and came running

at him like so many red devils. The main army was now formed in a hollow square around the town, and they pursued Hammond till they came in reach of us. We then gave them a fire, and they returned it, and then ran back into their town. We began to close on the town by making our files closer and closer, and the Indians soon saw they were our property. So most of them wanted us to take them prisoners; and their squaws and all would run and take hold of any of us they could, and give themselves up. I saw seven squaws have hold of one man, which made me think of the Scriptures. So I hollered out the Scriptures was fulfilling; that there was seven women holding to one man's coat tail. But I believe it was a hunting-shirt all the time. We took them all prisoners that came out to us in this way; but I saw some warriors run into a house, until I counted forty-six of them. We pursued them until we got near the house, when we saw a squaw sitting in the door, and she placed her feet against the bow she had to her hand, and then took an arrow, and, raising her feet, she drew with all her might, and let fly at us, and she killed a man, whose name, I believe, was Moore. He was a lieutenant, and his death so enraged us all, that she was fired on, and had at least twenty balls blown through her. This was the first man I ever saw killed with a bow and arrow. We now shot them like dogs; and then set the house on fire, and burned it up with the forty-six warriors in it. I recollect seeing a boy who was shot down near the house. His arm and thigh was broken, and he was so near the burning house that the grease was stewing out of him. In this situation he was still trying to crawl along; but not a murmer escaped him, though he was only about twelve years old. So sullen is the Indian, when his dander is up, that he had sooner die than make a noise, or ask for quarters.

Coffee reported 186 warriors dead (with 5 dead and 41 wounded among his own men) and noted that "without intention . . . a few squaws and children" had also been killed. Jackson passed the news on to the governor of Tennessee. "We have retaliated for the destruction of Fort Mims," he wrote.

Crockett went on to describe the battle's aftermath:

> [W]e went back to our Indian town on the next day, when many of the carcasses of the Indians were still to be seen. They looked very awful, for the burning had not entirely consumed them, but given them a very terrible appearance, at least what remained of them. It was, somehow or other, found out that the house had a potatoe cellar under it, and an immediate examination was made, for we were all as hungry as wolves. We found a fine chance of potatoes in it, and hunger compelled us to eat them, though I had a little rather not, if I could have helped it, for the oil of the Indians we had burned up on the day before had run down on them, and they looked like they had been stewed with fat meat.

✹

It wasn't just that I couldn't locate Tallusahatchee itself. I couldn't even find the two historical markers that commemorated the battle, though I'd read all about them in the Crockett tourist's bible, Randell Jones's *In the Footsteps of Davy Crockett*. It was starting to look as though the deaths of two hundred human beings had been erased from the American landscape.

Not quite, it turned out. I was just having a bad day.

My search had started well enough. The morning after my descent into Alabama, I drove to Anniston, where, a block up the street from the Public Library of Anniston-Calhoun County, I found a wonderful marker I wasn't looking for. In 1904, it noted, eighteen-year-old Tyrus Raymond Cobb "lived in a boarding house on this site while playing minor league baseball for the Anniston Steelers." Sitting in a local drugstore, young Ty—who would go on to become "the greatest baseball player of all time"—used various fake names to write the sportswriter Grantland Rice and tell him what a terrific find this kid Cobb was. Rice eventually took notice; so did the Detroit Tigers, and the rest is history.

Upstairs in the library's local-history room, I found a librarian almost as helpful as Grantland Rice. When I told Tom Mullins I was interested in the Creek War, he led me to the shelf of books most likely to be of use. When a Jackson base called Fort Strother came up in conversation, Mullins produced a cart full of documents assembled by a local man who'd been obsessed with the place. As soon as I mentioned Fort Mims, he showed me Gregory Waselkov's *A Conquering Spirit*—Waselkov is a historical anthropologist at the University of South Alabama, and his book is an in-depth study of the massacre—and I looked at it just long enough to know I needed to get my own copy.

As for Tallusahatchee, Mullins didn't know where it was, and he didn't think anyone else did, either. But he sketched out directions to the historic markers, and I headed north on U.S. 431 to look for the first one.

Several U-turns later, I was still looking. I'd been driving through nice, rolling countryside, some planted with corn, but it wasn't exactly unspoiled. Eyes peeled for history, I'd been distracted by tract mansions with ridiculous brick gates, signs for Bill's Flea Market and the Robert Trent Jones Golf Trail, the inevitable Waffle House at the intersection of 431 and Alabama 144, and a King Kong–sized red-and-white blow-up monkey advertising an auto dealer's anniversary sale. Finally I glimpsed a brown sign across from the Crossroads Baptist Church, and there it was, right where Tom Mullins and Randell Jones had done their best to tell me it would be.

The marker used half as many words as Ty Cobb's had. "Creek Indian War 1813–14," it read. "Nov. 3, 1813—Gen. John Coffee, commanding 900 Tennessee Volunteers, surrounded Indians nearby; killed some two hundred warriors. This was first American victory. It avenged earlier massacre of 517 at Ft. Mims by Indians." That seemed inadequate: no women, no children, no burning houses, and no skepticism about that Fort Mims death count (historians have since cut it roughly in half). Near the marker stood a sign for Tallasseehatchee Farm. I might have ignored the PRIVATE PROPERTY NO TRESPASSING warning, but there was no door to knock on, just a long stretch of gated dirt road.

I found the next marker more easily. It was maybe three miles away, just off 144, and I drove past it only once before spotting it in a neatly fenced square of grass hidden in some trash-filled woods. "This stone marks the site of the Tallasahatchie Battlefield," it read, surprising me with its geographical certitude. "On this spot Lieut. Gen. John Coffee with Gen. Andrew Jackson's men won a victory over the Creek Indians, November 3, 1813." The Daughters of the American Revolution had put up this small stone memorial a century after the fact.

Did they know something I didn't?

Much more striking, however, was a larger, newer stone a few feet away. It commemorated not the many who had lost their lives here—or at least somewhere in the general vicinity—but a child who had survived.

I don't remember who first told me the story of Lincoyer (alternate spellings: Lencoya, Lincoya, Lyncoya), but I do recall being astonished by it. Mythmaking has twisted the facts, and the monument got some wrong, but the essential narrative is this: In the immediate aftermath of Tallusahatchee, someone found a dead Indian woman clutching her small, living son. The boy was brought to Jackson, who learned that it was the Creeks' custom to kill such orphans if they had no relatives to take care of them. The general intervened. Lincoyer ended up living at the Hermitage, Andrew and Rachel Jackson's home, as their adopted son. He died as a teenager, probably of tuberculosis. A newspaper obituary reported that Jackson had considered sending him to West Point.

By itself, it's a touching tale. Yet the longer I contemplated those twinned monuments at the purported site of Tallusahatchee, the angrier I got. To label as a simple "victory" the mayhem Crockett had described was bad enough, but to celebrate Jackson's compassion seemed obscene. Hadn't his men killed the boy's mother while fulfilling their general's desire to see the entire Creek nation "covered with blood"? Didn't he believe so strongly that Indians and whites could never, ever get along that his removal policy would force Cherokees from their land at gunpoint, causing thousands to die on the Trail of Tears?

The next morning, a talk with the Auburn University historian Kathryn Braund calmed me down. Braund had studied the Creek War from the Indian point of view, and she held no brief for Andrew Jackson—but she did point out a couple of things I'd missed. Jackson's view on the races not being able to get along didn't apply to Lincoyer's adoption, she explained, because at the Hermitage, "the child was not living as an Indian." More important, Jackson's father died before he was born, and his mother died when he was fourteen. "I think he had a tender spot for orphans," Braund said.

Back at that patch of grass in the woods, however, I couldn't stop fuming about the way the monuments distorted history. Not far away, a marble slab thanked the Vulcan Materials Company for "providing and maintaining the site of this park." I had noticed a fleet of dump trucks rumbling down McCullars Lane, and I decided to look around the neighborhood. Turning south off McCullars, I drove a quarter mile, parked, and pushed through thick brush to the edge of a man-made cliff. Below me was a Grand Canyon–sized gravel pit (by comparison to the memorial park, at least) out of which those dump trunks had been filled. It was Vulcan's Ohatchee Quarry, and if by any chance *this* was where Tallusahatchee had been, the bones of its dead had been hauled off long ago.

But wherever they died, I thought, we have David Crockett to thank that they're remembered at all.

Unlike Tallusahatchee, the Fort Mims massacre site has been preserved, but I wasn't going to get there anytime soon. It's in southern Alabama near the little town of Tensaw—more than four hours south of the Lencoyer monument—and I was headed back to Tennessee. But talking to Braund made me aware how very little I knew about the war that had proved to be a life-changing event for David Crockett, so I assigned myself some homework. As soon as I could get my hands on it, I plunged into Waselkov's Fort Mims book, and I followed up with a broader history by Frank Owsley called *Struggle for the Gulf Borderlands*. Reading them reminded me of the endlessly recyclable headline I used to offer my *Washington Post* editors when I filed a history-related piece: "It's More Complicated Than You Think!"

Take, for example, the widespread belief that the Creek War started with Fort Mims.

More complicated.

It actually started as an Indian civil war.

The roots of the conflict for which the twenty-seven-year-old Crockett volunteered lay in the relentless pressure on the Creeks to ditch their traditional culture and cede their hunting grounds in the process. Many succumbed to the pressure and some thrived, but others, in Owsley's words, "bitterly resented the acceptance of the white man's civilization by their brother Creeks." A conservative faction known as the Red Sticks arose, combining the revival of traditional religious beliefs with what Waselkov calls "rejection of most cultural elements derived from whites"—especially the push to convert Creek males from hunters to farmers. Discontent spiked when the white-influenced Creek council ordered the punishment of the warriors whose attack on settlers had inflamed Jackson. The result, as Owsley put it, was "a large-scale campaign of murdering the chiefs and warriors who had tried to keep the peace."

Got all that? Good. Now let's zoom in on some specific complications in the Fort Mims neighborhood.

Over the first decade or so of the nineteenth century, a cluster of settlements in what was known as the Tensaw district, not far north of Mobile, turned into a testing ground for the Can't We All Just Get Along theory of Indian assimilation that David Crockett, years later, would endorse. White settlers, as Waselkov shows, lived in harmony with a community of mixed-race people who identified as Creeks. Both groups functioned in a plantation economy based on slavery, so the Tensaw was hardly a multicultural Shangri-la. But the whites and the mixed-race Creeks were certainly getting along.

Then peace was shattered by the massacre, right?

More complicated.

It was actually shattered by a botched skirmish that *led up to* the massacre.

In the summer of 1813, word spread that some Red Sticks had gone to Florida to get arms and ammunition from the Spanish. Territorial militia leaders planned a preemptive strike. On July 27, a militia force surprised the returning Red Sticks (who had obtained some powder and shot but no guns) at Burnt Corn Creek, not far from the Tensaw settlements. The militiamen declared victory too soon and were routed by counterattacking Red Sticks. Fearful settlers gathered at the fortified plantation house of a man named Samuel Mims.

Bad move—though if a drunken incompetent hadn't left the gate open, things might have turned out differently.

One last batch of complications before David rejoins the narrative: Why did the Red Sticks attack Fort Mims and not somewhere else? Turns out it was *because* of the complex stew of ethnicity inside. Traditionalist prophets targeted it, Owsley explained, "not only to avenge the attack at Burnt Corn, but also because of their hatred for the large number of friendly Creeks and mixed bloods living at the fort." To confuse matters further, some mixed-race Creeks sided with the Red Sticks—including William Weatherford, who helped lead the attack. Weatherford is known to history as Chief Red Eagle, though it's unclear that anyone called him that when he was alive; the earliest printed mention of the name occurs in a romantic poem published in 1855.

All of which made me question whether it was really true—as I read at a wonderfully weird historical monument thirty miles south of the alleged site of Tallusahatchee—that Crockett and Weatherford had faced off at the Battle of Talladega just ten weeks after Fort Mims.

Talladega is a city of roughly sixteen thousand people that's best known today for the nearby Talladega Superspeedway. The battlefield monument is a block west of the town square, in a tiny park next to a Piggly Wiggly parking lot. Its marble roof sits on narrow, inward-curving arches that make the whole thing look like a landing module for a stone-age moon flight. Beneath this, arrayed around a small fountain, historical markers informed me that Red Eagle was a "Creek chief, whose 1100 braves commanded by the half-caste Bill Scott, here lost the Battle of Talladega" and that among the members of the victorious commander's "staff" were Davy Crockett, Sam Houston, and John Coffee. Davy is said to have been "almost killed at a fortified ditch" during the battle. But the most startling assertion on the marker is that "the same forces under Jackson, Houston, Coffee and Crockett drove the British from Pensacola, and on January 8, 1815, crushed the British with casualties two thousand to seven, at New Orleans."

Wow, I thought. Imagine if this historical mash-up were true. Davy would be so proud!

Sad to say, Crockett's account of Talladega mentions no sudden promotion or near-death experience. I've found no reliable source that confirms Weatherford's presence. By the time David got to Pensacola, the British were gone, and he never got anywhere close to New Orleans.

The Talladega fight took place just six days after Tallusahatchee, and it started—surprise, surprise—as part of the Creek civil war. Hearing that the Creeks in a nearby fortified village were inclined to side with the whites, a large band of Red Sticks set siege to the place. (Crockett, too, reports their number as 1,100.) Alerted by a friendly Creek messenger, Jackson and two thousand troops hustled south from Fort Strother, intent on surrounding the besiegers. His plan didn't entirely work: the majority of the Red Sticks broke through his lines and escaped. But Talladega was a major victory nonetheless, with several hundred Red Stick warriors killed as opposed to seventeen of Jackson's men.

Talladega is the point where Crockett's autobiography veers into fiction. What follows are the spurious accounts of the anti-Jackson mutiny and the two January battles in which David didn't fight. In reality, according to War Department records cited by Shackford, his enlistment expired on December 24, 1813.

Crockett stayed home for eight months. His autobiography is silent about this period. The government had paid him $65.59 for his service, a lot of money for a poor man but not enough to keep him out of debt. While he was home, it seems likely—though we can't say for sure—that Polly got pregnant again.

Then he reenlisted!

Why? He wrote only that "I wanted a small taste of British fighting." Once again, Polly asked him not to go, and once again, he ignored her: "Here again the entreaties of my wife were thrown in the way of my going, but all in vain; for I always had a way of just going ahead, at whatever I had a mind to."

Whatever his reasons, they didn't include protecting hearth and home from Indians this time. The Creek War was over. In March, Jackson had smashed the Red Sticks at Horseshoe Bend. In August, he had made the whole Creek nation pay—including the part that had fought on his side. Here's Jackson biographer Sean Wilentz summing up:

> As his price for defeating the rebellion and settling the civil war among the Creeks, Jackson, acting on the authority of President Madison, imposed a treaty that ceded 23 million acres of the Indians' land to the United States—more than half of the Creeks' total holdings, representing approximately three-fifths of the present-day state of Alabama and one-fifth of Georgia. The forfeited lands included territories held by Creeks who had resisted Red Eagle—many of whom had fought alongside Jackson—as well as territories held by Red Sticks. With this agreement, Jackson believed the Creeks would never again pose a military threat to the

United States. The treaty also completed a land grab that opened immense tracts of exceptionally fertile and long-coveted soil to American speculators and farmers.

The Talladega monument puts it more succinctly. "'Old Hickory' broke the Red Man's power in the Southeast forever," it reads, "permanently claiming this land for a greater nation."

If Crockett was looking for glory this time around, he didn't find it. He rode off to Florida in September 1814 with the idea of helping Jackson confront the British, who had troops there, and the Spanish, who owned the place. But Jackson had occupied Pensacola by the time David's cohort arrived, and the only "taste of British fighting" David got was a glimpse of the enemy's fleet offshore. The rest of his second army stint consisted mainly of going hungry for long periods and observing disturbing incidents of Indian-on-Indian violence. Once a group of Choctaws allied with the Americans killed a couple of Creeks, cut off their heads, and began whacking them with war clubs. After Crockett joined in the game, he wrote, the Choctaws "all gathered round me, and patting me on the shoulder, would call me 'Warrior—warrior.'"

Twice he passed near the ruins of Fort Mims. The more complicated parts of its history were invisible, but David was strongly affected by the tale of a survivor who had seen his parents and siblings "butchered in the most shocking manner." Later he visited the battleground at Talladega, which "looked like a great gourd patch; the sculls of the Indians who were killed still lay scattered all about." Finally he went home.

What he found there remains a mystery.

The anonymous author of *Sketches and Eccentricities* wrote that Polly died while Crockett was still in the army. Crockett himself states firmly that Polly and the children were "well and doing well" when he got back to Tennessee. Taking him at his word, it remains impossible to tell if he's talking about two children or three, because he says nothing about the birth of his daughter, which could have occurred before or after his return. (Some sources place Margaret "Little Polly" Crockett's birth as early as 1812, though I'm with Shackford in doubting this, because David referred to her as "a mere infant" at the time of her mother's death.)

He didn't tell us when Polly died, though it was almost certainly in 1815.

He didn't tell us why she died, either, though that hasn't stopped Crockettologists from speculating. Typhoid, malaria, cholera, malnutrition, and complications from childbirth have been mentioned as possibilities, along with a now-rare illness known as milk sick. A 1926 *Knoxville Journal* article, utterly unsourced, reached the conclusion that "dreary days of waiting through weeks and months for her husband's return, and the dread of the savage Indians and wild animals about their lonely cabin" had fatally undermined Polly's health.

Finally, David neglected to tell us where she is buried, though local tradition, in this case, is too strong to question.

The old neighborhood cemetery sits high on Buncombe Ridge, surrounded by farmland, roughly a mile east of the well Jim Hargrove showed me. A grove of trees—oaks, walnuts, and poplars, said Hargrove, who used to play there as a boy—gives it an isolated feel, as if it were its own separate hilltop. The inscriptions on most of the gravestones have worn off, though some from Hargrove's mother's family, the Masons, are still readable. Polly's six-foot marble marker is modern by contrast. It didn't go up until Disney's "Davy Crockett, Indian Fighter" shamed the state historical commission into action in the 1950s.

"It took me a long time," Hargrove said, to accept that his family cemetery had been renamed for Polly. Now he helped maintain it. Not long before, he had recruited a neighbor to cut up some fallen trees. "Then I called the sheriff's department and they sent me some trustees down there and cleaned it up and helped me put the fence back."

I visited twice. Both times, I was alone. The first time, in the middle of the afternoon, small white butterflies flitted around the graves. The second time, at sunset, yellow light slanted beneath dark clouds and cut through the shade created by the trees. I thought about David standing on this ground after enduring "the hardest trial which ever falls to the lot of man," in which death "entered my humble cottage, and tore from my children an affectionate good mother, and from me a tender and loving wife." I tried to imagine the real feelings behind that elegant, ghosted prose. And I was reminded of the tale of Lightfoot, the Indian who shared his food.

"His son is buried up there in Polly Crockett Cemetery," Hargrove had said.

⊰ 5 ⊱

Go West, Poor Man

Seventy-five miles west of Polly Crockett's grave, I found myself alone at another Crockett site, staring up at a statue of David and marveling at how quickly a life can change.

It was a gray Sunday morning in Lawrenceburg, Tennessee, and I had the town square to myself. Crockett stands on the south end, opposite a Mexican War memorial. Life-sized, bronze, decked out in hunting gear, he cradles a rifle in his left arm and waves a broad-brimmed hat with his right, as if acknowledging a cheering crowd. I saw no sculptor's name on the statue, which went up in 1922, but the pose is instantly recognizable—to the Crockett-obsessed, at least—because it's lifted from a John Gadsby Chapman portrait done in 1834, at the height of David's pre-Alamo fame.

And speaking of fame: If not for Lawrence County, Crockett might never have known any. It was here, as he modestly put it, that he "began to take a rise."

Within months of his arrival, this unschooled thirty-one-year-old—a struggling farmer far more skilled with rifle than plow—launched a political career that would end up carved in stone. There it was on the base of his statue: justice of the peace, member of the first commission of Lawrenceburg, state legislator from

Lawrence and Hickman Counties, and three-time congressman from west Tennessee. And that's not all. Between 1817 and 1821, as the statue's text fails to mention, David Crockett came as close to breaking out of his lifelong poverty as he ever would.

How did this happen?

Well, it started with a second wife who could bring more to a marriage than a few cows and calves.

Left with three children to care for, David sensibly recruited his youngest brother's family to come live with him, but the arrangement did not succeed. His thoughts then turned to one of his Bean's Creek neighbors, Elizabeth Patton, a mother of two who had lost her husband in the Creek War. "She was a good industrious woman, and owned a snug little farm and lived quite comfortable," David wrote, so he began to hint that a merger might be in order. The resulting marriage was advantageous to both—it wasn't easy to be a widow with children on the frontier—but in economic terms, the groom got the better of the bargain. Elizabeth had both land and enough cash (Shackford cites a rumor that it was $800) to make her solidly middle class.

Child-care problem solved, finances bolstered, Crockett soon went looking for greener pastures. The trip almost killed him.

Once again, his destination was Alabama. This time, he and a few neighbors went south to scout land for possible settlement. Somehow they lost their horses. Pursuing the strayed beasts on his own, Crockett walked what he estimated as fifty miles in a single day—unlikely though that number may seem—then fell seriously ill, almost certainly with malaria. Passing Indians found him lying by the side of a trail in such bad shape that, after offering him food he couldn't manage to eat, they "signed to me, that I would die and be buried."

Reading this episode always makes me think: What if David Crockett *had* died then? On the one hand, his story was already remarkable. There was that amazing trek, at age thirteen, that had taken him to Baltimore and almost to sea. There was his push to overcome his father's legacy of failure, educate himself, and make a better life on the frontier. There were love, war, loss, and the will to keep going in the face of it all. On the other hand, Crockett was just one of innumerable poor strivers pushing west without leaving poverty behind, and if he had died in 1816, we would never have heard of him. History is unkind to those it judges downscale failures; as a rule, it makes them invisible.

But David, of course, did not die in Alabama.

One of the Indians helped him to the nearest house, a mile and a half away, carrying his rifle for him. His Tennessee companions found him there and tried to take him home, but he proved too weak to travel, so they left him with a family at another house. He didn't speak for five days, and it was two weeks before he began to mend. But eventually he made it back to Bean's Creek, astonishing Elizabeth, who had been told he was dead and buried.

"I know'd this was a whapper of a lie, as soon as I heard it," he wrote.

The next time he went land hunting, he looked west instead of south, moving his family into territory recently negotiated away from the Chickasaws by Andrew Jackson. For once, he could afford to buy. (Eventually he would own thirteen tracts of land in Lawrence County, totaling more than six hundred acres.) His new neighbors decided that he would make a dandy unofficial magistrate, despite the fact that he "had never read a page in a law book in all my life." When the county was formally established, the Tennessee legislature made the appointment official, naming him a justice of the peace.

Meanwhile, at some point, David Crockett acquired an office in Lawrenceburg.

An office! The King of the Wild Frontier!

I wouldn't have believed it if I hadn't seen it with my own eyes.

The modest hewn-log cabin is a block south of the statue, tucked into a shady lot next to a Cumberland Presbyterian Church. It's a replica, of course, and it's confusingly called DAVID CROCKETT'S HOME on the historical marker out front and DAVID CROCKETT MUSEUM on a green sign by the door. There was no one around to ask about this. But the door was open and a fluorescent light beckoned me inside, where I found a sketch of the original structure. It was titled "David Crockett's Office"; a handwritten note explained that it was "drawn from memory by Lillie Belle McLean Appleton April 29, 1969 at almost 82 years of age."

Looking around, I saw that all three Crocketts—man, legend, and myth—were on display.

An old rifle, a pair of leggings, a cloth shirt, a corduroy vest, and a purselike object labeled "Possible Bag Used to Carry Shooting Gear" hung in a case on one wall. Hand-lettered panels, ambered by shellac, laid out Crockett's life story. Among many framed pictures were one of the birthplace cabin, a portrait of David in formal attire, and a photo of an umbrella-wielding crowd surrounding the Lawrenceburg statue at its 1922 dedication. Black binders held newspaper articles, including one headlined "David Crockett as . . . a Businessman?" A white wooden sign listed all the Tennesseans martyred in San Antonio. It rested on flat cases filled with, among other things, a well-preserved ferret—I could find no explanation for this—and a copy of a 1967 poem by Linwood Polk Comer, the last stanza of which read:

> Oh, Hero of the Alamo!
> Though you left us years ago;
> You still live in memory,
> Down in Lawrenceburg Tennessee!

It was like walking around inside a Crockett time capsule. I didn't want to leave.

I finally tore myself away, but not before one last artifact caught my eye. It was an old program from an outdoor drama performed in nearby David Crockett State Park. Unlike *A Man Called Davy*, its east Tennessee counterpart, this one was an outdoor *musical* drama, and it turned out to be the work of a local high school teacher. Twenty-four hours later, I was sitting in her living room, hearing how she had scripted Crockett's days in Lawrenceburg—aka The Town Walt Disney Forgot.

"It was kind of a joke around here," Dolly Leighton said, laughing. "When Disney did his film, they just sort of drew this line through Lawrenceburg and kept going. They didn't say *anything*." So the place where Crockett began his famous "rise" made its only appearance as a dot on a map illustrating his westward movement through Tennessee.

An energetic woman in jeans and a brown blouse, Leighton looked like someone who could still handle an unruly English class, though she had recently retired from teaching. When I'd reached her on the phone, she'd told me she had a community theater meeting in an hour or so, but sure, come on by. After she answered all my questions and gave me two copies of *The Gentleman from the Cane: A Two-Act Musical Historical Drama*—one a spiral-bound script, the other a DVD from a 2006 performance—I thanked her, mentioning my gratitude that so many people on my Crockett tour seemed willing to help me on short notice. Amused by how naive a New Englander could be, Leighton offered the obvious explanation.

"You're in the South," she said.

How had she gotten into the Crockett drama business? Well, she had directed a lot of theater in addition to teaching English, and when the national bicentennial rolled around in 1976, "a lady in town asked me would I do a pageant." It was the wrong word to use with Leighton—"I picture this thing with little kids walking up over the stage and doing a little thing and walking off"—but still, she'd been staying home with her own children and needed something to stimulate her mind. I'm going to do a *play*, she thought and plunged into Crockett research. Then she did what any dramatist working with historical characters must do: she used her imagination to flesh them out, and she shaped their stories to put a premium on conflict.

Conflict between husband and wife, for example.

Leighton's David is a recognizable figure to anyone who's read much about him: a crack shot and skilled hunter, a friendly man with a good sense of humor, a husband who hates to hang around the house. Her Elizabeth, by contrast, seems more fleshed out than we've ever seen her. Leighton imagined the second Mrs. Crockett as a "large, strong, aggressive" woman who keeps the family going. She's the kind of wife who—after she and David invest in a gristmill, powder mill, and distillery—ends up running the business. But *The Gentleman from the Cane* also gives her an inner life. At the end of Act I, as David reminisces to new friends about his besotted courtship of Polly Finley, a spotlight comes up on Elizabeth, singing a solo lament called "The Shadow Between Us":

> *As soft as a whisper,*
> *As smooth as a sigh,*
> *She slips in between us*
> *And I can't get by.*

"He married Elizabeth out of convenience," Leighton said. "It was basically a marriage of 'Here, you take my kids!'" But what would that have felt like to her?

The playwright had political conflict to work with, too.

She dramatized a nasty fight over where the town of Lawrenceburg should be situated—near Crockett's land or someone else's?
(David lost, not gracefully.) And she included the more humorous
but still telling story, taken from Crockett's autobiography, of how
he had come to stand for his first elective office. It seems that a
certain Captain Matthews, who was seeking the position of colonel in the local militia regiment, asked Crockett to run for major,
in effect becoming Matthews's running mate and lending him his
Indian-fighter rep. But as David soon discovered, Matthews's son
was also running for major. "Why, that low down, ornery tail-end
of a skunk!" he exclaims in *The Gentleman from the Cane*, and he
follows up by deciding to run for colonel himself, instead of for
major, because "if I'm gonna have to run against the whole family
anyway, I may as well run against the head of the mess!" He beat
Matthews handily, and the victory made him "Colonel Crockett"
for the rest of his life.

The next thing Elizabeth knew, the colonel was planning
to run for the state legislature. "No! No! No!" is how Leighton
imagined her beginning the furious domestic argument that
followed:

> CROCKETT: But you and John Wesley can run the mills
> and distillery without me. You practic'ly run
> 'em now anyway!
> ELIZABETH: Sure, we do, 'cause you're already gone half
> the time.
> CROCKETT: Well, *some* of the time, yes!
> ELIZABETH: And I cain't see you spendin' the other half
> as representative up in Murfreesboro settin'
> in the middle of a room full of fancy, beruf-
> fled politicians.

But she had no choice. However strong the real Elizabeth may have been, she was no match for the irresistible force of her husband's restlessness—and she's no match for it in Leighton's play either. "I ain't never gonna be a stayin' home man," David tells her, "and the sooner you face up to it the better." By the end of the fight scene, she's holding David's hand as he sings of destiny, wanderlust, and his need to "follow a distant star."

Crockett won his election in August 1821. The next month, he rode off to a legislative session in Murfreesboro, then the capital of Tennessee. Before long—as Leighton's drama has it—the people who had sent him there were whooping it up over one of the most famous Crockett anecdotes ever. It's a highly visible part of most Crockett-related productions, be they biographies, musicals, or Smithsonian exhibitions.

Shackford told it this way: "Feeling ill at ease and awkward because of his ignorance of legislative procedure, Crockett rose to speak in behalf of some measure before the House." A fellow legislator, rising to oppose David, drew "a titter from some of the members" by referring to him as "the gentleman from the cane." (In other words, a hick: the allusion was to canebrakes, thickets dense with native bamboo that characterized poorer sections of the frontier at the time.) Furious, Crockett confronted the man "with the intention of pummeling an apology from him," but the man claimed he had meant no offense, forcing David to take his revenge more creatively. Back on the House floor, after his condescending colleague had spoken on some other subject, David stood to reply. Pinned to his coarse shirt was a fancy cambric ruffle just like the one affected by his enemy. Seeing it, the legislators "burst into prolonged laughter," driving the embarrassed offender from the chamber.

In one stroke, Crockett had turned an insult into an honorific and cemented his reputation as a backwoods pol not afraid to stand up to the "quality folks."

Or so the story goes.

Because after telling it at great length, as befits the kind of anecdote that seems to perfectly define its subject, Shackford backpedaled a bit. "As far as I know," he wrote, the story was first recorded in the unreliable *Sketches and Eccentricities*.

Translation: It has no solid source at all.

That doesn't mean it's false. The anonymous biographer may well have gotten the story from the horse's mouth. Shackford, seeking to bolster the argument for its veracity, plausibly identified David's foe as a legislator named James C. Mitchell (the *Sketches* author calls him "Mr. M——l") and reported that Crockett twice "used the phrase 'gentleman from the cane'" in his autobiography, "with just the implications that phrase would entail if the story were true." Yet Shackford doesn't have that last part precisely right. David didn't use the word "gentleman" in that context, though he did call himself "the man from the cane" and wrote about how he worked "to rise from a cane-brake to my present station in life." More important, if such a terrific story were true—as opposed to being entirely made up or, more likely, heavily reshaped—why wouldn't David have told it in his autobiography?

Good point or petty quibble, take your pick, but I'm about 175 years late in raising it. The "gentleman from the cane" anecdote is irresistible, and it's not going away. "When I found that story, I thought, 'Ah, there's my title!'" Dolly Leighton said, and she's right. It beautifully evokes the economic and social distances that an ambitious man like David had to cross to take his political rise.

"Mr. Crockett can do anything he sets his mind to," Leighton's Elizabeth says at one point. And what David set his mind to now was a new kind of American politics, one in which a backwoodsman could outsmart, outjoke, outbrag, and generally outcampaign the beruffled nobs who were accustomed to running things in Tennessee.

If winning meant he had to turn himself into a legend—well, he could do that, too.

✹

David Crockett State Park is one of the many Crockett-connected attractions that popped up after Disney Davy went viral. Dedicated in 1959, it sits just west of downtown Lawrenceburg on the banks of Shoal Creek, where the Crocketts first settled when they arrived in the county. Recreational options include camping, fishing, picnicking, swimming, biking, tennis, boating, and taking in shows at the amphitheater where early productions of *The Gentleman from the Cane* were staged. Exploring the park's winding, tree-shaded roads, my first impression was: What a wonderful place! If David accomplished nothing whatsoever beyond causing these thousand acres of woods and water to be set aside in his memory, we should still be grateful.

My second impression was: Sheesh, look at the deer!

White tails flashing, they ducked under a wire fence onto the green hillside facing the David Crockett Elementary School. Heads down, they grazed by the side of the road a few yards from where— as I later learned—Oklahoma-bound Cherokees had come through on the Trail of Tears. No fewer than six of Bambi's relatives eyed me calmly from the woods as I approached the park's visitor center and museum. Clearly, they had no experience of sharpshooting frontiersmen with long rifles—unless you count the outsized painting of Crockett that they could see through the glass if they wandered past the front door.

The museum burned down in 1969, and the rebuilt version doesn't have much in the way of original Crockett artifacts. But like its counterpart at Crockett's birthplace, it works hard to present a complex story in a small space. In the section on David's political career, I gravitated to an inspired wall display titled "A Manual of Dirty Politics or How to Get Elected in Crockett's Time." Packaged as a list of "rules" and drawn from several stages of his career, it added up to a kind of Davy's Greatest Hits album, filled with chart-topping electoral tunes covered again and again in the standard works of Crockettology.

I'd heard them all. By this time, I could pretty much croon them from memory.

"Make your opponent appear to be a rich aristocrat to the backwoodsman voters," one rule read, referring to Crockett's 1823 campaign for the state legislature against the likable-sounding Dr. William Butler. At one point, Butler invited David to his home for dinner. That proved unwise. Taking note of a luxurious carpet on the floor, Crockett informed the voting public that his aristocratic opponent routinely walked on material "finer than any gowns your wife or your daughters, in all their lives, ever *wore*."

"Speak and publish outright lies about your opponent," read another. That was from one of David's congressional races, in which a political foe accused him of drinking and womanizing. Crockett fired back with worse charges, all false. Infuriated, the man showed up at a campaign event with witnesses primed to prove that David was lying—but David preempted him by pleading guilty.

Lie about me, and I'll lie about you right back, was his message. The crowd loved it.

"Steal to buy liquor for the voters" referred to a hilarious tale in which Crockett, lacking the cash to treat some constituents to a round of whiskey, sold a coonskin to pay for it. When the whiskey-seller wasn't looking, David swiped the same skin back and resold it—then repeated the maneuver over and over until everyone's thirst was quenched.

I'll mention just one more, a rule enjoining politicians to "Discredit your opponent's morals." I think of it as "Did you hear the one about Davy Crockett and the farmer's daughter?" and I once heard the University of New Mexico historian Paul Andrew Hutton delight an audience with it at a Western Writers of America conference.

Crockett was running for Congress, Hutton began, against a man named Adam Huntsman, who had lost a leg in the Creek War and sported a wooden one in its place. The two were campaigning together in a county where "there was one wealthy farmer that pulled all the strings," and both stayed at the farmer's house. "As you would imagine, being a wealthy farmer, he had a beautiful young daughter. And she had a bedroom downstairs, and Huntsman and Crockett were upstairs." After Huntsman had gone to bed and started snoring, "Crockett picks up a chair and he goes downstairs to the young beautiful daughter's bedroom and he jiggles the door, calling out 'Honey, it's me, Adam! I'm here! I know you want me!' and she screams bloody murder. And then he takes—he's got that chair, remember—he goes running back upstairs. . . ."

Hutton rapped on the lectern—*thump! thump! thump!*—to imitate a man using a chair to imitate a man with a wooden leg. Then he finished up: "That farmer comes out with his shotgun and says, 'Huntsman, you son of a gun, get out of my house.' . . . Crockett wins his vote, gets the county's vote, goes to Congress. And God bless the American political system."

I knew enough by now to be a bit skeptical of this one. Just for starters, Crockett lost the only election in which he and Huntsman faced each other.

And yet . . .

As I revisited those stories on the wall at the museum, it struck me that they posed a more serious obstacle to Crockettologists than mere fact checking. Think of it as the Legendary Davy Syndrome, and think of me as its most recent victim. What had happened,

I suddenly realized, was that I had started to see all these tales as utterly characteristic of the man I was trying to understand—even the ones I doubted were true!

None of the stories mentioned above shows up in Crockett's autobiography, and they're all problematic in one way or another. The carpet episode, for example, is thinly sourced to begin with, and if you read Shackford's version carefully, you'll notice that he simply made up the "finer than any gowns" quote. (Crockett concluded his tale, the biographer avers, "with some such climax as this.") The coonskin theft is recounted in *Sketches*, whose normally scruple-free author introduces his own anecdote as one "which I do not altogether believe."

"Too good to check!" my newsroom colleagues used to exclaim gleefully when encountering dubious but wildly entertaining pieces of "news." But we *had* to check the darn things if we wanted to get them into the paper. I bring this up not to congratulate us on our professional skepticism—despite our best efforts, or sometimes for lack of them, plenty of unchecked whoppers got through—but to underline the deeply rooted human bias toward storytelling and entertainment over complex, eat-your-broccoli forms of information.

Crockett understood that instinctively.

In his autobiography, he described his first attempt at speaking to a political crowd, in which he started out tongue-tied but eventually found a way forward:

> At last I told them I was like a fellow I had heard of not long before. He was beating on the head of an empty barrel near the road-side, when a traveler, who was passing along, asked him what he was doing that for? The fellow replied, that there was some cider in that barrel a few days before, and he was trying to see if there was any then, but if there was he couldn't get at it. I told them that there had been

a little bit of a speech in me a while ago, but I believed I couldn't get it out. They all roared out in a mighty laugh, and I told some other anecdotes, equally amusing to them, and believing I had them in a first-rate way, I quit and got down, thanking the people for their attention.

Could Ronald Reagan have done it better? And we haven't even gotten to the part where David persuaded his listeners to bail on the speeches and join him for drinks.

Life on the frontier was hard. Humor was a balm. And there's little doubt that Crockett's natural ability to connect with voters through laughter—however exaggerated or invented individual examples of it may be—fueled his political rise. Richard Boyd Hauck, the author of a thoughtful 1982 study of David's life and legend, put it this way: "Crockett knew what folks liked to talk and joke about, and he understood perfectly how their humor offset the whole range of afflictions which weighed upon their lives. His audience included people who felt threatened by the complexities of authoritative or educated language and by official deceptions or maneuverings; they loved his humor because it deflated politics and politicians, law and lawyers, power and the powerful."

But let's put the political narrative aside for now. Because the David Crockett State Park museum has another dramatic story to tell.

✪

EXTREME DANGER KEEP OFF WATER WHEEL WORKS reads a bright-red-and-white sign near an old mill wheel standing against an outside wall. Inside the otherwise nondescript museum building, a few yards down from the political exhibit, visitors can check out the rest of the antique milling apparatus on display and learn about the *economic* rise Crockett took in Lawrence County.

The whole thing may have started, the park's interpretive specialist told me, because Elizabeth Crockett was trying to figure out a way to keep her husband home.

At twenty-nine, Rachel Lee radiated a kind of no-nonsense competence that made me think she could have *been* Elizabeth Crockett if she'd been born a couple of centuries before. She'd grown up in Lawrenceburg, taken a seasonal job at the museum, studied up on David, done a stint at a French and Indian War site in east Tennessee, then come home to continue her career as a ranger. The museum was closed for the season when I showed up, but Lee and a colleague had made time at the end of a long workday to give me a tour. As she hit the lights and switched on a video monitor that stood in front of the milling exhibit, a ghostly chorus began to echo through the hallways:

"Davy, *Davy* Crockett . . .

"Davy, *Davy* Crockett . . .

"Davy, *Davy* Crockett . . ."

I didn't recognize the performers, but whoever they were, they didn't shut up until Lee hit the play button and the saga of the Crockett family's business ventures began.

The video, milling machinery, and wall texts, along with Lee's informative commentary, offered a rich version of a story that Crockett told in two paragraphs. Whether or not Elizabeth was the instigator, she and David sank more than $3,000—much of it borrowed—into constructing three facilities essential to frontier communities: a powder mill, a gristmill, and a distillery. The mill complex was on Shoal Creek, a couple of stones' throws from the museum, near a spot now designated on park maps as Crockett Falls. The wheel would have been made of wood, Lee said, unlike the newer metal one outside. The moving parts would have been lubricated with hog fat. Most of the cornmeal produced would have gone straight to the distillery, because turning it into whiskey was an efficient way to reduce its bulk and get it to market.

I couldn't see the millstones in the museum's display. They were inside a wooden box, Lee explained, designed to keep ground corn "from falling out from the sides." But several stones that the Crockett mills had actually used lay on the ground just outside the front door. They included a "runner stone" and a "bedstone" from the gristmill, both in pieces, and a smaller, unbroken stone "that we suspect was part of the powder mill." Discovered in Shoal Creek five years earlier, they had been exposed when the water had started to wash away the sediment on top of them. Lee was working on getting the stones out and "all the archaeological stuff I had to deal with doing that" when the unbroken one disappeared. Someone had backed up a truck and stolen David Crockett's powder stone.

She could laugh about it now, and she did.

"I think they probably took it to be a planter or a mailbox holder," she said. She wrote an article for a local paper "about how bad it was to lose a piece of history" and the day it was published, the missing stone turned up in the parking area of a city park. Meanwhile, she borrowed a backhoe operator from the county road department and got the rest of the stones out of the creek in a big hurry. Since then, she said, she'd had to fight off attempts to have them moved to the Tennessee State Museum in Nashville or even to San Antonio.

So far, she had won.

Which is as it should be. After all, Lawrence County is the place where the Crockett mills stood. It's the place where "Mrs. Crockett did most of the milling," according to a much later newspaper interview with the "venerable William Simonton," who reported seeing Elizabeth in action when he was a boy. (Do I buy this? Yes. It seems totally in character for David to shun boring work.) And

Lawrence County is also the place from which Crockett set out in September 1821 to take his newly won seat in the legislature—only to hasten home, later that month, when he got some devastating, life-changing news.

The Crocketts' mills had been washed away in a flood, and with them David's hopes for a permanent rise from dirt farmer to frontier industrialist. The fact that the exact same thing had happened to his father did not console him.

The disaster, he wrote, "made a complete mash of me."

Elizabeth bucked him up. "Just pay up, as long as you have a bit's worth in the world," she told him, addressing the question of their crushing debts, "and then every body will be satisfied, and we will scuffle for more." He took her advice, for which he was grateful, but he wasn't prepared to keep scuffling in Lawrence County.

It was time to head west once again.

✴

I had floods on the brain as I drove out of David Crockett State Park. After holding off most of the day, the clouds had opened up. The rain reminded me of what Lee had said about how fast Shoal Creek had risen just a couple of weeks before. "Fifteen minutes later, the boat dock was under water. It happened like *that*," she told me—though the 2010 flood was nothing compared to the one in 1998 that had taken out the covered bridge above Crockett Falls.

Back on high ground, I clicked on the radio. A man and a woman were talking about the "thousand-year rain event"—as the Army Corps of Engineers called it—that had devastated Nashville on May 1 and 2, 2010, the same days the creeks rose in Lawrence County.

WOMAN: For two straight days the skies opened up and
poured nearly twenty inches of rain.

MAN: Runoff water inundated homes far away from
the nearest streams. School buildings literally
floated away. And still the deluge continued.

WOMAN: The Nashville floods wreaked havoc on hundreds of thousands of lives; caused an estimated
one and a half billion dollars in damage; and
most tragically, dozens of people lost their lives.

MAN: The floods threatened to silence Music City.
But we tonight here at the Ryman Auditorium
are not going to let that happen, are we?

Loud cheering followed.

I had stumbled onto the live broadcast of a Nashville benefit for
flood victims. The actor James Denton (of *Desperate Housewives*)
and actress Kimberly Williams-Paisley were cohosting. Dierks Bent-
ley, Brad Paisley, Martina McBride, and numerous other country
stars had signed on to entertain. The opening lines of McBride's
"Anyway" seemed particularly apt:

> *You can spend your whole life building*
> *Somethin' from nothin'*
> *One storm can come and blow it all away.*

A hundred and fifty miles to the northwest, the Obion River
country—where the town of Rutherford bills itself as "The Last
Home of Davy Crockett"—had been hit hard by flooding as well.
Cruising the area's elevated highways, I gazed down at what looked
more like vast, muddy lakes than the drowned fields they really
were. After crossing the Rutherford Fork of the Obion on Route
105, I parked and walked back out on the bridge to look at the

fast-flowing river. I was so busy noticing how high it still was that I almost stepped on the skeletal remains of a dozen fish, stranded there when the water receded.

There were no bridges, of course, when Crockett showed up to explore west Tennessee—but there was plenty of water, as his account makes clear.

He made the trek from Lawrenceburg accompanied by his oldest son, fourteen-year-old John Wesley, and a youth named Abram Henry. They found a satisfactory home site just east of the river and set off to visit their nearest neighbors, who were seven miles away. The Obion "had overflowed all the bottoms and low country near it," Crockett wrote, and the water—freezing cold, because it was now winter—"would sometimes be up to our necks." John Wesley often had to swim "even where myself and the young man could wade," and the boy arrived at the neighbor's house "shaking like he had the worst sort of an ague."

But it wasn't only floods that made this the wildest frontier David Crockett had ever seen.

Ten years earlier, an exceptionally violent series of earthquakes had reshaped the landscape of his new home. Named for a town just across the Mississippi River, the New Madrid quakes began on December 16, 1811, and recurred repeatedly over the next two months, affecting ten times the area that would be hit by San Francisco's Big One in 1906. One eyewitness, Eliza Bryan, described the shock and thunderous noise of the first earthquake as being followed by "a complete saturation of the atmosphere with sulphurous vapor causing total darkness." People ran about aimlessly, not knowing where to go, as the earth was "torn to pieces." Their screams blended with "the cries of the fowls and the beasts of every species; the cracking of trees falling, and the roaring of the Mississippi," which, for a few minutes at least, ran backward. Sand, hot water, and "a substance somewhat resembling coal" spewed forth from deep fissures, some of which remained open while others immediately closed.

That was the bad news.

The good news was that by 1821, the New Madrid earthquakes had turned the northwest corner of Tennessee into a hunter's paradise. Massive tangles of downed trees combined with a decade's growth of underbrush to create impenetrable thickets that were fabulous habitats for, among other creatures, the American black bear. Judging from the space Crockett's autobiography devotes to bear hunting—which he was extremely good at and which obviously delighted him—a casual reader might be forgiven for thinking he did nothing else for years.

Once again, he had Andrew Jackson and the Chickasaws to thank for the chance to make his move. In 1818, Jackson had persuaded the tribe to sell west Tennessee and part of Kentucky for $300,000, not counting all the bribes it took to cement the deal.

David's book leaves the impression that he started entirely from scratch when he left Lawrence County. That was not quite the case. It's true that he sold his holdings there to pay debts, but once again, being married to Elizabeth gave him a leg up. Her father, a Revolutionary War veteran from North Carolina, held a warrant that entitled him to a thousand acres of land in west Tennessee, some of which ended up in David's hands after the mill disaster.

Still, he never again approached the economic status he had achieved before the flood and seemed financially underwater most of the time. "What Crockett needed to do," as William Davis wrote in *Three Roads to the Alamo*, was to "stay put, work his farm, and try somehow to put his personal affairs in order."

Didn't happen.

Instead—after he'd put up a cabin, planted some corn, trekked back to Lawrenceburg, and moved his family west—he determined to continue his political rise.

David's version of his decision to get back into politics is, to my mind, a little suspect. He wrote that the notion of his running for the legislature again came up while he was drinking with acquaintances in the town of Jackson, where he'd gone in February 1823 to sell some skins and buy a few necessities. He told his companions he couldn't possibly do it, but the next thing he knew, the local paper had announced his candidacy. Someone appeared to be having a joke at his expense, and that annoyed him enough that he decided to go ahead and run. Maybe I've lived in Washington too long, but this feels like the sort of "I'm not like all those other politicians" camouflage that's often used to hide deep-rooted ambition.

Be that as it may, Crockett went on to win his first west Tennessee election. That was the one in which he faced Dr. Butler, the man with the fancy rug, and yet another great story comes with it. Encountering his opponent at a public meeting, David couldn't resist spelling out exactly why Butler was bound to lose:

> I told him that when I set out electioneering, I would go
> prepared to put every man on as good footing when I left
> him as I found him on. I would therefore have me a large
> buckskin hunting-shirt made, with a couple of pockets
> holding about a peck each; and that in one I would carry
> a great big twist of tobacco, and in the other my bottle of
> liquor; for I knowed when I met a man and offered him a
> dram, he would throw out his quid of tobacco to take one,
> and after he had taken his horn, I would out with my twist
> and give him another chaw. And in this way he would not
> be worse off than when I found him.

This story is a red flag for fact-checking Crockettologists, because it's so often repeated as the literal truth. That hunting shirt never existed, they say—David was telling a tall tale!

But it's totally in character all the same.

When I pulled up in front of the David Crockett Cabin Museum in Rutherford, I found Joe Bone, the museum's volunteer curator, waiting for me on the porch. Five minutes later, the subject of old-time string music came up, and Bone popped a CD into an old boom box that sat on a desk inside. He and some friends had recorded "kind of a bluegrass version of 'Lorena,'" he told me. "Are you familiar with 'Lorena'?"

Then he pulled out a harmonica and started playing along with himself.

Thus began a morning filled with musical education. Before it was over, I'd been treated to Bone's rendition of "Go Ahead, a March Dedicated to Colonel Crockett," a catchy tune that dates back at least to 1835, and I'd shelled out ten bucks for a CD of Crockett-themed songs by Riders in the Sky. "You probably *need* that," Bone told me, and he was right: at the time, I did not yet own a single recording of anyone singing all twenty verses of "The Ballad of Davy Crockett." Best of all, I'd learned a fabulous new word for people who play banjos, guitars, and mandolins. All the musicians on that recording of "Lorena," Bone said, were members of an organization called the Jackson Area Plectral Society.

Plectra-what?

"That's a ten-dollar word for pickers," he explained.

But I'm getting off track here. Joe Bone taught me a lot about David Crockett in west Tennessee, too.

A compactly built man with a green-checkered shirt and a few wisps of white beard, Bone had been the unofficial keeper of Rutherford's Crockett flame for more than fifteen years. When I met him, two days before his seventy-seventh birthday, he said he was more than ready to turn the job over to a younger volunteer—he just hadn't found one yet.

The museum itself kept David's flame alive in a couple of ways.

The building preserved the story of the real man by letting visitors see what one of his cabins looked like. A two-story replica of the Crocketts' second log house in the area, it seems modest in size today, but Bone said it would have been large for David and Elizabeth's time. Inside the cabin, meanwhile, a patchwork of facts, legends, random antiques, amateur artworks, and pop-culture ephemera offered an expanded version of the Crockett saga. Like the Lawrenceburg office, the place had a bit of a time-capsule feel. It seemed far less selective, though, more like an attic crammed with all the stuff your eccentric Aunt Martha couldn't bear to take to the dump.

But really, I thought, as Bone showed me around, what would you want to get rid of?

Surely not the furry cap with the cute little raccoon face that Fess Parker wore as grand marshal of Rutherford's annual Davy Crockett Days parade in 1992. ("We didn't think he would come, you know? But we found out all we had to do was call and ask him.") Or the photograph of the severe-looking old woman who turned out to be David's youngest daughter, Matilda. (Bone's grandmother was a neighbor of hers.) Or the copy of *Davy Crocketts Eventyr ved Obion*, one of a series of Danish children's books on Crockett, whose cover shows him thigh-deep in an ice-covered river. (A Danish boy named Gert Petersen got hooked on the series in 1956; astonished to discover that its hero was a real person, he'd been pursuing the historical Crockett to places like Rutherford ever since.) Or the painting of the tree-shrouded cabin, done by a local art teacher, with the smiling frontiersman hidden in the branches. ("Can you find Davy Crockett in the picture?" Bone asked. It took me a while.) How about the old wooden storage chest in the corner, the one with the handwritten label that says, "This chest is from the Alamo, donated by the late Mr. J. A. Hadley"? Chances are that the generous Mr. H. got sold a bill of goods here—but who would want to take the chance and throw it out?

If it were up to me, I thought, I'd keep everything, even the squat, half-finished log sculpture of Davy that stands under the stuffed goose. And I'd certainly keep the portrait of the silver-haired priest from Fall River, Massachusetts, though I'm going to wait a few chapters to explain what *he* was doing on the wall of the Crockett Cabin Museum.

"Now, if you don't mind riding in my truck . . ."

Bone interrupted my meditations and herded me out the door. The museum's brochure listed three Crockett cabin sites within a few miles of where we stood, and he wanted to make sure I didn't miss any of them.

We headed east through the block-long strip of stores that constitutes downtown Rutherford, and I asked him what had been happening in the Last Home of Davy Crockett lately. "Well, the local industry folded up," he said. Then he amended his statement: "It didn't fold, they closed up, and all the manufacturing was overseas. And then last year they were bought out by some investors group and closed up completely."

The Kellwood Company had operated out of a big brick plant just across North Trenton Street from the museum. "They made clothing originally for Sears Roebuck. Later on they started making it for Levi's, London Fog, L.L.Bean, Lands' End—a lot of different people," Bone said. "I was there for thirty-eight years; my wife was there for forty." Both had been lucky enough to retire before the plant shut down, but Joe's son from his first marriage had not. "I think he got twenty-six years before they closed. He was a receiving supervisor, but right now he's working for another company as a forklift operator on the third shift, so that's not good. But it's a *job*."

We were out of downtown by now, driving through farm country east of the Obion. Spring greens mixed with the browns of last fall's harvest. Two miles northeast of the museum, we turned onto a dead-end road and pulled up by a hand-carved sign that read FIRST CABIN SITE OF DAVY CROCKETT. The farmer who used to work the fields beyond the sign, Bone said, had once showed him traces of the spring, now dried up, that had most likely caused David to settle here. I tried to picture the land as it would have looked in 1822: heavily forested, except for the patch David had cleared to plant his corn, with a creek behind it flowing toward the river. On one corner of the sign—which had been donated by a Crockett fan from Michigan—Bone had attached an aid to the imagination: an enlargement of an old postcard, circa 1900, that showed a tiny, nearly windowless structure that was the smallest Crockett-related building I'd encountered to date.

The second cabin site, maybe three miles farther east, left even more to the imagination; all I saw was high ground near some tall trees. But in 1934, Bone told me, this had been the scene of a heroic rescue operation. Hearing that the owners of what was believed to be Crockett's old house were about to tear it down, a Rutherford banker named Fred Elrod "went out there and asked them what they were going to do with the logs. And they said, 'We're going to use them to repair this old barn.'" Elrod gave them $25 to buy other materials instead. He and a friend then made a sketch of the floor plan and had the logs moved to the schoolyard next to where the museum now stands. After the replica cabin finally went up in 1955, its promoters proudly announced that it had been built from the salvaged logs.

Unfortunately, that wasn't true.

"Some carnival workers burned a lot of those logs one chilly night, and some others succumbed to termites, I think," Bone explained—though the cabin did include logs from a house David's mother had lived in. Rebecca Hawkins Crockett and other family members had followed David west, and she was living with David's sister and brother-in-law when she died, sometime around 1834.

There was another glitch in the way the rebuilt cabin was marketed, too, though it wasn't anyone's fault. Further research revealed that the cabin was not, in fact, a replica of Crockett's last dwelling in Tennessee, the one from which he had ridden off to Texas. Several years earlier, beset with "a lot of cash flow problems," he had sold out and moved to a third cabin, built on rented land not far away.

Once again, there wasn't much to see there, just a field of brown corn stubble across from a tiny chapel. And once again, Bone brought the landscape to life.

"The place where they had the big going-away party, the big barn dance and all that, was right out here," he said, referring to a frolic the departing Crockett is said to have thrown for himself. I didn't immediately recall where I'd read a description of that party, which was probably just as well: doubt about the sourcing might have spoiled my visions of meat roasting in a barbecue pit, men filling drinking gourds at a liquor barrel, and David entertaining neighbors with tall tales and fiddle tunes.

By now it was lunchtime. We bought thick sandwiches at a store run by the local Mennonite community, and as we worked our way through them, I asked Bone how he'd gotten so involved in preserving the Crockett story. After he stopped laughing, he told me.

One evening, heading home from the Kellwood plant, he'd gone by the cabin "and there was a big Coca-Cola machine sitting on the front porch, all lit up. I said, 'You know, something's not right here,' so I started asking questions." The Rutherford Lions Club was responsible for the museum at the time. It seems that maintenance was required but funds were short, and someone had had a bright idea. "I said, 'Now look, we don't want a Coca-Cola machine on the front porch of the David Crockett Cabin.' So I got a few more people felt like I did and we organized an old-time music concert and dance" that raised $1,800.

The Coke machine went away.

So did the Lions in the end—a town commission took responsibility for the cabin off their hands. Bone retired from the Kellwood Company in 1994, and he's been Rutherford's number one Crockettologist ever since.

Speaking of old-time music: I could have spent the rest of the day listening to Joe Bone talk, and I almost did, but eventually it was time for him to take his leave. He and some Plectral Society friends were playing that evening in Jackson, down at the Old Country Store. Would I like to come? Or how about the following morning, when he'd be performing with a different set of pickers at the Tennessee Welcome Center out on I-55 near Dyersburg? I said I'd see him at one place or the other. As it happened, I made it to both.

In Jackson, a gaggle of string bands had set up on the edge of the Country Store parking lot, where the Red Cross was taking donations for flood relief. I found Bone sitting inside a circle of musicians—there were two fiddles, two guitars, a string bass, a mandolin, and a hammered dulcimer—blowing intently on one of the seven harmonicas he carried on his belt. At the Welcome Center, I got to hear him join in the harmonies on "I'll Fly Away," "You Win Again," and a favorite of mine, "Remember Me," which I knew from the singing of Tim and Mollie O'Brien. Joe and his wife, Sue, had brought along a small Crockett display for the tourists as well. It featured a Davy Crockett Days banner, a snapshot of Fess Parker signing autographs, and the painting of the cabin that I'd already seen, the one with the ghostly green face hidden in the trees.

I found Davy right away this time. And I'm pleased to say that there was no trace of a Coke machine on his porch.

The I-55 Welcome Center sits on a bluff above the Mississippi River flood plain, and, driving west that morning, I had missed the exit. Before I knew it, I was on a bridge crossing the Mississippi, which gave me a chance to contemplate its muddy vastness and implacable force. Flooding seemed to have doubled its size. Uprooted trees swept downstream like twigs. It was impossible to imagine this liquid colossus reversing course, even for a second. And it was equally impossible for me—a man whose experience with river navigation was limited to paddling down the placid Saco in southern Maine—to comprehend the enormity of the risk that Crockett had taken here in the late winter or spring of 1826.

The previous year, he had given up his seat in the legislature to run for Congress but lost. Out of politics, at least for now, he cooked up another entrepreneurial scheme: he would manufacture a large quantity of barrel staves, load them on newly constructed flatboats, and float them down the Mississippi for sale in New Orleans. Hiring some men to help him, he got started in the fall of 1825—but, being David, he soon got distracted.

There were simply too many bears in the woods.

The full story of that year's hunting takes Crockett twenty pages of autobiography to tell. We see him respond happily to news that the bears were "extremely fat, and very plenty" around Obion Lake and whistle up his dogs for a hunt. We see bears climb trees and take cover in earthquake cracks trying to escape him, and we see him follow one bear into such a crack, where, after putting a hand on the bear's rump, he "felt for his shoulder, just behind which I intended to stick him." By the time he was ready to cut the region's bears a little slack, he had killed, by his own count, no fewer than 105, though he may have included some brought down by hunting companions.

One hundred five bears!

Before I left Tennessee, I had the chance to ask David's great-great-great-great-granddaughter about this feat.

"Have you ever heard of dog heaven?" Joy Bland asked. "It's an old southern saying: 'They must have been in dog heaven.' And he must have been in dog heaven when he found all that wild stuff to shoot."

Bland, a white-haired woman whose style belied both her name and her grandmotherly appearance, brought a delightful edge to her Crockett talk. She would lower her voice to a whisper, say something provocative, then let loose a laugh that began as a kind of astonished gasp. We met at the public library in Paris, Tennessee, a quarter mile from where her great-great-great-grandfather, David and Polly's son John Wesley, rests in the town cemetery. Asked about the Direct Descendants and Kin of David Crockett, the family organization she helped launch in the 1980s, Bland joked about the tug-of-war between Tennesseans and Texans for bragging rights to the Hero of the Alamo. "Texans are—Texans," she said, as if no further description of Lone Star exceptionalism were required. "I tell my cousins that he just came to Texas to die." Later, she mentioned that she had a large supply of "David Crockett 1810" posters—clones of the one I'd seen that made her ancestor look like Elvis—stashed under her bed. The Hollywood filmmaker and Crockett obsessive David Zucker had shipped them to her long before, she said, as part of a promotion for a movie he never quite got made.

Then, in a whisper: *"I'm trying to get rid of them."*

Throughout the conversation, Bland tossed out ideas about the kind of man she thought the real David Crockett was. They added up to a warts-and-all portrait all the more persuasive for its informality.

A few excerpts:

"He was something else. But he was a man, and he was not all myth. . . . He made enemies, but he also fought for good stuff. . . . He had had some really hard knocks—you know, his father loaned him out; that would have left its scar on you, and prepared you for life. . . .

"He was a lot of fun. . . . He liked to be the center of attention. . . . He was quick on his feet. . . . You read about him on political campaigns, how quick he was to come back, how quick he was to *think*. . . .

"He was a wanderer. . . . He wasn't home a lot. . . . There was a family man to him some, too, it was just kind of—as he came through the *house*. . . . Polly needed him really bad that last trip through, and I'm just sorry he didn't stay. But he didn't. . . .

"He never gave up. . . . He obviously wasn't easily discouraged. With all the things that happened to him, he bounced right back. . . . You know, that would have finished me up, losing everything going down the Mississippi. Wouldn't that have finished *you* up?"

Bland was referring to what happened when Crockett went back to his barrel-stave scheme. He and his hired men loaded thirty thousand staves into two crudely built flatboats and floated them down the Obion to the Mississippi. Next stop, New Orleans! But as David belatedly realized—he may have been a quick thinker, but planning ahead was not his style—no one on board had a clue when it came to piloting flatboats down mighty rivers.

The rest of the story would be comic if it weren't so frightening. Crockett and his crew couldn't even manage to steer their boats to shore. Resigned to running all night, they lashed them together to prevent their getting separated, and David retired to a cabin below. He was just thinking "how much better bear-hunting was on hard land, than floating along on the water" when the boats slammed into "an island where a large raft of drift timber had lodged."

Water flooded into his cabin.

The only way out was through a hole in the side. It was too small. David stuck his arms out and yelled.

His companions yanked him out, naked and "literally skin'd like a rabbit." Thirty thousand barrel staves disappeared down the river. He took refuge in the nearest town, which happened to be Memphis.

And there—could it be that the Goddess of Pigheaded Stubbornness and Dauntless Courage had finally taken notice of David Crockett?—he met a man who fueled his next political rise.

At the corner of Jackson and North Front Streets, on what was the original Memphis waterfront, stands a historical marker dedicated to Marcus Winchester. From it I learned that Winchester had set up first a store, then a post office at this site; that in his role as a land agent, he had been "largely responsible for the early growth of the town"; that he had served as its first mayor; and that he had "persuaded David Crockett to enter national politics."

Well, not quite. As we've seen, Crockett had already run for Congress once. Winchester's contributions were encouraging his nearly drowned new acquaintance to try again and putting up some crucial seed money for David's 1827 campaign.

Crockett needed all the help he could get. He'd been born poor, and after a lifetime of striving, he was a poor man still. But so were a lot of people whose votes he was seeking, and he was smart enough to turn their shared poverty into a campaign theme. Take, for example, the open letter to one of his opponents, the incumbent congressman Adam Alexander, that was published in the *Jackson Gazette* on May 5, 1827. "I envy no man his wealth," Crockett wrote. But when the rights of poor citizens "are threatened by monopolizing institutions, for the advantage and convenience of the wealthy," he refused to "remain a silent and submissive spectator."

The letter went on for a while. Clearly, the candidate had gotten some assistance with grammar and spelling. But in the end, he summed up his platform in four short words.

He was running for Congress, he wrote, as "the poor man's friend."

⚹ 6 ⚹

Crockett Goes Rogue

Back in my elder daughter's Crockett phase, I remember taking the girls to the National Portrait Gallery, where we admired their favorite presidents—the place was littered with paintings of Andy and Abe—and dropped in on Davy, too. The portrait then on display in a small side gallery is one of the best we have of Representative David Crockett of Tennessee. Painted by Chester Harding in 1834, it shows an attractive, sharp-nosed, rosy-cheeked fellow in formal dress who doesn't look as if he ever saw a bear, let alone killed one before he was kindergarten age.

Lizzie showed not the slightest interest in him.

It's not easy for Crockett fans of any age to imagine him in Washington, D.C. We're used to picturing the man outdoors, fighting Indians, wrestling bears, or swinging his long rifle like a Louisville Slugger as Mexican soldiers swarm into the Alamo. People who have Fess Parker's Davy imprinted on their brains do have a Crockett-in-Congress image to hang on to—the one in which Davy gives a fiery speech to save peaceful Indians from being booted off their land. But the Disney version is deeply misleading on at least two counts.

First, of course, neither Crockett's oratory nor anything else stopped Andrew Jackson's Indian Removal bill or kept the Cherokees off the Trail of Tears. Second, and more important, at least when it comes to understanding Crockett: the most dramatic speech the real David ever gave in Congress had nothing to do with white people exploiting Indians.

It was about rich people exploiting the poor.

In January 1829, when Crockett stood on the floor of the House and denounced the public lands policy advocated by his fellow Tennessee Democrats as a "swindling machine" calculated to defraud his constituents, he was speaking to the single issue on which he would stake his political career: keeping impoverished frontier families in western Tennessee from losing their homes.

The legislation under discussion was known as the Tennessee Vacant Land Bill, and it surfaced in many shapes and forms during Crockett's time in Congress. It is a fiendishly complex bit of political and economic history involving squatter's rights, states' rights, North Carolina, Tennessee, the federal government, Revolutionary War veterans, massive speculation in public land, and rampant fraud. After doing my best to wrap my brain around it, I knew I'd need expert help.

Fortunately, that help was just an area code away.

Allen Wiener agreed to meet me at White Flint Mall, not far across the Maryland line from D.C. We found each other in the history section of the mall's chain bookstore—Wiener spotted me flipping through an Alamo book—and settled in to talk Davy over industrial-sized salads at Bertucci's. Given our topic, the surroundings felt surreal: White Flint is a nature-free landscape, sculpted to meet the needs of upscale consumers in cars, that would have been inconceivable to someone accustomed to watching oxcarts navigate the muddy track in front of the Crockett Tavern.

The coauthor of *David Crockett in Congress: The Rise and Fall of the Poor Man's Friend* turned out to be a cheerful, lightly bearded man in his midsixties with roots in Union City, New Jersey. Now retired, Wiener had spent thirty-two years at the Department of Transportation working on international issues, and he told a story about a visitor from Mexico encountering a giant Alamo poster on his office wall. ("We both pretended it wasn't there.") Before I started grilling him on the context of Representative Crockett's inflammatory House speech, I asked the obvious question: How did a DOT bureaucrat who grew up a few miles from Times Square end up as the world's leading expert on the Tennessee Vacant Land Bill?

"Same old story: Fess Parker and Walt Disney," Wiener began. Eleven years old when "Davy Crockett, Indian Fighter" aired, he'd already discovered cowboys, but Davy's sense of humor and anti-authoritarian tendencies immediately struck him as different: "He's crossing swords with Andrew Jackson, and nobody's controlling him. It might have been like an early-fifties teen *rebellion* thing going on there." Wiener had never heard of the Alamo, so he was shocked when friends told him that Davy was doomed. "I said, 'No, that can't be right. Hopalong Cassidy doesn't die, and Gene Autry doesn't die.' I'm not sure it had totally registered on us that he was a real person." He looked up Crockett in the encyclopedia and found a strange-looking portrait of a politician in a suit.

Fast-forward fifty years or so: after slogging his way to the dissertation stage of a political science Ph.D., Wiener had traded grad school for his DOT job, married, and raised a daughter. Maintaining his interest in all things Davy, he'd found himself writing a book on—John, Paul, George, and Ringo. "My mind runs chronologically," he said, explaining how he had gotten started on *The Beatles: A Recording History*; after John Lennon's death, he'd had the idea of "tracing their music and sound, their whole story" through a detailed chronology of every recording they'd ever made. He ended up publishing three editions but doubts he made a profit, "because

I spent so much money on records and CDs." Done with the Fab Four at last, he took a long break from his routine of working till 2:00 A.M. ("I felt like I'd gotten out of jail"), but then, as retirement approached, he realized that he needed a new project.

He had a notion about Elvis, but it didn't work out.

What about a book on Alamo-related songs?

Wiener headed over to the Library of Congress just to "see what they've got."

Around that time, he began to meet other Crockett fans, both through the Internet and on visits to San Antonio. He got to know fellow New Jerseyan and Crockett obsessive Bill Chemerka—the founder of the Alamo Society and publisher-editor of both the *Alamo Journal* and the *Crockett Chronicle*—who asked if he'd like a coauthor on the music book. Sure! And he struck up a friendship with a Florida-based sound engineer and avocational historian named Jim Boylston who had recently taken on a task no academic had managed to get done: collecting and publishing every one of David Crockett's surviving letters. Would Wiener be interested in helping? Hell, yes! For the next year or so, he worked on two books at the same time.

"I'll never do that again," he said, laughing.

Music of the Alamo came out in 2008. The letters project, which became *David Crockett in Congress*, took longer. Boylston and Wiener finished tracking down all the letters they could—Boylston had already done considerable work on it—then set out to annotate them. The annotations morphed into essays on "the major issues Crockett addressed and what the letters actually tell us about them," and when they divvied up topics, Wiener volunteered to take on the land bill. He planned to proceed the same way he always did, lining up the evidence in chronological order and seeing what it added up to.

The better part of a year later, he was still adding.

Hoping to find a shortcut to the explanation I needed, I tossed out the kind of hypothetical question trained professional journalists keep in reserve for situations like this. I know it's complicated, I told Wiener, but suppose you were on a panel and had to explain the whole darn Tennessee land thing in two minutes—what would you say?

Wiener just stared at me.

"My *God*," he said.

The roots of the "swindling machine" that David Crockett would spend his political life fighting went back to the late stages of the Revolutionary War. Six years before David was born, the government of North Carolina—needing more troops and lacking funds to pay them—came up with a bright idea: Why not lure volunteers with the promise of western land? The land in question was in territory that would eventually become Tennessee. Thousands of military "land warrants" later, millions of acres had been given away—and more than half that acreage had been snapped up by speculators for a song.

John Finger minces no words in describing those land grabbers. Tennessee "was a society shaped by aspiring elites, covetous men of vast ambition who saw the acquisition of land as the means of economic and social advancement," the historian wrote in *Tennessee Frontiers*, an eye-opening 2001 book that features a hat-waving Crockett on the cover. "With the Revolution finally won, land speculators circled Tennessee's landscape like vultures, seeking to profit from the end of British control." It was a cinch to persuade impecunious veterans—especially those with no desire to move west—to sell their warrants "for a fraction of their value," and it was perfectly legal. Less savory maneuvers by speculators included "bribery, forgery and enrolling nonveterans for bounties."

Americans have a pleasant vision of their frontier past in which hardy pioneers surge west and stake claims to free government land. Is this a myth? Not totally—but the free land part didn't come along until Congress passed the Homestead Act in 1862, by which time the frontier had moved well past Tennessee and Crockett had been dead for twenty-six years. In the meantime, it was the hardy pioneers with cash and political connections who prospered.

Take the North Carolina politician and land jobber William Blount, "whose position on a soldiers claims committee," Finger wrote, "offered unrivaled opportunity for contact with warrant holders." Blount's empire building went well beyond scooping up military warrants and is too complex to detail here. But consider the glimpse Finger offers of this well-connected speculator in 1790, the year North Carolina ceded its western lands to the federal government, making Washington responsible for those warrants. The newly ceded territory needed a governor. Blount got himself appointed. And "with typical candor he rejoiced because the office had 'great Importance to our Western Speculations.'"

More than three decades later, Crockett's constituents lived in fear of what Blount-like men wielding land warrants could do to them.

Like David, most had moved west without the resources to purchase their farms. Many had settled on government land not yet claimed by holders of North Carolina warrants. Those squatters, as they were known, cleared fields, built homes, and hoped for the best. Maybe they could save enough to buy the land they'd improved. Maybe no one with a warrant would ever force them to leave.

They could never be sure, though.

You might think that, forty years after the Revolution, the

government's obligations to veterans would have been taken care of. But no: those North Carolina warrants had a miraculous way of proliferating. Old warrants, whether genuine or forged, could be used to oust not only squatters but the holders of more recently issued warrants. And in a bizarre legal twist, a single warrant could be used over and over again. As Wiener and Boylston put it, if a warrant holder didn't like the land he'd obtained in east Tennessee, he "could buy his warrant back from the state for a mere 12½ cents per acre" and use it to acquire better land farther west—whether or not that land was occupied by squatters.

"Who gave a crap about these poor farmers?" Wiener asked rhetorically.

Well, David Crockett did.

He knew about being landless. Yes, he had benefited from Elizabeth's family's warrants, but he hadn't stayed well off for long, and he retained the poor man's chip he carried on his shoulder. There was no question whose side he would take in this fight.

But there was no guarantee he would be remembered for it either.

Even as he plunged into the land battle, his carefully cultivated backwoodsman persona had started to define him. Today's Crockett fans may know the "gentleman from the cane" story, but they are unlikely to be aware of anything else that happened while he was in the Tennessee legislature. Yet his record there foreshadows two important arguments that Wiener and Boylston made about his later career: first, that the historical David's image as a clueless, easily manipulated legislator is greatly exaggerated, and second, that being "the poor man's friend" was much more than just a slogan for him.

To take just one example: Less than two weeks into his first term in Murfreesboro, Crockett was already working to eliminate an egregious aspect of the warrant system that hurt the people who'd elected him. That was the provision under which warrant holders could split their claimed acreage into multiple parcels, allowing them to acquire only the best land while leaving a patchwork of lesser parcels unclaimed. The Tennessee House and Senate would eventually make Crockett's position law. In *Three Roads to the Alamo*, William C. Davis drew the obvious conclusion: "However much the pose of bumpkin suited his purpose when seeking votes from those who were truly ignorant of the forms of governing—and suspicious of those who knew too much—he revealed a ready grasp of parliamentary procedure."

Crockett, however, had a bigger hurdle to face than procedural nitty-gritty.

Most of his new colleagues, including the Andrew Jackson protégé and future president James K. Polk, were upscale types from middle and east Tennessee, and they simply didn't share his concern for western squatters. Still, for the time being, he accepted Polk's and the legislature's strategy on Tennessee's vacant land. The idea was to get Congress to cede the land to the state, which would then sell it and use the profits to fund schools. Crockett's hope, apparently, was that Tennessee would set the price low enough to give his constituents a shot at purchasing their farms.

Polk was elected to Congress in 1825, and two years later Crockett followed him to what was then known as Washington City. But David almost didn't live to take his place in the House. He fell ill as he traveled east, most likely with a recurrence of the malaria he had contracted in Alabama; had to spend a month recuperating with Elizabeth's family near Asheville; and was still sick when he finally reached the capital in November 1827. What passed for medical science in those days didn't help: a doctor "took two quarts of Blood from me at one time," he wrote a friend, adding that "I am much reduced in flesh and have lost all my Red Rosy Cheeks that I have carryed So many years."

Twice he thought he was dying, but each time he pulled through, using up two more of what seemed like an infinite supply of lives. Polk, meanwhile, had introduced his version of the Tennessee land bill. When H.R. 27 came up for debate in the spring of 1828, Crockett quite naturally backed the leader of his state's congressional delegation.

He had some issues with Polk's bill, but he was being a good Tennessee soldier.

For now.

"He not only goes along with Polk's bill, he speaks in favor of it. That's *very* important! There's not any controversy among the Tennessee delegation—they all backed it, and it lost. It lost big-time!"

Wiener was talking fast now, doing his best to oblige my absurd request for a quickie summary. I appreciated the effort, but the need for context soon derailed it.

So why did Polk's bill lose?

"There's a paragraph in our book somewhere—it's probably in that first land chapter—saying that Crockett and Polk had walked into a national controversy on land." Trying to grasp the controversy's nuances, Wiener spent hours on the phone with the University of Tennessee historian Daniel Feller, author of *The Public Lands in Jacksonian Politics*. But we're in our two-minute drill here, so let's just say sectional differences shaped attitudes toward the issue. One difference: easterners didn't like the idea of giving vast tracts of federally owned land to western states for free, something for which Polk's bill would appear to set a precedent—and never mind the fact that those North Carolina warrants made Tennessee such a special case that Feller had to leave it out of his book.

Time to move on. What happens next?

"Crockett now sees that that is not going to work. So he goes to Polk—and this is important; he *doesn't* go off on his own, he's *trying* to work with them." He goes to Polk and the rest of the Tennessee delegation and asks them to try a new approach. Why bother ceding the federal land to the state if that notion upsets enough people to keep a bill from passing? Let's eliminate the middleman and turn over some acreage straight to those hardy pioneers who've already camped out on it!

And how do Polk and the others respond?

"They stonewall him. They won't even listen to him. Screw you, you know, *we'll* tell you what to do about this." When the next session of Congress begins, they start trying to pass the same old Polk bill again.

But then Crockett . . . amends it?

"Technically it's an amendment. But the amendment says: Strike out everything and put this in. It's really a whole new bill." And when David Crockett rises to speak on its behalf, he makes his views—which will be recorded in the *Register of Debates in Congress*—extremely clear.

Yes, the Tennessee legislature wants its representatives to follow Polk's lead, but his own constituents feel differently, and his loyalty is to those "hardy sons of the soil; men who had entered the country when it lay in cane, and opened in the wilderness a home for their wives and children." No, he doesn't think it fair that the state might sell land from under them and use the money to build colleges: "The children of my people never saw the inside of a college in their lives, and are never likely to do so." By the way, cranking out land warrants in the names of long-dead Revolutionary War vets isn't fair either; it is "unjust and oppressive." What's more, "if a swindling machine is to be set up" to dispossess the people who sent him to Congress, "it shall never be said that I sat by in silence, and refused, however humbly, to advocate their cause."

Extra! Extra!

David Crockett goes rogue!

Stay tuned for furious colleagues' reactions. But first, a crucial point that Wiener credits Feller with explaining to him: Crockett is not just asking the federal government to give squatter families title to the land they've actually been working. He is asking that each of them be granted 160 acres—far more than they need to grow their own crops.

What's *that* about?

"These people all wanted to be speculators themselves! The speculators were the ones making the *money* off the land. Land was the key to wealth. So yeah, you wanted your little farm, but you wanted three times as much so that you could rent it, sell it, or whatever—*this* was the way you made money. So he's making them speculators!"

Every man a speculator: it sounds a little too Wall Street–ish, at least to modern ears. But there are high-minded ways to think about Crockett's amendment, too. He's promoting Jeffersonian democracy, a political system in which free men with small farms are what he calls "the bone and sinew of the land." And he's trying to level the American playing field. "Crockett believed that the poor could not, on their own, elevate themselves, regardless of how hard they worked and that the government owed them a leg up" is the way Boylston and Wiener put it.

Fair enough?

James K. Polk and the rest of the Tennesseans don't think so. Sure, they've got policy differences with Crockett—it's true, they really *don't* give a crap about those poor farmers—but that's the least of their beef with him.

"It's about control. Polk wants to control his delegation. Crockett is a pain in the ass—he's an embarrassment!" Wiener said. That's especially true in January 1829, because Andrew Jackson's supporters have finally seen their man elected president after he was, from their point of view, "screwed out of the election of 1824" by a "corrupt bargain" between John Quincy Adams and Henry Clay. Tennessee Democrats know that the Adams and Clay backers in Washington's political establishment will be gunning for Old Hickory. "The last thing they need is a guy from his own state going up against him." Worse, to judge from the reaction of other House members on the floor, Crockett may be about to win on the land issue: "He has reason to believe that he has sufficient support and he can get this thing through."

So what can Polk & Co. do?

Well, they can move that consideration of Crockett's amendment be postponed a week or so, on the grounds—according to the *Register of Debates*—that it has so muddied up the land question that "some might inadvertently give a vote which they would afterward regret." They can spend that week shoring up support for their side of the argument. And they can watch Crockett's amendment soundly defeated when a vote is finally taken.

Then they can start trying to take him down.

Two days after the vote, Polk dictates an angry letter about Crockett's off-the-reservation behavior and posts it to some of his Tennessee allies. Not intended for publication, it's the opening shot of what will become a six-year anti-Crockett vendetta by the Jacksonians. Shackford found a copy in the Library of Congress, and Wiener and Boylston included the letter in their book.

"Rely upon it he can be and has been opperated on by our enemies," Polk wrote. "We cant trust him an inch."

Was Polk right? Had Crockett made himself the unwitting tool of the anti-Jacksonians? Should we see him as a courageous, independent figure who knew what he was doing or a naive country boy seduced by fast-talking Washington City pols? The question has been debated for 180 years, but a consensus has not been reached.

Let's take the Davy Was Duped theory first. It comes with plenty of evidence.

Crockett ran for Congress as a Jackson man. "I am opposed to this man from the Yankee states called John Q. Adams; I am opposed to the conduct of the Kentucky orator, H. Clay," he proclaimed, while trumpeting his Creek War service under "the immortal Old Hickory." Oddly, however, one of the first things David did after winning the election was to call on Henry Clay's son-in-law James Erwin in Nashville and ask for an introduction to Jackson's archenemy. Erwin shot off a letter warning Clay what he was in for—but he also explained why cultivating Crockett might be a good idea.

The downside: "He is not only illiterate but he is rough & uncouth, talks much & loudly, and is by far, more in his proper place, when hunting a Bear, in a Cane Break, than he will be in the Capital," Erwin wrote. The upside: "He is independent and fearless & has a popularity at home that is unaccountable," which makes him "the only man that I now know in Tennessee that Could openly oppose Genl Jackson in his District & be elected to Congress."

In Washington, Crockett took a room at Mrs. Ball's Boarding House on Pennsylvania Avenue, where a number of other congressmen resided. The most important connection he would form there was with Representative Thomas Chilton of Kentucky, a fervent anti-Jacksonian whom Crockett would later enlist to help write his autobiography.

David also befriended Joseph Gales and William Seaton, the publishers of an anti-Jackson newspaper called the *National Intelligencer* and of the *Register of Debates in Congress*. (The *Register* was not a word-for-word account of congressional proceedings, like the *Congressional Record*; it summarized "leading debates and incidents" between 1824 and 1837.) Polk believed that Gales was one of several anti-Jacksonians who helped Crockett by "dressing up and reporting speeches for him, which he never delivered as reported." That the undereducated David got speechwriting help from somewhere is irrefutable, as a quick look at his private correspondence confirms.

Viewing Crockett as a dupe suggests answers to some otherwise problematic questions. Couldn't David see how absolutely furious the public dissing of his Tennessee colleagues would make them? Couldn't he imagine how foolish he would look offering to vote for absolutely anything any House member desired if that member would only vote for his land bill? Well no, he couldn't. He was just a poor, naive bear hunter who'd been led astray.

William Davis, whose portrait of Crockett in *Three Roads to the Alamo* is generally sympathetic, offers this gentle version of the Davy Was Duped theory:

> It is not hard to fathom what was happening to Crockett. He never felt truly accepted as a member of his own delegation. From the moment of his departure for the first session of the House, members of the opposition had been at least as friendly as his own party, and perhaps more so. . . . Now when he simply tried to do what he knew to be right, his colleagues all abandoned him, and suddenly the only friends he seemed to have were men like Gales. . . . A man of the world might have seen their motives as questionable, but a simple man of the canebrakes, a man who said and meant what he thought and felt, and who took others likewise at their word, saw only open hands of friendship from men whose agreement with his amendment only proved that he was right to go ahead.

Shackford makes the same point more harshly, writing that "the complete blindness of this simple, wayfaring man to the machinations of the Thieves of Jericho is amazing."

There's more. Some of the strongest arguments for the Davy Was Duped theory come from later in his career, in particular from the 1834 Crockett book tour sponsored by his anti-Jackson allies. But right now we need to give equal time to the Davy Was No Fool alternative.

Allen Wiener summed it up nicely. "I don't buy the whole line of Crockett being naive," he told me. "I think it was symbiotic." Jackson's foes may have been using him, but he was using them, too. "Crockett may have been naive to think that he could survive in politics while remaining so fiercely independent," Boylston and Wiener concede, but that didn't mean he was the total doofus he was made out to be. His reputation as a political naif was "at least partly the result of his disaffected Tennessee colleagues repeatedly spreading that image of him in the press in order to tarnish him at home."

Prompted by Wiener's skepticism, I started to generate Davy Was No Fool arguments on my own.

Sure, Crockett ran for Congress as a Jackson man in 1827. Why wouldn't he? The Hero of New Orleans—despite his own status as a member of Tennessee's plantation-owning elite—had become the living symbol of the expansion of American democracy, a game-changing trend that had been eliminating property requirements for voting and expanding the political influence of common men like Crockett. That didn't mean David flip-flopped when he got to Washington. He had sometimes voted against Jackson's supporters in the Tennessee legislature, and one time he had voted against Jackson himself in a Senate election.

Independent guy, that Crockett!

And remember, Old Hickory hadn't yet been elected president, and his victory the following year wasn't a foregone conclusion. That makes it possible to see David's 1827 visit to Clay's son-in-law in a different light. What if Jackson lost? Wouldn't it be good to have friends on the winning side? Smart! And even if Crockett's overture meant that he planned to join the anti-Jackson camp no matter what, that doesn't necessarily brand him as a fool.

As for the land bill: From his point of view, Crockett was totally in the right. He'd come to believe that if the federal land were turned over to the state of Tennessee, as Polk and the others advocated, rich men in the legislature would set a price on it that his constituents couldn't afford. Besides, Polk's bill was never going to pass anyway! The House was too worried about the precedent-setting thing.

Why not try it his way for a change?

Yes, he got carried away rhetorically. And yes, there were negative consequences. Representative Pryor Lea, a Polk ally, kicked off the Jacksonians' anti-Crockett campaign with an anonymous letter in the *Knoxville Register* charging that David had "changed his course, abused his State, and co-operated with her enemies." Crockett called the letter writer a "contemptible sneak"; Lea outed himself as its author; and the escalating spate of charges, counter-charges, and name-calling almost led to a duel.

Yet none of that appeared to have hurt Crockett in his home district. Sensibly refraining from attacking Jackson directly, he won reelection by a landslide—6,773 to 3,641—in the summer of 1829. And what did this supposedly naive politician do next? He compromised! He went straight to work to negotiate a deal with the Tennessee delegation that might get *some* land bill passed that would help his poor constituents, even if it wasn't a perfect one.

"He tried to reach out to Polk," Wiener said.

First Crockett got himself appointed chairman of a special committee on the issue (something he couldn't have done, of course, without help from the anti-Jacksonians). The committee produced a bill that both Crockett and the other Tennesseans could support. The state would get some land to sell for schools. Squatters would get a "preemption right" to buy 160 acres at 12½ cents per acre. By compromising, Crockett wrote to one supporter in January 1830, "I have united my whole Delegation," and he urged the man to explain to his constituents that he'd done "the best that I could do for them."

Can't we all just get along?

Alas, the Davy Was Duped theory can easily deal with this heartwarming episode. For starters, the compromise bill didn't win, though the entire Tennessee delegation did vote for it. Congress just wasn't buying federal land giveaways. Second, as soon as the bill failed, Crockett destroyed any goodwill he'd built up by frantically pushing an amended version much like the one that had infuriated his colleagues in the first place. Finally, he seems not to have noticed that the Polk forces hadn't ever really been behind him. They'd simply decided that opposing him openly would hurt them with Tennessee voters. No member of the delegation other than David stood up in the House to speak in favor of the compromise bill.

Dupe or no dupe, they wanted him gone. They would try again—much harder—to defeat him in 1831.

Meanwhile, just weeks after his land bill went down, Crockett found himself holding a stick of political dynamite. It was time to vote on Jackson's Indian Removal bill. If David opposed it, his enemies would surely light the fuse.

✯

Here's a game biographers play: What if you could cross that bridge to the past just one time and watch your subject in action on just one day—which day would you choose? Would I want to see Crockett on that wharf at Baltimore? At Tallusahatchee? At Polly's deathbed? On a bear hunt? Inside the Alamo on March 6, 1836?

Rejecting that last option wouldn't be easy. Still, I'd be tempted to pick the afternoon of May 19, 1830, on the floor of the House of Representatives, when David Crockett got up to explain why he was voting against the Indian Removal bill.

It wouldn't be because his speech was a dramatic one. Compared to his land bill oratory, it was subdued. And it wouldn't be because I thought his precise words (unknown to us today) would reveal something I didn't know about his reasoning. There's plenty of evidence about Crockett's arguments, though it gets interpreted in different ways.

No. It would be to hear David's voice and watch his body language at what feels to me like one of the most emotionally and politically complicated periods of his life.

Sixteen months earlier, in January 1829, Crockett had written a letter to his brother-in-law George Patton, in which he was unusually direct about his feelings. He had recently built another mill in Tennessee—a small one, in which the millstones were turned by horses or oxen yoked to a spokelike arm—and word had just reached him in Washington that his niece had been killed by it. "She was with my children in my horse Mill walking Round after the oxen," he wrote, and the end of the arm had "caught her head a gainst the post and mashed it all to peaces Poor little dear Creature never knew what hurt her. . . . I hope she is this day in eternal happiness whare I am endevouring to make my way."

The religious content of this passage was unusual for David—and there was more. "I have altered my cours in life a great deal sence I reached this place," he told Patton. "I have not taisted one drop of Arden Sperits since I arrived here nor ever expects to while I live nothing stronger than Cider. . . . I have never made a pretention to

Religion in my life before. . . . I have been reproved many times for my wickedness by my Dear wife who I am certain will be no little astonished when she gets information of my determination."

It's important not to read too much into a single letter. Crockett probably didn't stop drinking for long, and there doesn't appear to have been much religion in his future. Still, I think it's reasonable to assume serious tension with Elizabeth over these issues and others, including his chronic debt and refusal to be a "stayin' home man." It's also easy to imagine David, gregarious though he was, feeling lonely and out of place in a city where personal connections were inextricable from political ones and you couldn't leave politics behind by whistling up your hunting dogs.

And by the time May 19, 1830, rolled around, Crockett's political life was going very badly indeed.

His attempted compromise on the land bill had ended in bitterness. The possibility that the bill might never make it through Congress in any form may finally have sunk in. Now came President Jackson's attempt to bludgeon the so-called civilized tribes out of their homelands and force them across the Mississippi River. Crockett had come to dislike almost everything about Tennessee's imperious favorite son, but he still wasn't attacking Jackson directly, and he knew beyond any doubt that west Tennessee voters strongly favored getting rid of the Indians.

Why, then, did he oppose Indian Removal? What was he thinking?

Crockettologists have not been shy about weighing in. He was following the lead of his anti-Jacksonians pals, they've argued. . . . No, no, he had real sympathy for the Indians. . . . But wait: Indians killed his grandparents! He fought them in the Creek War! . . . Yes, but they also saved his life that time in Alabama, and besides, the man had a capacity for moral growth. . . . But the Tallusahatchee passage in his autobiography showed him being totally callous about the massacre, so his vote had to be all about politics. . . . Actually, the passage showed him being horrified by Tallusahatchee, so he was voting his guilty conscience. . . . Perhaps his hatred for Jackson got so irrational that he just wanted to hurt the guy any way he could. . . . Maybe he saw the conflict as one of class, not race, with poor Indians getting ripped off just like his poor white constituents. . . .

Oh, and one more wrinkle: according to his best-known biographer, Crockett never actually gave that Indian Removal speech.

The *Register of Debates* includes nothing from him on the subject, Shackford argued, and though something claiming to be "A Sketch of the Remarks of the Hon. David Crockett" did show up in an 1830 collection of removal oratory, it was easily explained. "Evidently someone wrote a speech for Crockett that he never got around to delivering." And why would someone do that? "Evidently the inclusion in that volume of a spurious speech by David was part of the Whig plan to build him into an anti-Jacksonite of national proportions."

There's virtue in Shackford's repeated use of the hedge word "evidently." Biographers, historians, and journalists often draw conclusions that they honestly believe but that are not provable with available facts. Relying on words and phrases such as "must have," "no doubt," or "evidently" is a common solution—mea culpa! see the use of "reasonable to assume" a few paragraphs back—but a careful reader will treat all such words and phrases as red flags for uncertainty. I'm strongly tempted, for example, to write that "evidently, Shackford leaped to his conclusion about the speech because it fit the Davy Was Duped theory so well," but I don't really know that.

What I do know is that Shackford was wrong.

Crockett did give that Indian Removal speech. Allen Wiener proved it.

Wiener had been searching digitized newspapers at the Library of Congress, he told me, and he was about to call it a day when he noticed a small news item on Crockett in the May 25, 1830, *United States' Telegraph*. If he'd been using predigitization research techniques—flipping through physical newspapers or scrolling through microfilm—he would likely have missed it, because "your eye can only do so much with those narrow columns from nineteenth-century newspapers, and his name isn't in the headline." But there it was in the text, highlighted in yellow. Crockett had written to correct the *Telegraph*'s earlier paraphrase of his Indian Removal speech! The paper, he complained, had falsely reported him as saying that "he was opposed in conscience to the measure; and such being the case, he cared not what his constituents thought of his conduct."

Not so. "I never hurl defiance at those whose servant I am," David insisted. "I said that my conscience should be my guide . . . and that I believed if my constituents were here, they would justify my vote."

"Most exciting moment in my life, probably," Wiener said, laughing.

There are many possible reasons the speech didn't make it into the *Register of Debates*, he explained, but there's no need for me to go into them here. It is worth noting, however, that a version of the speech—very close to the one in the book Shackford mentions—also appeared in the *Jackson Gazette*. Wiener and Boylston think Crockett himself may have sent it to the west Tennessee paper in order "to head off his political enemies, who would surely have exposed any effort to conceal it."

Assured that the speech was real, I sat down later to read carefully through it.

I wasn't expecting much. For one thing, it seemed likely that Crockett had had help writing it. For another, what appeared in print was a paraphrased report, not a first-person transcript, which further distanced it from David's actual voice. Finally, I already knew the arguments he had made: he thought giving Jackson $500,000 for removal with no accountability was dumb; he saw Indian tribes as sovereign peoples; he would happily vote for removal if it really were voluntary, not coercion in disguise; and so on.

What was left to learn?

Plenty, it turned out, if only I could have watched the speech live.

"Mr. Crockett said, that, considering his very humble abilities, it might be expected that he should content himself with a silent vote," the paraphrase begins. Other congressmen have talked "much more ably" than he has. "He had been told that he did not understand English grammar. That was very true. He had never been six months at school in his life." I can imagine David sounding genuinely downcast here, like a man just whipped on a vote he cares about who's feeling overmatched. Yet he goes on to say that he "raised himself up by the labor of his hands"—which reads more like pride—and that on no account will he "yield up his privilege as the representative of forty thousand free men on this floor."

Humble or proud? Dupe or no man's fool?

I'd love to have been there to judge for myself.

"He knew that he stood alone, having, perhaps, none of his colleagues from his state agreeing in sentiment," the paraphrased speech reports. Yet: "If he should stand alone amidst all the people of the United States, he should not vote otherwise; and it would be a matter of rejoicing to him till the day he died, that he had given the vote."

Lonely and isolated? Righteous and independent? What about the numerous other congressmen who spoke against the bill? Was David independent of them, too?

I read the speech at least five times, with shifting reactions. One time I'd notice the quiet eloquence with which David said, over and over, that he would answer only to God for his vote. The next time through, I'd recall his biographer Mark Derr's assertion—unproven but plausible—that Crockett's friend Chilton, a Baptist preacher as well as a congressman, was the man responsible for those religious references. Yet I never stopped admiring the way Crockett brought his brief remarks to a close: "He had been charged with not representing his constituents: if the fact was so, the error (said Mr. C) is here (touching his head) not here (laying his hand upon his heart). He had never possessed wealth or education, but he had ever been animated by an independent spirit, and he trusted to prove it on the present occasion."

If Crockett spoke those words and didn't mean them, then count me among the seriously duped, because I'm giving him the benefit of the doubt. Poor but proud, willing to trust to his heart—never mind if being "independent" meant following the lead of Jackson's enemies—David was right about Indian Removal. The vote was close, so his opinion mattered. If three other Tennesseans had broken ranks and joined him, they might have rewritten a shameful chapter in U.S. history.

There's a question I'd really like to ask him, though.

Crockett certainly stood out from his Tennessee contemporaries when it came to treating Indians as human beings—yet he did not stand out in his attitude toward slavery. If there is a record of David's thoughts on the subject, I haven't come across it. But we do know a few things about his actions.

For the first three decades of his life, he was too poor for the question of owning slaves to arise. Some of his neighbors were slave owners, however, and on Bean's Creek, Elizabeth Patton may have been one of them. Her father, Robert Patton, worked his substantial North Carolina farm with slave labor, and we know that he gave David and Elizabeth three slaves as a gift not long after Crockett was first elected to Congress.

Earlier, when David was a justice of the peace in Lawrence County, one of his jobs was to certify the bills of sale when slaves were sold. At the time of the flood that wiped out his mills, as he wrote in his autobiography, he "had some likely negroes"; the context suggests that he might have sold them to help pay his debts, but we don't know for sure. In an 1829 letter, Crockett wrote of declining to buy a ten-year-old boy a relative had offered for sale, in part because the prices for such boys were lower in Washington. In 1831, a year after his Indian Removal speech, he sold a slave girl named Adaline for $300. Below Crockett's signature on the bill of sale, according to Shackford, "are the words 'Be allways sure you are right then Go, ahead,'" seemingly the first link between David and the motto that would come to be "inseparably associated with his name."

Historical figures, it is rightly said, must be judged in the context of the times and places in which they lived. Tempting though it may be, it is a mistake to impose contemporary attitudes and beliefs on them. Slavery was a largely unquestioned fact of life in west Tennessee in Crockett's time, and although much of the slave population was concentrated on relatively few large plantations, many small landholders owned slaves as a well. Acquiring a few "likely negroes" would have looked to David—assuming that he ever stopped to think about it—like a normal way for a poor white pioneer to "take a rise."

Still, he did stop to think about the rights of Indians.

And if I could magic my way back to May 19, 1830, a day David Crockett stood tall against injustice, I would want to ask him about Adaline.

✫

The House passed the Indian Removal bill by a vote of 102 to 97 on May 24, 1830. The Senate having passed it earlier, Jackson signed it immediately. The Cherokees in particular resisted removal, delaying their forced exile for years, but their effort was in vain. Thousands would die on the Trail of Tears. In November 1838, some seven hundred Oklahoma-bound Cherokees would pass through downtown Lawrenceburg, a few yards from where Crockett's bronze statue stands today.

As the second year of the congressional term began, Crockett repeatedly tried to get the House to take up his land bill again. No dice. By February 1831, he was openly proclaiming his opposition to Jackson. He wrote one Tennessee supporter that because he had refused to wear a collar inscribed "my dog" with Jackson's name on it, as Democratic partisans were expected to do, he had been "herld from their party."

Yes, he had. And in his reelection campaign, furious Jacksonians *really* sicced the dogs on him.

They pulled a classic dirty political trick, advertising Crockett speeches all over his district without informing David, then showing up themselves to attack the absent headliner as a turncoat and a coward. Jackson himself weighed in, writing friends in west Tennessee that he hoped the district's voters "will not disgrace themselves longer by sending that profligate man Crockett back to Congress." One Jacksonian wit, Adam Huntsman—he of the farmer's-daughter anecdote, though Huntsman wasn't running himself in 1831—unleashed a biblical parody featuring "David of the river country" and his betrayal of Andrew, the "chief ruler over the children of Columbia."

"In those days there were many occupants spread abroad throughout the river country: these men loved David exceedingly, because he promised to give them lands flowing with milk and honey," he wrote. "But the wise men from the south, the southeast, the west, and the middle country, arose with one accord, and said, Lo! brethren, this cannot be done. . . . If we give the lands away, it must be to the tribe of Tennessee; so that they may deal with the occupants as it may seem good in their sight." Hearing this, David became "exceedingly wroth" and allied himself with Andrew's enemies, "wicked men . . . of the tribes of Maine, Massachusetts, Rhode Island, Kentucky and Missouri." The people of the river country then booted him out in favor of a certain "William, whose surname is Fitzgerald"—exactly what would come to pass in real life.

The campaign got so nasty, according to one report, that Fitzgerald had to pull a gun on Crockett in self-defense.

Shackford traced this tale to a newspaper article from forty years after the election, carefully noting that it was inaccurate on a number of points. Nonetheless, he believed it had "substantial basis in fact." The rhetorical warfare between the candidates, he wrote, had escalated to the point where "Crockett threatened to thrash Fitzgerald" if he repeated certain charges. Sure enough, when Fitzgerald did so in his next speech, Crockett got up from the audience and started coming at him. But Fitzgerald had taken the precaution of hiding a pistol under a handkerchief on the table in front of him. He retrieved it, pointed it at Crockett, and said he'd shoot if his opponent came closer.

Sensibly, Crockett retreated, but it cost him: "That incident, according to this account, 'decided the election.'"

Too good to check!

Back to the more certain facts: The election was close. Relentless Jacksonian attacks, combined with the Indian Removal vote and Crockett's failure to get any kind of land bill passed, might have been enough to do him in even if the pistol-pointing humiliation never happened. In any case, he lost, and he took it badly. He tried to challenge the results (Congress wouldn't bite) and referred contemptuously to Fitzgerald as "a perfect lick spittle" and "the thing that had the name of beating me."

During the campaign, as David wrote shortly after it ended, he had been "compeled to sel my land where I live to try to pay my debts." He leased twenty acres nearby and built the last of his three west Tennessee cabins. At age forty-five, he was a dirt-poor tenant farmer once again.

Not much would be heard from Crockett over the next eighteen months, before he set out to retake his House seat.

Or not much from the real Crockett, I should say.

Because over those same eighteen months, Legendary Davy would come into his own.

⊰ 7 ⊱

"Don't Get Above Your Raisin'"

Americans in the twenty-first century are all too familiar with celebrity culture. We know what it can do to people who become well enough known—never mind why—to have their lives contorted in its funhouse mirror.

But David Crockett didn't have a clue.

How could he?

A person could be famous in early-nineteenth-century America, of course. Andrew Jackson's military renown opened the way to the presidency, and his rise was viewed as a triumph of democracy because he earned his ruling-class status rather than inheriting it. But pure celebrity—defined as widespread public recognition in the absence of significant accomplishment—didn't exist as a concept in 1830, when an actor named James Hackett sponsored a contest for a new play to be built around an original American character.

Hackett's prize went to a romantic comedy called *The Lion of the West*, whose title character was a Crockett parody named Colonel Nimrod Wildfire. No one involved could have imagined that *Lion* would become the first half of a literary one-two punch—the second being *Sketches and Eccentricities of Col. David Crockett, of West Tennessee*—that would radically reshape David's image and his life.

Lion and *Sketches* transformed a defeated congressman who never got much done into a living legend riding the greased pig of fame into the sunset of immortality.

By 1830, Hackett had already played a variety of backwoods characters onstage. He was good at it, and he sponsored the contest because he was looking for a new vehicle. The writer James Kirke Paulding—a friend of Washington Irving's and, of all things, a future secretary of the navy—took up Hackett's challenge. Paulding would later denounce as "malicious and unfounded" the notion that he had based Wildfire on Crockett.

He was lying.

It's true that the playwright had other sources to draw on. Portrayals of American frontiersmen as boastful "half horse, half alligator" types predated Crockett's arrival in Washington City by many years. Yet David's backwoods style had caught the attention of the press, which painted him as either a charming, forthright child of nature or a crude, ignorant buffoon, depending on the politics of the newspaper involved. Paulding knew that perfectly well. He gave the game away in a letter to a friend from whom he was soliciting raw material. Please send "sketches, short stories, & incidents, of Kentucky or Tennessee manners," he wrote. "If you can add, or *invent*, a few ludicrous Scenes of Col. Crockett at Washington, you will be sure of my everlasting gratitude."

The Lion of the West opened at New York's Park Theatre in April 1831, but Hackett thought it needed major revisions, and he didn't take it on tour until later in the year. The only surviving version dates from 1833, but from what we know of the others, Hackett's Colonel Nimrod Wildfire remained a constant: an illiterate but good-hearted Kentucky congressman who saves the day as part of a farcical plot pitting right-thinking Americans against scheming Europeans.

Wildfire was the most memorable thing about the play, and

the most memorable thing about him was his outrageous manner of speaking—especially his ritualized frontier bragging. A classic Nimrod brag, transcribed by an unidentified playgoer, turned up in the newspapers in the fall of 1831, by which time the real colonel was adjusting to private life in west Tennessee. In it Hackett's character trades insults with a Mississippi boatman, then describes the fight that ensues:

> He was a pretty hard colt, but no part of a priming to such a feller as me. *I put it to him mighty droll*—in ten minutes he yelled enough! and swore I was a ripstaver! Says I, *"An't I the yaller flower of the forest!"* . . . Says he, *"Stranger you're a beauty!* oh, if I only know'd your name, I'd vote for you next election." Says I, "My name is Nimrod Wildfire—half horse, half alligator and a touch of the airthquake—that's got the prettiest sister, fastest horse, and ugliest dog in the District, and can outrun, outkick, outjump, knockdown, drag out, and whip any man in all Kaintuck."

Legendary Davy talks just like that, as I learned from the brags Nicolas Cage delivers on that Rabbit Ears CD we got for Lizzie. It's no coincidence, either. Even if Paulding had been telling the truth about not basing Wildfire on Crockett, it wouldn't have mattered, because the theatergoing public promptly linked the two. And in December 1833, when Hackett took a version of the play to Washington, the real man confirmed the connection by showing up at the theater to see himself mirrored onstage. Here's the journalist Benjamin Perley Poore re-creating this weirdly postmodern scene:

> At seven o'clock the Colonel was escorted by the manager through the crowd to a front seat reserved for him. As soon as he was recognized by the audience they made

the very house shake with hurrahs for Colonel Crockett, "Go ahead!" "I wish I may be shot!" "Music! let us have Crockett's March!" After some time the curtain rose, and Hackett appeared in hunting costume, bowed to the audience, and then to Colonel Crockett. The compliment was reciprocated by the Colonel, to the no small amusement and gratification of the spectators, and the play then went on.

Man meets legend! They bow to each other!

No red-blooded Crockettologist could pass this up, even if there weren't contemporary newspaper reports to confirm that it really happened.

Legendary Davy's second punch landed early in 1833, before Wildfire's Washington debut but more than two years after his creation. As noted earlier, *Sketches and Eccentricities* was first published as *Life and Adventures of Colonel David Crockett*, etc., and had its title changed after it sold out and needed reprinting. The anonymously written celebrity biography appropriated Crockett's image for its own purposes, just as *The Lion of the West* had done. But the real David reacted differently this time.

He hated *Sketches*.

It made him so mad that he set out to produce a celebrity bio "written by himself."

Who stole David Crockett's life story? Crockett said he didn't know. Many have been skeptical of that claim, because *Sketches* includes large chunks of early Crockett history that could have originated only with David. But his biographers haven't agreed on the identity of the culprit—offering, instead, two prime suspects.

Matthew St. Clair Clarke, clerk of the House of Representatives, is Shackford's candidate and an integral part of the broader Davy Was Duped argument. Clarke's motive, the biographer believed, was to help "reelect David Crockett to Congress as an anti-Jacksonian" and to "increase his usefulness through a multiplication of his fame." A graduate seminar in historiography could be built around Shackford's obsession with this theory and its widespread, lasting influence: Clarke's authorship was presented as almost certain fact by one important Crockett biographer four decades after it was first proposed.

The second option is James Strange French, obscure author of a long-forgotten 1836 novel called *Elkswatawa, or, the Prophet of the West: A Tale of the Frontier.* French would be a long shot except for one thing: he obtained the copyright for *Sketches.* A handwritten contract with his publishers is reproduced in Boylston and Wiener's book.

Wait, wait! Why is that not conclusive?

Well, if you're building up Crockett as an anti-Jackson puppet (as Shackford's argument goes), you don't want to be seen pulling the strings. So you need a useful idiot like French as your front man.

There's more. Much more. But I gave up on parsing the dueling authorship scenarios after a while. Better to read *Sketches* carefully myself, I thought, and see what light the book itself might shed on the argument.

Three pages into the introduction, I was ready to hurl the thing across the room. I couldn't, though, because I was reading it online.

Sketches starts with almost twenty pages of desperately purple prose, as though the writer were trying to establish highbrow credentials before taking on a lowbrow subject. Sample passage (take a deep breath):

The Past tells me that here, but a few years since, nature slept in primeval loveliness: her forests had never echoed to the sound of the axe; her rivers had never been disturbed by the noise of a steamboat; there was nothing to break in upon the stillness of evening, save the loud whoop of her children, the long howl of some hungry wolf, the wild scream of a famished panther, or the plaintive notes of some gentle turtle, weeping for one that's far away.

You *really* have to want to know about David Crockett to get past that weeping turtle.

Things calm down after this baroque outburst, though. The sentences get more straightforward, as in: "While David was yet young, his father moved from Greene to Sullivan county, and settled upon a public road for the purpose of keeping a tavern." Anyone who's read Crockett's autobiography will find much of what ensues quite familiar: here's David leaving home on that first cattle drive, almost going to sea in Baltimore, falling in love with the Quaker's niece, and so on. There are many discrepancies—David was not the "ninth child" in his family, for example, and as we've seen, the *Sketches* version of the Margaret Elder courtship puts him in a less flattering light—but in the first half of the book, at least, the factual similarities outnumber the differences. And though Mr. Highbrow's attempts to enter Crockett's world can be comically awkward, he appears to admire his subject. Consider his description of David during the Creek War:

No man ever enjoyed a greater degree of personal popularity, than did David Crockett while with the army; and his success in political life is mainly attributable to that fact. I have met with many of his messmates, who spoke of him with the affection of a brother, and from them have heard many anecdotes, which convince me how much goodness of heart he really possesses.

What's not to like?

Well . . .

Sketches eventually loses the momentum that the narrative of Crockett's early life provides. There are some lengthy hunting yarns. There's a visit to the colonel's west Tennessee home, reported in enough detail that we're persuaded it really happened. But then Mr. Highbrow turns into Mr. Scavenger and starts tossing in whatever he can find that might titillate readers or at least fill space. Some of this material is weird but harmless, including a series of anecdotes said to be told by Crockett in faux-Dutch dialect. But some is not harmless at all. Take the recycled newspaper story purporting to describe uncouth behavior by David at a White House dinner. (A waiter takes his plate, he demands it back as though it's been stolen, and so on.) When this slanderous tidbit first appeared, it upset Crockett so much that he recruited fellow dinner guests to write denials. *Sketches* printed the denials, too. But from Crockett's point of view, why bring it up?

And for God's sake, why reprint that Adam Huntsman "David of the river country" parody?

Worse, perhaps, is the fact that Mr. Anonymous proves tone deaf when it comes to mixing his subject's real and legendary selves. It was one thing for Crockett to indulge in "I can whip my weight in wildcats" hyperbole on the campaign trail, because he did it in a way that his listeners understood to be humorous, or for Nimrod Wildfire to proclaim himself "half horse, half alligator," because Wildfire—however Crockettesque he may have been—remained a fictional character. It was quite another thing to put this stuff into David's mouth in a book marketed as his true story. The mashed-up Crockett of *Sketches* rides streaks of lightning across the sky but has a real wife who dies; saves the world from Halley's Comet by wringing off its tail but loses real mills to real floods; grins awed raccoons out of trees but hunts and kills real bears. To confuse things further, he does a "yaller flower of the forest" brag that's straight out of *The Lion of the West.*

By the end of the book I was convinced that French was the author, if only because *Sketches* is such an incoherent portrait. Wouldn't a conspirator have come up with a cleaner hagiography? But I was equally convinced that the authorship fuss obscures a bigger point.

Legendary Davy was out of control—and the real David wanted his story back.

In 1833, the newspapers were full of Crockett. It wasn't because he was running hard for his old House seat—he ended up beating Fitzgerald by 173 votes, despite the fact that the Jackson machine had gerrymandered the district—but because editors nationwide mined *Sketches* for amusing excerpts. David complained of meeting hundreds of people who, knowing him only through "that deceptive work," seemed astonished to find him "in human shape." Back in Washington, he wasted no time in recruiting his friend and colleague Thomas Chilton to help him remold his image and, not incidentally, start cashing in on his own celebrity. Late in December, he announced his intentions to the world. "I know not why my humble name should have excited any general interest," he told a Washington newspaper, but since it had, "that interest shall be met by a plain and unvarnished history of myself, prepared under my own notice, and submitted to the public by my own authority." His autobiography would present him "as I really am, *a plain, blunt, Western man,* relying on honesty and the woods, and not on learning and the law, for a living."

Here comes that time-travel fantasy again: I'd love to drop in on Representatives Crockett and Chilton at Mrs. Ball's Boarding House and ask them what the phrase "prepared under my own notice" actually means. Was Chilton a full-fledged ghostwriter, especially valuable because he had a Kentuckian's ear for the rhetorical style of the frontier? Should we take Crockett at his word that he simply asked Chilton to "correct" what he wrote? Doesn't it seem odd that Crockett would assign half his book's copyright to a collaborator with only a minimal role? Ah, but isn't there reason to believe that David—desperate for cash, as usual—*sold* that half share to Chilton?

I'd say "maybe," "no," "yes," and "yes," but I'm going to defer to a veteran Crockettologist whose middle-ground position makes a lot of sense to me. Richard Boyd Hauck argues in *Crockett: A Bio-Bibliography* (good book, horrible title) that Crockett supplied the stories while Chilton took care of "the technical details of writing." Yet Hauck adds that the autobiography's greatest strength— the consistently "credible language" that makes its first-person voice "artistically true to the style of both Crockett and his public image"—should be credited to the partnership, rather than to either partner individually.

Next question: Did *A Narrative of the Life of David Crockett, of the State of Tennessee* tell the totally real, utterly nonlegendary story Crockett promised it would?

Of course not. It's a political memoir!

As we've seen, Crockett included politically motivated falsehoods about his Creek War service. Some of his hunting tales cross the credibility line as well, though they're told in that consistent frontier voice Hauck talks about, which allows for storytelling exaggeration. But to understand the image David was trying to project—as Joseph Arpad, another important Crockettologist, has noted—it is equally important to consider what he left out.

Two examples should suffice. First, Crockett says nothing about the crucial role Elizabeth's modest wealth played in his "rise." Second, and more surprisingly, he makes no mention of what Arpad calls his "heroic effort" to pass a land bill that would have made his poor constituents secure. It's possible that he simply didn't want to call attention to this politically damaging failure. But Arpad, in his 1970 dissertation on Crockett, offers a more complex interpretation. The autobiography, he argues, was "a shrewd and subtle masquerade of backwoods originality" intended to enhance "the legend that had already been established" about Crockett's character.

In sum, David knew that his image as a frontier eccentric—incongruously combined with "his elevated status in society"—was what "marked him as an original." And he knew that tales of legislative maneuvering would muddy that image up.

Political document though it was, the book also established its author of record as a literary original. The Crockett-Chilton collaboration, as Arpad somewhat long-windedly puts it, produced "a colloquial style that did not particularly call attention to itself as humorous, but which permitted a vigorous expression of sentiment and humor, allowing the vernacular persona to be more forcefully revealed than by either crude dialect or genteel diction." Nothing comparable would turn up in "a sustained work of American literature until Mark Twain's *Adventures of Huckleberry Finn.*"

Not bad for a semiliterate frontiersman. Now all Crockett had to do was sell the thing.

With Chilton's help, he found a publisher, Philadelphia's Carey and Hart. On February 3, 1834, he put his only copy of the manuscript in the mail. But even before that, he'd started planning his book tour. "I may take a trip through the eastern States during the session of Congress and sell the Book," he wrote his oldest son on January 10. He intended "never to go home until I am able to pay my debts," and "a great many have perswaded me" that the exposure gained from taking his act on the road would help him accomplish this objective.

Three months later, Representative Crockett abandoned his congressional duties in midsession, hopped on a stagecoach, and headed north on what Arpad calls "perhaps the first 'promotional tour' in book-selling history." David's anti-Jackson friends, by now formally organized as the Whig Party, had helpfully scheduled it for him. There would be appearances in Baltimore, Philadelphia, New York, Boston, and Lowell.

And if the newly minted author were to take a few whacks at "King Andrew" along the way—well, that was part of the Crockett Tour's agenda, too.

✦

What was going on in David Crockett's head when he boarded that Baltimore-bound stagecoach on April 25, 1834? The whole Davy Was Duped versus Davy Was No Fool debate appears to hinge on this point—yet there is no way for us to know.

The chief source on Crockett's three-week adventure in political bookselling is a memoir that appeared under his name the following year. *An Account of Col. Crockett's Tour to the North and Down East,* like his autobiography, was published by Carey and Hart and states on the title page that it was "written by himself." David's real contributions were so limited, however, that he wrote his publishers to ask if they could describe the thing instead as having been "written from notes furnished by my Self."

No chance. Bad for sales.

The actual author, a congressman from Pennsylvania named William Clark, went uncredited when *Col. Crockett's Tour* was published the following year. Clark was no Chilton, and his faux-Crockett voice rings almost entirely false. The book is also heavily padded with anti-Jackson rhetoric; it reproduces no fewer than a dozen Crockett speeches, all of which sound pretty much alike.

A brief sample: Jackson believes in the "government of one man" and "wields both sword and purse" to that end. . . . By threatening vetoes that can be overridden only by a two-thirds majority, the president is saying "My will shall be the law." . . . David would prefer to be "politically damned" than to be "hypocritically immortalized" with Jackson's collar around his neck. . . . Jackson-worship leaves a stench like that of "a skunk getting into a house—long after he has cleared out, you smell him in every room and closet, from the cellar to the garret." Think what you may of these political views, it's impossible to read twelve variations on them without nodding off. That's why, when the tour book was later reprinted as part of a package of "autobiographical" Crockett material, a wise editor cut out every speech.

What was left is a remarkable tale—especially when you remember that the last time David had passed through Baltimore, he had been an anonymous thirteen-year-old who hoped to run away to sea.

Thirty-four years later, he spent the night at Barnum's Hotel at the corner of Calvert and Fayette Streets, where the Equitable Building now stands, and if he walked down to Fell's Point to look at the wharf, his ghostwriter doesn't say. The next morning he was off to Philadelphia, conveyed by steamboat and train. Crockett had never been on a train before. When the spark-spewing locomotive spooked some horses, which then smashed the wagon they were pulling, he couldn't help bursting into laughter.

Steaming into Philadelphia, he was stunned to find "the whole face of the earth covered with people" who had turned out to cheer him. His Whig hosts hustled him into an "elegant barouche" and spirited him away. Over the next few days, besides delivering a lengthy anti-Jackson harangue, he toured the city's mint, waterworks, asylum, naval hospital, and navy yard. Admirers presented him with a seal for his watch chain that was inscribed "Go ahead," and the young Whigs of Philadelphia solicited specifications for a fine new rifle they planned to have made for him. One night he took in a minstrel show at a Walnut Street theater. Musicians in blackface improvised Crockett references into a popular song called "Zip Coon," a published version of which, according to "Music of the Alamo," included the following verse:

> *Dat tarnal critter Crockett, he never say his prayers,*
> *He kill all de wild Cats, de Coons and de bears,*
> *And den he go to Washington to make de laws,*
> *And dere he find de Congress men sucking deir paws.*

The Chestnut Street hotel to which David retired after the performance is long gone. But the splendid Greek Revival building across the street, completed in 1824, still stands, and it's filled with resonance from Crockett's time.

The Second Bank of the United States was Jackson's archenemy. As a National Park Service marker outside now explains, it was "the center of the bitter financial and political struggle in which the bank's head, Nicholas Biddle, and his ally, Henry Clay, contended with President Jackson for control of the nation's monetary system." Crockett was a bit player in this war, most of which took place while he was out of office: by 1834, Jackson had vetoed the renewal of the bank's charter and pulled all its federal deposits.

That didn't stop David from filling his tour speeches with a probank vehemence that seemed straight out of the Davy Was Duped playbook.

What the poor man's friend was doing on the barricades with the aristocratic Biddle is hard to understand. Was he simply sucking up to the probank Whigs, who, after all, were wining and dining him and giving him fancy rifles? Had a blind hatred of all things Jackson robbed him of his judgment? Might his stance be connected to the $500 he'd borrowed from the bank and hadn't yet repaid? "I hope you will extend all the liberalitys in your powar," Crockett wrote a

Bi ldle minion in 1832. "I did come out in the late election in fa-
vour of the renewal of your charter," and, by the way, "I still hope to
be in Congress again before there is a vote taken on that subject."

Even Crockett's admirers concede that this looks bad.

Yet, as Boylston and Wiener point out, Biddle never forgave
Crockett's loan; he merely extended it. More important, there
was—and still is—a strong argument that Jackson greatly over-
reached in his assault on the bank, selfishly ignoring the damage it
caused to the economy and confirming the opposition's belief that
he was a menace to American democracy. "I think Jackson's our
first president who's pretty much a sociopath," a Park Service ranger
told me, standing in front of a big-haired Andy portrait. "I mean,
he *really* seems unhinged."

That's exactly what Crockett thought. And whether he was right
or wrong, it's hard to believe that a $500 loan would have been
required to purchase his opinion.

Leaving Philadelphia for New York, he was again greeted by a
cheering crowd and a committee of young Whigs "appointed to
wait upon me." After an evening spent watching the actress Fanny
Kemble "play in grand style," he heard a cry of "fire, fire," leaped
up to help fight the blaze, and was smugly informed that "we have
fire companies here, and we leave it to them." At Peale's Museum,
a boy born without hands or arms "took a pair of scissors in his
toes, and cut his name in full, and gave it to me." More travels by
elegant barouche ensued. Returning from an excursion up Broad-
way to the "new part" of New York, Crockett asked to have a look
at a Democratic stronghold called Five Points, which he described
as filled with drunks "too mean to swab hell's kitchen"—a remark
sometimes credited with giving the neighborhood a new name.
One morning he crossed the Hudson to Jersey City, where he happily joined "a great many gentlemen shooting rifles."

Then it was on to Boston.

Until my daughter's infatuation with him, I had no idea that David had ever been to Massachusetts, much less stayed in a tavern within walking distance of Fenway Park. (Okay, it would have been a long walk, and Fenway itself wouldn't have been there—the place is not *that* old.) That made me especially fascinated to read about the New England portion of the tour. Yet the more I read, the more uncertain I was of Crockett's true feelings about it all.

As reported in the book that bore his name, he checked out Faneuil Hall and Quincy Market—the prices were a bit steep— and visited factories that made shoes, India-rubber clothing, and carpets. He drank "the best of wines," with "the Champaigne foaming up as if you were supping fog out of speaking-trumpets." At the Charlestown Navy Yard, he joked about the newly carved likeness of Jackson on the figurehead of the USS *Constitution*, known as "Old Ironsides," which still anchors there today. (It was no joking matter to local Whigs; two months later, according to the *New York Times*, someone chopped Jackson's head off to use as "a surprise centerpiece" for "a banquet of Boston Brahmins.") Moving on to the Bunker Hill battlefield, Crockett paid his re- spects to the men "who fell in that daybreak battle of our rising glory." He found himself wishing he could "call them up, and ask them to tell me how to help to protect the liberty they bought for us with their blood."

His own daybreak battle was less than two years away, and those words were enough to give me chills. But were they really David's?

One afternoon, according to *Col. Crockett's Tour*, some gentle- men invited him to Cambridge, "where the big college or university is." He refused to go. "I did not know but they might stick an LL.D on me," he explained, and his constituents might assume those let- ters stood for "lazy lounging dunce." Ha, ha, ha. The whole episode rings false and may have been cooked up in response to the fact that Harvard had given Jackson an honorary degree in 1833.

Yet the account of Crockett's visit to the Perkins School for the Blind has a different feel, even if the words are Clark's. A blind boy shows up at David's Tremont Street lodgings to issue an invitation. He leads the way through the streets of Boston to the Pearl Street mansion in which the school is temporarily housed. A blind girl reads a passage from the Bible by using "letters stamped on the under side of the paper." Other pupils play flutes and clarinets and sing beautifully. Their visitor's astonished verdict: "I never saw happier people in my life."

It's a sweet scene, and David's sincerity is palpable. The farther north I followed him, however, the more I found myself contemplating metaphorical blindness along with the physical kind.

The northernmost point Crockett reached on his tour—and in his whole life, for that matter—was the famed mill town of Lowell, Massachusetts. Founded a decade earlier by wealthy Bostonians who dreamed of a utopian capitalism that would put England's "dark Satanic mills" to shame, the Lowell of 1834 was dense with brick-walled textile factories and the young women recruited to work in them. It was the most incongruous context I could imagine for a bear-hunting politician from west Tennessee. This made me eager to explore Lowell National Historical Park, though I wasn't expecting to find specific Crockett traces there.

Wrong, wrong, wrong. I should have known better, by this time, than to underestimate the power of celebrity harnessed to propaganda.

"I know about Davy Crockett!" said Jen Burns, the first park employee I asked. Burns, a summer hire cheerfully answering tourists' questions in the park's Boott Cotton Mills Museum, then pointed me toward a large plaque featuring "one of his quotes about Lowell." The quote was from *Col. Crockett's Tour,* and, not surprisingly, it didn't sound much like David. "I wanted to see the power of machinery, wielded by the keenest calculations of human skill," it read in part. "I wanted to see how it was that these northerners could buy our cotton and carry it home, manufacture it, bring it back, and sell it for half nothing; and in the meantime be well to live, and make money besides."

Good question. The park's introductory slide show helped me get a handle on the history involved.

It begins with a well-connected Bostonian named Francis Cabot Lowell. "In 1810, Lowell sails to England, where he gains access to a number of major factories and memorizes the fundamentals of the new power looms." In the 1820s, associates use the fruits of Lowell's industrial espionage to transform a tiny village on the Merrimack River into "a huge laboratory for experiments in water power, engineering, textile chemistry and machine design." The new city is about "more than cloth and machines," however. To operate their looms and spindles, the factory owners turn to "a new source of willing, unskilled workers: the daughters of New England's Yankee farmers."

Here's where the utopian part comes in: Lowell's capitalists don't want to replicate the "squalor and misery" of British factories. They pay their young women fairly by contemporary standards (a bit more than schoolteachers), build them boardinghouses to live in, hire matrons to supervise them, and encourage them to attend lectures and otherwise improve their minds. The women, in turn—who mostly range in age from fifteen to thirty—welcome the chance "to earn decent wages in a clean and morally upright environment" and to broaden their intellectual and social horizons.

Judging from the tour book, Crockett found Lowell just as advertised. Walking briskly to dinner, "the girls looked as if they were coming from a quilting frolic." When David questioned some on a factory floor, "not one expressed herself as tired of her employment, or oppressed with work; all talked well and looked healthy." Was his opinion influenced by the fact that he'd driven up from Boston "in a fine carriage"; that one of the mill owners, a Mr. Lawrence, had made him a gift of a handsome broadcloth suit; or that he had been toasted at dinner by a hundred "young gentlemen of Lowell," whom he entertained with a political speech?

It seems likely. So a reality check is in order.

I asked Jen Burns what a Lowell factory floor would have been like in the 1830s. "Well, it would have been about ninety degrees in there," she said. "Almost a hundred percent humidity, because they would keep the windows shut so the cotton threads wouldn't break." Work would begin at 4:00 A.M., with the women roused by the clanging of the factory bell. Latecomers would find the factory gate locked against them. According to the park slide show, the women worked "some 73 hours a week—thirteen hours a day Monday through Friday and eight hours on Saturday."

And that was in the good old days, before competition drove the price of cloth down and mill owners—forced to choose between profits and utopian ideals—slashed wages, sped up production, and increased workloads.

Before I left the old brick mill that housed the museum, I took in a small exhibit on the link between slavery and the textile industry. It quoted Senator Charles Sumner of Massachusetts decrying the "unholy union" between "the lords of the lash," who supplied Lowell's raw material, and "the lords of the loom." Outside, a restored wooden bell tower rose over the courtyard. A short walk through Boarding House Park took me to a smaller museum where, at the replica of a room barely big enough to hold two beds, I heard the recorded voices of four fictional occupants debating the pluses and minuses of their mill-girl lives.

"The corporation takes advantage of us," one voice complained. "We work morning till night, the machines going faster all the time, and we're paid no more for it—"

"I don't find it a terrible strain," another countered. "After all, any work has its unhappy conditions, and factory work isn't half the drudgery as *domestic* service—"

But the most surprising thing I encountered in either museum was a simple historical time line on a wall near the bedroom display. Always on the lookout for traces of Crockett, I checked the entry for 1834.

"Mill girls' strike," it read.

Thomas Dublin's *Women at Work,* a social history of early Lowell, filled me in. Three months before the congressman's visit, it seems, the mill owners announced a reduction in wages and eight hundred women walked off the job in protest. A Boston paper reported that they formed a procession and "marched around town," with one leader delivering a fiery address on "the rights of women and the iniquities of the monied aristocracy" in the style of the feminist icon Mary Wollstonecraft. The 1834 strike was the first in Lowell's history, and though it quickly failed—within a week, the strikers were either gone or back to work—it was a harbinger of bitter strife to come.

Apparently, no one mentioned it to David.

Up to this point, I had been working hard to keep an open mind on the Duped/No Fool dispute. I kept trying. Crockett defenders argue that he saw the mill workers as poor people, just like the squatters in his district, but with one key difference: Lowell's poor had decent, reasonably secure jobs. Why *wouldn't* the poor man's friend approve? This argument is buttressed by a broader one that No Fool proponents invariably make. Crockett, they say, was congenitally independent but needed Whig help with his land bill. He saw the relationship as: you use me and I'll use you.

There is another, just conceivable explanation for Crockett's re-action to Lowell. It mixes obscure fact with speculation yet seems worth noting nonetheless.

Decades before David toured the mills, according to Bible rec-ords reproduced in a Crockett family newsletter, his debt-ridden fa-ther had sent one of David's sisters into domestic service. Margaret Catharine Crockett had been "served out to old Genl. Taylor at Jonesborough by her papa to settle duns," a descendant wrote. Trag-edy ensued. The young woman got pregnant, presumably by the old general; the general's wife kicked her out; and John Crockett "would not let her come home." Taken in by a compassionate min-ister, Margaret Catharine had her baby and "went to be with the Lord later in the day." I've found no record of David mentioning his sister's death, let alone of whether he knew the details. But if he did, I can see why those supervised New England boardinghouses might have struck him as a good idea.

Still, the more I thought about Crockett's travels in the North-east, the more I realized that I was trying far too hard to make excuses for him. Because there is, of course, a simpler explanation for his infatuation with the lords of the loom and for his blind en-thusiasm about the tour as a whole.

The man was duped. The foaming champagne of celebrity went to his head.

Yes, the tour gave him a national soapbox, and yes, it produced a barrage of newspaper stories that helped sell A Narrative of the Life of David Crockett. But his Whig sponsors got by far the better end of the deal. For the price of a rifle, a watch seal, a suit, some hotel bills, and a few weeks' worth of fancy dinners, they got to wind Crockett up like a mechanical frontiersman doll and turn him loose on their archenemy, Jackson.

And, unlike David, *they* didn't have to worry about how it would play with voters on the actual Tennessee frontier.

By May 15, 1834, Crockett was off the road and settled back in at Mrs. Ball's. Six weeks later, he would head home to west Tennessee by way of Philadelphia, where he would share Fourth of July speaking duties with Daniel Webster and collect his custom-made rifle from the city's young Whigs. But for now he was back in his Washington digs on the southwest corner of Sixth Street and Pennsylvania Avenue, where—according to the most intimate glimpse we have of him during his living-legend phase—tourists sometimes came to call just so they could say they'd seen him in the flesh.

That glimpse comes courtesy of the portraitist John Gadsby Chapman, who painted Crockett twice in 1834 and who was fascinated enough by his subject to write down nine pages of reminiscences. Chapman had set out to do a small portrait, "a study of his head alone," but Crockett didn't care for the result. It was a picture, he said, "like all the other painters make of me, a sort of cross between a clean-shirted Member of Congress and a Methodist Preacher." Bor-*ing*. Why not take a fresh approach? "If you could catch me on a bear-hunt in a 'harricane,' with hunting tools and gear, and a team of dogs, you might make a picture better worth looking at."

Chapman said he'd try, and David really got into it.

He searched all over Washington for props: leggings, moccasins, a hatchet, a butcher knife, and, in Chapman's words, "a well worn linsey-woolsey hunting shirt, a good deal faded and soiled by use, of a prevailing color harmonising with that of the woods and thickets during the hunting season." Everything had to be positioned on his body correctly, with the knife, for example, "in easy and prompt reach of his right hand." He borrowed an appropriately battered rifle from an old hunter who lived by the Potomac. He insisted on authentic mongrels, not purebreds, as models for his hunting dogs, informing Chapman that there were "plenty of first-rate fellows to be found about the country carts any market day." With the painting well under way, he suggested a crucial change in his overly static pose, demonstrating what he was after by raising his broad-brimmed hat above his head and giving "a shout that raised the whole neighborhood."

Talk about a man conscious of how his public saw him! And Chapman's observations don't stop there.

One day, he reported, he was talking with David "at his rooms on Pennsylvania Avenue" when some visitors were announced. Two were said to be "strange gentlemen" staying at the hotel across the street; the third was a local man prone to giving informal Washington tours. "'Show 'em up,'" Crockett said with a "comical air of resignation . . . putting on his hat, and throwing one leg over the arm of his chair." He greeted the strangers, who had come "expressly to pay their respects to Colonel Crockett," treated them to "several of his best stories," and bade them a cordial farewell. Then he "shook himself out of dramatic pose, replaced his hat upon the table, and, as it were, thinking aloud, murmured, 'Well!—they came to see a bar, and they've seen one—hope they like the performance.'"

The site where this scene played out is now home to the Federal Trade Commission. At the east end of the building stands a pair of limestone statues, each depicting a shirtless man tugging on the bridle of a recalcitrant horse. Feet planted firmly on the ground, he has yanked the horse's head in his direction. "Man Controlling Trade," the twin statues are called, and they're supposed to evoke a heroic FTC reining in monopolies—but they make me think of David trying to control his image in 1834.

And when I look at reproductions of that first Chapman painting, the one David said looked like all his other portraits, I have to disagree. I see a very human legend caught with his guard down. His lips are tense, his gaze is distant, and there is something haunted about his eyes.

Image making wasn't all that concerned Crockett that year, of course. He had his share of other worries.

Chapman portrays him as a generally cheerful man, but two less-than-upbeat moments stand out. One time, David showed up for a sitting with a crumpled letter in his hand. He carried himself, the painter noticed, in a way that was "less erect and defiant" than usual, and there was "a subdued expression in his face that I had never before seen there." Had he received bad news? "No, 'spose not," Crockett said, "only a son of mine out west has been and got converted. Thinks he's off to Paradise on a streak of lightning. Pitches into *me*, pretty considerable. That's all."

The letter was from Crockett's son John Wesley, but it may have reflected wider family tension. Surviving letters from David to family members are rare, and if he wrote any to Elizabeth, they have yet to be found. Some historians think the two had separated by that time, though the evidence is far from conclusive.

On another occasion, Chapman ran into an exhausted-looking Crockett at the foot of Capitol Hill. "*[S]uch nonsense* as they are digging at up yonder, it's no use trying to—I'm going home," he said.

There's no telling what caused that particular outburst, but the larger context is perfectly clear. Political reality was catching up to David Crockett—and no amount of image manipulation was going to reverse that trend.

He was never going to get his land bill passed; before long, he wouldn't even be able to mention it on the House floor without being shouted down. Meanwhile, Andrew Jackson's presidency was stronger than ever. Old Hickory had smashed the Second Bank of the United States, and it looked as though he'd be able to handpick a successor, his vice president and longtime consigliere, Martin Van Buren, whom David despised.

It's true that, early in 1834, there had been a faint Whig-generated buzz about Crockett running for president himself. David appeared to have enjoyed that—there's some joking about it in his autobiography—but not to have taken it very seriously. By the end of the year, he was promoting the candidacy of a fellow Tennessean, Hugh Lawson White, as a way to stop Van Buren. Either way, he was waving a red flag in front of the already furious Jacksonian bull.

Worst of all, west Tennesseans were starting to tire of Crockett's celebrity act. That image-making portrait of the hat-waving bear hunter with his dogs wasn't aimed at them; they already knew who their congressman was. Or thought they did. Because the David Crockett *they* knew, "the gentleman from the cane," used to make *fun* of rich people, not traipse around after them scarfing fancy dinners and swilling champagne.

Crockett's enemies lost no time exploiting his book tour politically. Wasn't he supposed to be devoting himself to the people's business? Why was he off hobnobbing with rich Yankees instead? His playing hooky from Congress, Boylston and Wiener write, "enabled the competition to portray him as a man more concerned with personal advancement than looking out for the welfare of his constituents." As a Nashville newspaper put it that summer, the people of west Tennessee had not sent him to Washington "for the purpose of his there writing his life."

But his real sin was the hobnobbing.

You could sum it up in the old saying "Don't get above your raisin'," a piece of country wisdom strongly associated with the physical and psychic landscape in which David had his roots. It means don't forget who you are; don't leave your people behind. Lester Flatt and Earl Scruggs used to do a song about it—Ricky Skaggs has a more recent version—and there were times, as I drove around the recession-scarred vicinity of Crockett's last Tennessee home, when I couldn't get Flatt's lyrics out of my head:

Now I got a gal that's sweet to me,
She just ain't what she used to be

Just a little high headed
That's plain to see
Don't get above your raisin'
Stay down to earth with me

The northeast tour "was the blunder of Crockett's career," Shackford wrote. Unlike some of the biographer's judgments, this one has gotten no serious argument from other Crockettologists. It won't get one from me either.

Still, there's another way to think about it.

Like most of us, David Crockett was neither simple nor consistent. Yes, he knew where he came from, and no, he had not forgotten. Over and over, in his pursuit of his land bill, he had proved that he wanted to be the poor man's friend. But he had also spent his whole *life* trying to get above his raisin'.

Wasn't that what you were supposed to do in America when you were born anonymous and dirt poor?

Crockett's opponent in the 1835 congressional race was none other than Adam Huntsman, the author of the biblical parody, possessor of the wooden leg, and alleged victim of the farmer's-daughter stunt. If David really did pull off that hilarious trick, it would have been during that campaign—but it didn't help. Huntsman knew that Crockett was in trouble before he decided to run, and he summed up his view of the situation in a letter to Polk: "If he carries his land Bill it will give him strength. Otherwise the conflict will not be a difficult one."

Huntsman was wrong about the difficulty. The race turned out to be close. Among other issues, as the author of *Adam Huntsman: The Peg Leg Politician* pointed out, David's rival used the tour as a club to beat him with. He reminded voters, Kevin McCann wrote, that their elected representative "dined at elegant banquets, made speeches, accepted gifts from Whig admirers, and hawked his autobiography while still collecting his salary. 'Whatever may be the fashion of those who breathe the atmosphere about Washington,' Huntsman scolded, 'we of the West consider that no man should take a tour of pleasure for three weeks, *and then charge us eight dollars per day for it.*'"

Crockett ended up losing by 252 votes. The exit poll hadn't been invented in 1835, but it seems likely that at least 127 of his constituents thought he'd gotten above his raisin'.

Always optimistic about his political prospects, at least in public, David had never conceded that Huntsman was likely to win. Still, long before the returns were in, he had a Plan B in mind. It was the same plan he had used over and over, earlier in his adult life, when something had halted his forward progress:

Go west. Go ahead.

Six months after the loss to Huntsman, Plan B would send him riding into San Antonio. (The town's full name at the time was San Antonio de Béxar, which was often shortened simply to Béxar.) A month later, it would place him behind the walls of the Alamo on the morning the Mexicans attacked. History records, however, that before David left Tennessee, Plan B also allowed him get off one of the great exit lines in the annals of American politics.

"Since you have chosen to elect a man with a timber toe to succeed me," he is said to have told his constituents, "you may all go to hell and I will go to Texas."

Reportedly, he said something like that even before he was defeated. Reportedly, he said it at the farewell barbecue he threw for himself at his last Tennessee home. Reportedly, he also said it in Jackson, Tennessee, where the town square boasts a historical marker to that effect, though when I saw it, the date was off by four years. Reportedly, he said it again at a drunken revel in Memphis, as recorded by an untrustworthy local historian nearly four decades after the fact. And reportedly, he recycled the line at the first fancy dinner he attended in Texas.

But the details really aren't important here.

All we need to know is that at forty-nine years of age, David Crockett—half man, half legend—was setting out on the last great adventure of his life.

⨝ 8 ⨞

"The Richest Country in the World"

The first shots of the Texas Revolution rang out on October 2, 1835, some seventy miles east of San Antonio de Béxar. They came in a confrontation between the Mexican army and the Texians—as the Anglo settlers of this far northeastern frontier of Mexico were known—over a six-pound cannon. The cannon belonged to the army, which, in happier times, had bestowed it upon the settlement of Gonzales for use against warlike Indians. Now, with Mexican-Texian tensions on the rise, the Mexicans thought it might be prudent to get it back.

Good luck with that.

Stephen Hardin lays out the ensuing comic opera in the first chapter of his classic *Texian Iliad*, a military history of the revolution. Texians bury cannon to keep it safe! Then they dig it up again! They load it with scrap metal! They wave a flag featuring a picture of the cannon and the words COME AND TAKE IT! They fire the thing! By the time they get it reloaded, the outgunned Mexicans have sensibly abandoned the field. The only Texian casualty has a bloody nose suffered in a fall from his horse. Does that stop the encounter from going down in history as "the Lexington of Texas"? Hell, no. And once I get over my Yankee annoyance at the comparison—eight patriots were *killed* at Lexington, folks, and those New England minutemen went on to rout the most formidable army in the world—I have to concede that it's reasonable enough. At least one Mexican was dead, and, as Hardin put it, "a fatal step had been taken. There could be no turning back." Three weeks later, Texian volunteers under Stephen F. Austin would be marching on Béxar to take on the Mexican force occupying the town. The serious fighting was about to begin.

But David Crockett didn't know that when he planned his Texas adventure. "I want to explore the Texes well before I return" was all he said in his last letter from Tennessee, written on October 31, the day before he saddled up.

Crockett would become the best-known American to cross the Texas border in 1835. Fame aside, he had much in common with many of those moving in the same direction. Things were not going well for them at home, for whatever reason. They were in debt. They had family problems. In some cases, they had trouble with the law. Texas offered a fresh start.

And for David, as for most other emigrants, the key to that fresh start was land.

Different perspectives on Texas real estate had fueled the conflict toward which he rode. From the point of view of Mexico, which had won independence from Spain in 1821, Texas was a vast empty space (if you didn't count the Comanches and other native tribes) that was difficult to populate. From the United States' point of view, it looked like God's gift to an expanding population—a place to go once all the territory from which Indians had been removed had been gobbled up. At first, this seemed a happy convergence of needs: the Mexicans invited foreigners to Texas, and thousands of Americans took them up on it. Then the Mexican government started to worry that the Anglos might take the place over, and in 1830, it banned further immigration from the United States. The ban worked about as well as U.S. immigration bans work today. In 1834, Mexico gave up and reopened the border.

Think demographics might be destiny? The evidence here is persuasive. Between 1821 and 1836, the population of Texas (again, not counting the Indians) rose from 2,500 to more than 40,000. At least 35,000 of that number were immigrants from the United States and their slaves. Americans on both sides of the border assumed that it was just a matter of time before Texas split from Mexico and joined the United States.

Antonio López de Santa Anna begged to differ.

Santa Anna personified opportunism and ambition. By 1834, he had seized dictatorial power as Mexico shifted from federalist to centralist rule. In May 1835, he put down a revolt by federalists in the state of Zacatecas with astonishing brutality. The general rewarded his troops "by allowing them two days of rape and pillage," Hardin wrote, during which "more than two thousand defenseless noncombatants were killed." The news filled Texians with "dismay and foreboding," but it seems not to have reached west Tennessee: Jackson and Van Buren remained the chief villains in David's world.

"I do believe Santa Ana's Kingdom will be a paradise, compared with this, in a few years," he wrote in August, just after his bitter electoral defeat.

Crockett may not have known about Zacatecas or about the Texian army's advance on Béxar, but that's not to say he wasn't aware of broader Texas trends. He had crossed paths with his old Tennessee acquaintance Sam Houston in Washington the previous year, and it's easy to imagine Houston offering a sales pitch on the future Americanization of Texas and the opportunity it offered David to become a landowner once again. He would soon learn more about the military situation—where and when is not entirely clear—but the evidence of his letter, along with later family testimony, shows that he wasn't looking for a fight when he left home.

He headed south with three companions: a neighbor, a nephew, and a brother-in-law. Their route took them through Jackson, where a sign at an out-of-the-way cemetery now points to the grave of CONG. ADAM HUNTSMAN WHO DEFEATED CONG. DAVID CROCKETT AUG. 6, 1835. They rode on to Bolivar, where David's host compared him to "a passing comet, not to be seen again." Memphis was next. There, according to the local historian, Crockett went barhopping. At Neil McCool's place, friends hoisted him onto the counter and he did his go-to-hell-I'm-going-to-Texas routine.

If any trace of McCool's remains in downtown Memphis, I didn't find it. Before I left town, though, I did manage a trip to Graceland, where I fantasized—I know this is completely nuts—about an alternative universe in which David and Elvis could hang out. Just think of it: two of the most celebrated Americans who ever lived, belting down drinks in the Jungle Room, taking potshots at the human-shaped targets in the firing range, comparing notes on the costs and benefits of fame.

Sadly, the King of the Wild Frontier never got to meet the King, and Elvis died even younger than David did. I bought a refrigerator magnet and hit the road.

Crockett's road took him through Arkansas. By mid-November, if not before, he had gotten some updated Texas news: a Little Rock newspaper reported that he was en route "to join the patriots of that country in freeing it from the shackles of the Mexican government."

My road took me to the airport. From what I'd read, few traces remain of Crockett's Arkansas trek, so I'd developed a Plan B of my own: I would fly to Dallas, drive northeast, and pick up David's trail at the point where he crossed the Red River into the future Lone Star State.

Not that I knew for sure where that was.

The truth is that nobody knows exactly how David Crockett made his way from Arkansas to the Alamo. Crockettologists have been known to fake it, bluffing themselves into certainty, but I didn't want to do that any more than I wanted to get stuck (as I did) in rush-hour traffic on U.S. 75 in Plano. Most of my previous experience of Texas had involved big cities and interstates, and I was looking forward to finding some back roads and poking uncertainly around.

One thing I did know was that the hunt would take a while. Crockett fans tend to think of David as heading straight from the Texas border to San Antonio, but in reality, he spent a couple of months exploring this wild new world—just as he'd said he would—hanging out with a diverse assortment of Texas pioneers and seemingly unconcerned with any timetable at all.

A hundred miles or so beyond the gridlock, I found Farm Road 410. It was the kind of winding two-lane on which you can cruise for twenty minutes without seeing another car. Spring flowers yellowed the fields, cumulus clouds whitened the horizon, and I got to watch a coyote lope across the road near the Howdy U ranch. It wasn't the wilderness you'd have seen if you'd ridden through here 175 years ago, but it wasn't suburban Dallas, either. And look, here was my man Davy, coming across the river at Jonesboro, just where I thought he would!

Or so a historic marker informed me—though there was no river in sight.

No, I had not entered the twilight zone. The town of Jonesboro really did once sit on the south bank of the Red River, and in the early nineteenth century, it really was an entry point for emigrants to Mexican Texas. But Jonesboro became a ghost town and the river shifted its course. To complicate things further, the tiny road-side park I was now visiting—a jumble of historic markers sharing space with a sprawling prickly pear cactus—couldn't even be built on the original town site because the site's twentieth-century owner wouldn't play ball. That's why the hallowed spot where "Sam Houston (1832) and David Crockett (1835) entered Texas" had to be commemorated half a mile away.

But with all due respect to the well-meaning folks who put up the Crockett Was Here marker, Jonesboro is only one of many places where David might have made his Texas debut.

One student of this vexing question is Manley F. Cobia, Jr., a supremely dedicated Crockettologist who spent years research-ing David's route to the Alamo. "There are at least four different points where Crockett is believed to have crossed the Red River," Cobia wrote in his 2003 book, *Journey into the Land of Trials*. At two of them, David would have crossed straight from Arkansas; at the others, he'd have gone through part of Oklahoma first. Cobia doesn't come right out and say so, but he appears to favor the Jones-boro scenario. He credits Judge Pat B. Clark of nearby Clarksville, the author of a regional history published in 1937, for the argument that Crockett rode west to Fort Towson, Oklahoma, then turned south and "caught the ferry at the old Jonesboro crossing."

I'd go with Jonesboro, too, if forced to choose. But I'm sorry to report that my judgment can't be trusted—because I've fallen head over heels in love with an important source.

She's a handsome woman of thirty named Isabella Clark, wid-owed in 1827 and now remarried. She's fully at home in the kind of trackless, barely populated terrain where, if you're trying to give a stranger directions, you point him toward a distant clump of oaks and tell him to go on from there. By 1835, she and her husband,

James, have moved south from Jonesboro to pioneer the town that will soon bear their name. And in late November of that year, when Isabella hears that Crockett and some friends have crossed the Red River and headed west, she has to act fast.

West of Clarksville is Indian country. James Clark, in fact, has just set out with a group of armed men to drive a Comanche band away from the settlement.

What to do?

Isabella jumps on a horse and follows David's trail, risking her own life to perhaps save his.

She will be telling this story, with variations, until she is almost ninety years old. Picking up "two other spirited young matrons along the way," as a version later retailed by a newspaper columnist has it, "she galloped after the Crockett party," finally overtaking them at sunup at the isolated home of some settlers she knew.

"Mrs. Clark, what in the name of God brings you here at this hour?" someone asked.

"My horse fetched me!" snapped Isabella. "What's for breakfast?"

You go, girl!

What did she make of the famous man she'd tracked down? According to some purple prose later published in Isabella's honor, each admired "the glowing patriotism that burned in the bosom of the other." Isabella herself praised David in more vigorous language. "It has always disgusted me to read these accounts of Crockett that characterize him as an ignorant backwoodsman," she told a reporter from Dallas in 1894. "He was a man of wide practical information and was dignified and entertaining."

Ah, but did he heed her warning? We're well beyond the realm of the provable here—as Cobia points out, even Judge Pat, who was Isabella's grandson, told more than one version of her story—but it sounds as if David paused long enough to find a local guide before continuing west. When he did, he is said to have run into James Clark and told him, without knowing the two were related, about the woman who'd thundered after him on horseback to warn him about Comanches. "That was my wife, for no other woman could do a thing like that," James replied.

Cobia conscientiously reports that knowledgeable local historians dispute that part of the story. They could be right. I'm not sure I want to know.

James Clark died a couple of years later, but not before he and Isabella had equipped a company of volunteers to fight in the Texas Revolution. Isabella married a family friend and went on to run Clarksville for half a century. She donated land to settlers, churches, and storekeepers; paid to have the town's first courthouse built; and "through her liberality and enterprise," as her grandson put it, "ensured that this place enjoyed its steady growth." In the words of another chronicler: "Politically, financially, and socially, she reigned supreme."

She's buried in the St. Joseph Cemetery on Main Street, where a decent-sized stone marks her grave. But if you ask me, she deserves a statue in the town square.

✷

In downtown Paris, Texas, thirty miles west of Clarksville, there's a six-foot-high portrait of Crockett heading into uncharted territory. He rides a white horse, holds a rifle across his saddle, and gazes intently out of the frame as if scouting for Comanches on the horizon. It's one of four striking murals, done in the 1930s, that hang in the Paris public library, but what really tips off informed viewers to its Paris setting—though the town didn't exist in 1835—is the oak in the background. David has carved his initials on the trunk, just as local tradition says he did when he camped at a spot now known as Crockett Circle.

Crockett traditions are thick on the ground in northeast Texas.

One of my favorites, from a newspaper column called "Backward Glances" recommended by an archivist at Paris Junior College, concerns David's stay at the home of a man named Matthias Click; to appreciate it, you need to know that Mat had a daughter named Louisa who had a suitor named Abner. Here's *Paris News* editor A. W. Neville, writing with great confidence a century after the event:

> The story goes that Davy Crockett . . . stopped at Mat's and stayed for a week or so. It is reasonable to believe that Davy did linger there for it is likely that the hilarious Abner was fooling round there courting Miss Louisa, and the still was handy there, two impelling not to say compelling motives to linger—good company and good licker. For one must remember that back in the pioneer days when men had to work hard and live hard, taking a drink was not the disgrace that it is now. We can imagine that Abner and Davy had a glorious time, roving through the thickets, killing a buck every day and eating venison and fiddling all night— for Davy was a fiddler, you know.

There's more: While staying with the Clicks, according to Neville, Crockett built a sledlike object called a "lizard" or a "spider" out of the hard wood of a bois d'arc tree. Used to transport water or game, it became known as "Davy Crockett's Lizard" and "lay around the Click place about sixty years" before, regrettably, disappearing.

Crockett Circle turned out to be a disappointment, offering no hint of David beyond his name on the street sign. More rewarding were a couple of non-Crockett attractions I'd read about. One is an elegant statue of Jesus wearing cowboy boots that graces a memorial in a cemetery south of town. The other is a dramatic sixty-five-foot hunk of metal that rises skyward beside the Love Civic

Center. Who could resist a giant model of the Eiffel Tower with a bright red cowboy hat on top? Especially when, as this story goes, the hat was added to make the Texas tower taller than a rival Eiffel in Paris, Tennessee?

I had to tear myself away, though. The Crockett trail called.

The specifics of David's movements during the five or six weeks he spent wandering around the northeast corner of the state are extremely hard to verify. The best evidence comes from a letter he wrote to his daughter Margaret and her husband from San Augustine, east of Nacogdoches, after arriving there in January. It is the single Crockett letter from Texas that survives (we have only copies, not the original, but historians generally agree that it is genuine), and it is important for, among other things, a clue-filled, punctuation-free passage describing the glorious landscape he had recently explored. "I expect in all probilaty to settle on the Bordar or Chactaw Bio of Red River that I have no doubt is the richest country in the world," he wrote. "Good land and plenty of timber and the best springs & good mill streams good range clear water—and every appearance of good health and game plenty it is in the pass whare the Buffalo passed from North to South and back Twice a year and bees and honey plenty."

Crockettologists have argued, as Cobia reports, that David intended "Bordar" to refer to Bois d'Arc Creek in what's now Fannin County and that "Chactaw Bio" is the Choctaw Bayou, a large, ill-defined swath of prairie in the same general vicinity. As for those plentiful bees, that clue could hardly be clearer: it said Honey Grove was the place to check out.

I tried to keep my mind on Crockett as I drove west on U.S. 82, but it wasn't easy. Practically the first thing I saw was a lovely old passenger airplane parked randomly in a field just north of the highway. It turned out to be a Martin 404, a remnant of an aviation museum run by a Paris-born pilot who used to fly in Hollywood films such as *Midway* and *Catch-22*. Not long after spotting the Martin, however, I ran into a 2,100-acre preserve of native grassland that helped take me back in time. I could imagine David on that white horse, traversing the green prairie, despite the roar of the eighteen-wheelers barreling past.

Honey Grove proved even more startling than an out-of-place airplane or a Stetson-wearing Eiffel Tower. It's not as though I hadn't seen plenty of small towns with decaying cores, but this one was a gorgeous, ghostly archetype. Smith Feed-Seed & Hardware still did business on the corner of Market and Sixth, yet rows of empty storefronts, missing many bricks on their facades, lined the street to the south, and the whole place had the feel of a lavishly constructed film set abandoned a century before.

The Bertha Voyer Memorial Library was open, though, so I ducked in to search for David there.

The commonly accepted story about Crockett and Honey Grove is that he named the area in December 1835, when he and an unknown number of companions camped at a grove of trees—some of them hollowed out and filled with honey—just north of what would become the town square. As usual, however, there are alternate versions. I found one, in a nineteenth-century history of Fannin County, that talked about some hunters from Arkansas exploring the same territory two decades before. They were said to have camped at a beautiful spot that, due to "the immense quantity of honey found in the timber," they had given "the appropriate name of Honey Grove."

Hmm. No David in that version—though he still could have passed through later on.

It was late and I was hungry, but before I packed it in for the day, I remembered my stroke of luck in finding the Man Who Knows Everything in Tennessee. So I asked librarian and Crockett fan Patsi Tindel if she knew anyone in town who was deeply into local history.

"Woody Austin," she said immediately.

Half an hour later, I was scarfing a milk shake in a local eatery with a boarded-up front window—someone had driven a car through it—as a lean, tall gentleman in jeans and cowboy boots gave me his take on David's Texas Tour. A longtime manager of auto dealerships who had most recently lived in Irving, he had chosen to retire in Honey Grove in part because of its irresistible past.

"Crockett crossed the Red River and came into Clarksville," Woody began, echoing the tradition I'd already heard. Passing through the future Paris, he headed northwest toward what's now the town of Sumner—that was news to me; Sumner is a few miles north of the roadside airplane—because "he had a good friend that had a farm there." The friend had just left on a hunting trip, so David and his entourage headed after him. They spent a night near where "the Blue River runs into the Red," turned south, then camped at "a place called 'the honey grove.'"

At that point, Woody began to laugh. "The honey grove is right behind my house," he said. "We know Crockett was there long enough that he carved his initials in a tree stump. A man named James Fletcher Black found it when he was twelve years old. Now whether that was a stump Davy carved or whether he'd spent the previous three nights carving it himself, nobody will ever know. But he found it."

Right behind his house! I was dying to see the place. But before I could say so, we started talking about the history of Honey Grove the town, which was settled six years after Crockett allegedly wandered through. "I can take you through one of those old buildings," Woody said. Pretty soon we'd scrambled up to the kind of vast, unfinished second-floor loft space that big-city artists would kill for. Light flooded through the nearly floor-to-ceiling windows, and from them I could gaze down at the remnants of a place that used to be—something else.

It started, Woody said, with a couple of settlers who'd known Crockett in Tennessee; Honey Grove tradition says they'd received a letter from David extolling the virtues of the area. Small farming drove the economy at first, but within a few decades, cotton boomed and the town expanded like crazy. "The businessmen on the square took up a collection and hired a road gang to extend fifth street all the way to Ladonia," a dozen miles to the south, "so that people down there could come up here and spend their money"—but that was just the beginning. Ladonia was on a rail line to Dallas, so at some point, those ambitious nineteenth-century businessmen paid the railroad to build a spur to Honey Grove, bought an engine and a few passenger cars, and hired an engineer. By that time the town boasted "four hotels, a number of restaurants and four opera houses, and we were on the circuit for all the traveling shows and singers."

Honey Grove was a *destination*. "Our peak was seven hotels and seven opera houses," Woody said. "There was quite an aristocracy here."

So what changed?

"Boll weevil is what did it."

The weevils drove the cotton economy west. The train from Ladonia chugged into Honey Grove for the last time in 1944. A few decades later, highway traffic was rerouted north of town. At some point, along came "a Walmart in Paris and a Walmart in Bonham," each an easy drive from Honey Grove's town square.

Woody's house is just northwest of the square. I admired its old-fashioned wraparound porch as we drove past on our way to Crockett's campsite. West of the road was a field lush with pecan trees.

"Go up here to this next bend, and you can look back to the south and you'll be looking right down the throat of the grove," he said. I drove around the bend and parked. The light was fading, but I could still make out the low-lying patch of green Woody pointed out. We couldn't walk down to it, though, because the field between it and us was occupied by cattle and buffalo. Yes, buffalo. The herd belonged to rancher friends of Woody's. Even from behind a fence, we seemed to make them nervous; when one of the shaggy bulls broke into a run, he accelerated a lot faster than I would have expected.

What must it have felt like, I wondered, to explore this landscape when such creatures were truly wild?

It's easy to romanticize the weeks Crockett spent in northeast Texas, if only because we know what happened next. Beyond that surviving letter home, he left no paper trail to help take us inside his head. That said—and bearing in mind that David was here in December, not the balmiest month of the Texas year—I suspect he had a fabulous time. Why wouldn't he? It was the kind of risk-heightened adventure he had always loved, and his hunting companions, however many there were, would have asked nothing from him beyond camaraderie.

Politics? Family pressure? Debt? War?

All gone, at least for now.

Alas, he had to turn back. It's unclear whether he had already fixed on Béxar as a destination, but even if he had, it would have been unsafe to head straight southwest. Too many Comanches, as many people besides Isabella would have told him by now. So he turned east again, most likely picking up a well-traveled path called Trammel's Trace that would eventually take him south to Nacogdoches.

I had one last Crockett site to seek out before I followed him there. Lost Prairie was a settlement on the Red River, a few miles below Fulton, Arkansas. Some Crockett scholars think it's where he first crossed; others think he stopped by later on his way south. Like Jonesboro, it's a ghost town now, though it lacks helpful historical markers. Long story short, I didn't find it—which is ironic, because it's the only place on the whole river through which we're truly certain David passed.

That's because a Lost Prairie man mailed David's watch back to Elizabeth after the Alamo. Her husband had been short of funds when they met, Isaac Jones wrote, and had traded the timepiece for Jones's plainer one plus $30 in cash.

On December 4, 1835, while David Crockett was still happily wandering the prairie west of Clarksville, a man named Benjamin Rush Milam rode into a Texian camp outside Béxar and got seriously pissed off. Milam's anger had enormous consequences for the Texas Revolution—and for Crockett. Without it, David wouldn't have died defending the Alamo, and few of us today would know his name.

That's what I think, anyway. Let me explain.

The Texian force besieging Béxar wasn't really an "army" in the normal sense of the word. The men were all volunteers, and as such, they came and went as they pleased. They elected their officers, and they had a habit—admirable in some ways, problematic in others—of disregarding direct orders and making military decisions democratically. That was a good thing in late October, when, flushed with a modest victory won en route to Béxar, the inexperienced Texian commander, Stephen F. Austin, ordered his outnumbered troops to pursue some retreating Mexicans into the fortified town. Wiser heads prevailed. It was less of a good thing a few weeks later, when Austin ordered his considerably strengthened force to assault Béxar and a majority of the men refused. And it appeared utterly disastrous on December 3, when the men rejected a similar order from Edward Burleson, who had replaced Austin in command.

Hardin evokes the chaos in *Texian Iliad*. "Between 250 and 300 volunteers departed for home; others berated their officers; and more than a few got blind drunk," he writes. "On December 4, with his army melting around him, Burleson announced his decision to abandon the siege and go into winter quarters at Goliad."

Then Ben Milam showed up.

A forty-seven-year-old soldier of fortune, entrepreneur, and now Texian officer who had been off on a scouting expedition, Milam couldn't believe what was happening. Enlisting the support of Frank Johnson, a colleague with similar views, he stormed into Burleson's tent and emerged with a deal: he could call for volunteers, and, if enough men responded, he could lead an attack on the town.

"Who will follow old Ben Milam into San Antonio?" he demanded. (He meant the town of Béxar itself, not the Alamo, a run-down Spanish mission complex on the town's outskirts.) Four days of intense house-to-house fighting followed, and on December 9, the Mexicans—under the command of Santa Anna's brother-in-law—were forced to surrender. Milam wasn't around to share the triumph, though. Two days earlier, a Mexican sharpshooter had put a bullet through his head.

Historians will tell you that what-if scenarios are the road to madness. It's hard enough to establish what actually happened in the past, they say, without running through an infinity of questions like "What if Ben Milam hadn't led that assault on Béxar?" or "What if Stonewall Jackson had been at Gettysburg?" The correct answer is "We'll never know"—or, as more than one Civil War historian has been known to say in response to the Stonewall question, "He'd have smelled very bad, because he'd have been dead for six weeks."

Fair enough. But I can't help myself here.

If not for Milam, there would have been no Texian garrison in Béxar in the winter of 1836, and it's easy to spin the what-ifs forward from there. What if Santa Anna's decision making hadn't been clouded by the urge to respond to military and family humiliation? What if, instead of laying siege to the Alamo—the strategic importance of which has been disputed—the Mexican dictator had marched his army straight into the heart of the Anglo settlements? What would that have meant for the ragged Texian rebels and the high-profile Tennessean who had just joined them?

Repeat after me: we'll never know. Because of course Milam did lead the assault, and the Texians occupied Béxar, and the last Mexican soldiers in Texas were sent packing—and three hundred miles to the northeast, it put the leading citizens of Nacogdoches in a festive mood. When Crockett rode into town on (most likely) January 5, they promptly invited him to a dinner party, where he was said to have "added greatly to the pleasure of the company by his numerous quaint stories." His go-to-hell-I'm-going-to-Texas routine reportedly drew thunderous applause.

Then a remarkable Nacogdochian invited David home, and he settled in as a guest in a lovely wood-frame house you can still walk around in today.

✦

My route to the Sterne-Hoya House Museum and Library took me down North Street, formerly known as La Calle del Norte, which is sometimes called the oldest public thoroughfare in the United States. The claim refers to its use by Nacogdoche Indians, who showed up in the neighborhood sometime in the thirteenth century, not by the Spanish, who didn't settle there until the eighteenth. These days, North Street offers more in the way of chain restaurants than history, but I wasn't hungry. A couple of Texas-shaped waffles at the motel had taken care of that.

Crockett's temporary housing was a few blocks east of La Calle del Norte, on a quiet street just off what's now State Highway 21. Named after the only two families who ever owned it, the Sterne-Hoya House was built around 1830 by Adolphus Sterne, a German immigrant whose story is, in its own way, as astonishing as David's.

A few highlights: Born in 1801 to an Orthodox Jewish father and a Lutheran mother, Sterne decided at sixteen that he didn't want to be drafted into the military. He forged a passport, emigrated to New Orleans, worked as a peddler, and wound up as a merchant in Nacogdoches. In 1826, he took part in the Fredonia Rebellion, a bizarre insurrection sparked by a cranky land speculator that got Sterne sentenced to death. Somehow he got off. Before long, he and his wife, Eva, knew everyone in Texas worth knowing. Sam Houston was baptized a Catholic (as was theoretically required of all emigrants to Mexico) in the Sternes' parlor. When the Texas Revolution broke out in 1835, Houston asked Sterne to go to New Orleans and recruit volunteers. Sterne spent $10,000 to help outfit the 120 or so men of the New Orleans Greys, many of whom would die at the Alamo or at the massacre in Goliad that followed. One company of Greys stopped at Nacogdoches on their way to the siege of Béxar; they drank champagne and feasted on roast bear ("draped with its hide and carried to the banquet table," a pamphlet informed me) in the peach orchard opposite the Sternes' house.

I learned more about Adolphus and Eva from the enthusiastic, well-informed Carlie Howard, who greeted me inside. But my mind kept coming back to the fact that I was walking in Crockett's footsteps. Literally. The walls, ceilings, mantel, and floorboards in the room where Howard and I stood—it had been the Sternes' bedroom, which they had sometimes turned over to guests—were original.

I hadn't yet been in a real building where David had spent the night, and it was eerie to think of him wandering around this one. I felt as though I were four years old again and, like my daughter, sti'l believed that a historical pal could walk out of the past and introduce himself.

"Do we know where he slept?" I asked.

Howard showed me two possible rooms besides the Sternes', one on each side of the "dogtrot," the wide central passage dividing the two main parts of the house. Then she pointed to a staircase behind an open door.

"These are the original stairs up to the attic," she said. "So Davy Crockett certainly saw those stairs."

The Sterne children slept in the attic when they were young. One of the boys was six when Crockett came to stay. When that boy was in his nineties, "some sweet young thing sat him down and had him dictate his memoirs," which included a passage about David. "Apparently he was one of those people who didn't say, 'Go away, kid, and don't bother me,'" Howard said, laughing, as she went off to find a copy of Charles A. Sterne's unpublished Crockett memories for me to read.

"David Crockett was a guest at my father's house for a week or ten days. My father introduced me to him & he put his hand on my head and said 'Judge what a fine boy you have,'" Charles recalled in 1924. "He was very distinguished looking, fair in complexion, medium in height and size. . . . I remember the horse he rode: a large black horse, fine looking horse. I remember it for he stayed at my father's house & the horse was in our horse lot."

At the time Charles told that story, I realized, my own father was eight years old. More strangeness: How can 1836 seem so long ago when it's only two lifetimes away?

Part of the way through his week or ten days with the Sternes, Crockett saddled up his horse (which some say was not black but chestnut) and rode thirty-five miles east to San Augustine, a smaller settlement whose excited citizens fired off a cannon and hosted a dinner in his honor. There he began writing his final letter home. He told his daughter and son-in-law not only about that prairie paradise he had found, with its migrating buffalo and its "bees and honey plenty," but about the decision he had just made to fight for an independent Texas.

"I have taken the oath of government and have enrolled my name as a volunteer," he wrote.

In his letter, he gave a pragmatic reason for this choice: army volunteers got to send representatives to the upcoming convention that would decide the future of Texas, and he had "little doubt of being elected a member to form a Constitution for this province." Crockettologists interpret this, reasonably enough, to mean that David was eager to revive his political career. Some go further. His political ambition, they argue, along with his land hunger—Texian troops could anticipate being paid with land grants—was his true reason for signing up, and we should disregard the patriotic rhetoric about fighting for freedom that was attached to his name after the Alamo fell.

That seems too harsh.

There's no question that Crockett was looking for political and financial renewal. Not only do those motives make psychological and practical sense, but he acknowledged them plainly ("I am in hopes of making a fortune yet for myself and family") in that last letter home. And if you eliminate everyone with personal financial or political motivation from the pantheon of Texas heroes, it would be empty. Did I mention that Ben Milam was a land speculator? Heck, the Founding Fathers could never have met that standard.

So yes, David wanted to get back into politics. But as his hatred of the autocratic Jackson showed, he had strong views about the kind of politics with which he wanted to be associated. He demonstrated this once more when he went before Judge John Forbes to take his oath. Asked to swear "true allegiance to the Provisional Government of Texas or any future Government that may be hereafter declared," he refused. The "future Government" part was there because Texas was still almost two months from officially declaring its independence, but never mind that: Crockett would swear to support only future *republican* governments, he said.

Judge Forbes made the necessary change.

Tradition has this minidrama taking place in a building known as the Old Stone Fort, then the center of public life in Nacogdoches. The original is gone, but I toured a replica on the campus of Stephen F. Austin State University that now houses a history museum. It had exhibits on Spanish Nacogdoches and the lives of pioneer women but nothing on David. Looking for someone to tell me what the town was like when he came through, I tracked down a historian, Scott Sosebee, with whom I spent a happy hour learning things I hadn't known.

Those east Texas pines I'd heard so much about, for example? Mostly not here in 1836. "This was hardwood virgin forest. *Very* thick," Sosebee told me. The Nacogdoches Crockett experienced was truly a frontier town, not because it was primitive but because it was isolated from the rest of Texas by distance, many hard-to-ford rivers, and that dense forest. It was one of the biggest towns in the province, yet fewer than a thousand people lived there, not counting the farms and horse-raising operations on the outskirts.

Sosebee filled me in on Adolphus Sterne and the Fredonia Rebellion ("Sterne had his fingers in everything; that guy was something else"). He speculated about what the heck Sam Houston was doing while Crockett was holed up in the Alamo, and he marveled at the fact that no one but Houston seems to rate higher in the Heroic Texan Sweepstakes than David, despite David's having spent barely three months "alive in the confines of the state." The professor also assigned homework. If I really wanted to understand what went on in those three months, he said, I had to read Paul Lack's

*The Texas Revolutionary Experience: A Political and Social History,
1835–1836.*

I thanked him and went off to follow Crockett out of town.

From the Sternes' house, Crockett would have picked up the Old
San Antonio Road—aka El Camino Real, the King's Highway;
now Highway 21—which would have taken him right past the
Stone Fort. An unforgivably hideous bank now occupies the site.
On a plaque across the street, I found a poem called "Nacogdoches
Speaks," by Karle Wilson Baker, that evokes the shades of hard-
edged, dream-fueled horsemen riding by:

> I was The Gateway. Here they came, and passed,
> The homespun centaurs with their arms of steel
> And taut heart-strings: wild wills, who thought to deal
> Bare-handed with jade Fortune . . .

No one knows how many homespun centaurs rode west with
Crockett on or around January 16, 1836. Only one of his original
west Tennessee companions—his nephew William Patton—was
still with him by that point, but I've seen estimates ranging from
sixteen (frequently cited) to fifty-one (an extreme) for the size of
David's party, and the numbers will continue to fluctuate (mostly
by shrinking) in unreliable reports of his journey to Béxar. Apparently the men started calling themselves the Tennessee Mounted
Volunteers, though many were not from Tennessee and Crockett
was not formally in charge.

One volunteer who almost certainly left Nacogdoches with him
was the twenty-one-year-old Kentuckian Daniel Cloud. In an earlier

letter home, Cloud had summed up his reasons for fighting in three eloquent sentences that show how readily pragmatism and idealism could mix. "If we succeed, the Country is ours. It is immense in extent and fertile in its soil, and will amply reward all our toil," he wrote. "If we fail, death in the cause of liberty and humanity is not cause for shuddering."

The El Camino Real of 1836 could better be described as a network of trails than as a single road, but it served as the main drag between Louisiana and Mexico City, passing through San Antonio de Béxar on the way. The Daughters of the American Revolution planted pink granite King's Highway markers along it in 1918, and as I made my way toward the town of Crockett, sixty miles west of Nacogdoches, it seemed that I saw one every five minutes. In between came a plethora of other historical information. A small graveside marker read: MOTHER OF CHILD THOUGHT TO HAVE BEEN FIRST ANGLO-AMERICAN BORN IN TEXAS. Another marker noted the location of an Angelina River port built in the 1830s to ship cotton to New Orleans. A massive, grass-covered Caddoan Indian mound rose above the site of a village where people were living a millennium before Crockett rode through.

Maybe four miles past a dirt road leading into the Davy Crockett National Forest, I pulled up beside a marker for the first Spanish mission in east Texas, established to convert Tejas Indians in 1690. Part of the news here was that " 'Tejas,' a Spanish rendition of the native word for 'friend,' " gave the state its name. But I also learned that the mission had lasted just three years and that among the reasons it failed was "the insincerity of the Indians," who "took the Spaniards' gifts but not their religion."

Oh, those insincere Indians! For shame!

The town that bears Crockett's name dates back to 1837, when members of an early pioneer family, the Gossetts, donated land and suggested that the settlement be called after him. Residents have been proud of their connection with David ever since, despite the fact that he spent no more than a day in the area. It was no ordinary day, if local tradition is to be believed: separated somehow from most of his party, David was accosted by angry settlers, accused of being a horse thief, and nearly lynched. He escaped death only because one of the Gossetts happened along and recognized him.

Crockettologists, as we have seen, take many local traditions seriously. This is not one of them.

I walked around downtown Crockett for a while. It seemed to have survived Walmart—at least Davy Crockett Drug was still open—though there were hand-lettered signs of distress in the window of an antique store. (GOING OUT OF BUSINESS SALE, one read. WE HAVE RATS IN CONGRESS AND WE NEED TO EXTERMINATE, another proclaimed.) A few blocks away, I ran across a music venue called the Camp Street Cafe and was disappointed to learn that I'd be missing a performance by the David Crockett Dulcimer Society that weekend. Then I went looking for the town's main Davy location.

David Crockett Spring turned out to be a roadside park on the way out of town—or, more precisely, a funky old water fountain with a plaque claiming that it "marks the camp site of the famous Texan on his historic journey to the Alamo." A brightly colored mural beside it showed a familiar buckskinned figure in a wilderness setting along with three people I couldn't identify. The skeptical-looking guy whose hand Crockett was trying to shake may have been a Gossett. But who were the long-haired kid and the foppish fellow in the dress coat and top hat, both of whom seemed to be camping out with David?

Here was another Crockett mystery. I had more important ones to worry about, though.

What, for example, had David's orders been when he left Nacogdoches? Did he even *have* orders at that point, or was he hoping

Sam Houston would tell him what to do? Was he planning to overtake Houston at the town now known as Washington-on-the-Brazos, which would require a detour south from the King's Highway? It's all guesswork. But to understand the political and military craziness Crockett was dealing with, I had to back up a bit and get some context.

And the professor was right: reading Paul Lack's *The Texas Revolutionary Experience* was a huge help, especially the chapter titled "Into Anarchy."

Consider the "government" to which Crockett had just sworn allegiance. It was the brainchild of a November 1835 gathering of Texian elites called the Consultation, which Lack described as dominated by "scores of old personal jealousies, regional suspicions, and factional quarrels." The members of this extremely contentious body seem never to have looked in a mirror; otherwise, how could they have invented a system of governance so dependent on pie-eyed optimism about human nature? Here's how it was supposed to work: The Consultation would choose a governor. Local delegations would select an amorphous body called the General Council to "assist" him. Council members would have little authority unless "in their opinion the emergency of the country requires it."

In their opinion—got that?

The governor turned out to be a man named Henry Smith, who, while not without his virtues, "had always displayed flamboyant, controversial, and partisan tendencies as a politician." Within a month or so, the council was overriding Smith's vetoes of its actions—which, in the opinion of its members, were definitely required—and the governor was trying to have his most powerful council enemy deposed. Failing, he vented his rage "in rambling letters that leave the impression of derangement," then suspended the whole council, which promptly impeached him and declared Lieutenant Governor James Robinson acting governor. Smith refused to leave office or to turn over executive documents; a citizens' posse refused the council's order to seize them; Texas was left with dueling governors; and Robinson began comparing his rival to tyrants such as Caesar, Napoleon, and Santa Anna himself.

Who, unbeknownst to the participants in this farce, was already marching toward Béxar.

Now consider the "army" the Consultation had created to deal with the Mexican threat. In theory, it was to be commanded by Houston and made up of soldiers who would commit to serving for two years. In practice, it didn't exist. Volunteers were the whole ball game, and the Consultation ordered its new commander in chief to leave the volunteers alone. "Gen. Houston will not be authorized to command them," Robinson blithely explained, "unless it is their wish fully expressed." The result, Lack noted, was that "Texas had two military forces: a regular army on paper, with discipline, a single commander, and civil direction but no soldiers; and another consisting of several hundred volunteers who showed but a minimum of respect to any authority, submitted occasionally to an officer of their own choosing, and constantly debated such matters as whether, when, or where to fight." And that was before some of those chosen officers came up with one of the most boneheaded ideas in military history.

Don't have enough men to defend Texas? Hey, no problem. Let's invade Mexico.

The target was Matamoros, a Mexican port at the mouth of the Rio Grande. The leaders of the proposed attack emphasized the town's strategic position and argued that Mexican federalists there would welcome armed Anglo liberators (whether flower throwing was predicted is unknown). Less openly discussed was the fact that some attack proponents had speculated in land south of the Texas border and stood to lose their holdings unless military action secured them. It's hard to summarize the politico-military chaos sparked by "Matamoros fever"—among other things, it became central to Smith's feud with the General Council—but historians agree that the result was disastrous. As Craig Roell put it in the Texas State Historical Association's *Handbook of Texas Online*, the Matamoros expedition led not just to the pointless deaths of many involved but "to the fall of the provisional government and to the near destruction of the Texas army in 1836."

A couple of Crockett-related points stand out. The first is that David may have left Nacogdoches thinking *he* was headed to Matamoros. In his letter home, after noting that he had taken his "oath of government," he went on to say that he would "set out for the Rio Grande in a few days with the volunteers from the United States."

The other is less speculative and more horrifying. A few weeks after Ben Milam turned defeat into victory at Béxar, Matamoros fever stripped the town's garrison of defenders. The expedition, Lack wrote, "took two-thirds of the three hundred men and the bulk of all available draft animals and supplies."

In mid-January, Sam Houston got an update from the officer left to pick up the pieces in Béxar. "The men all under my command, have been in the field for the last four months," James Neill wrote. "[T]hey are almost naked . . . and not less than twenty will leave to-morrow, and leave here only about eighty efficient men under my command." At one point, the General Who Couldn't Give Orders had been ordered to lead an attack on Matamoros himself; now Houston did his best to talk the volunteers out of their folly. But by the end of January, he had begun a monthlong furlough, during which he traveled to east Texas to negotiate a nonaggression pact with some Indians that may or may not have been necessary and shouldn't have taken that long. What he was actually doing while Santa Anna completed his march north and laid siege to the Alamo remains mysterious.

In any case, he wasn't around to give advice when Crockett rode up Ferry Street into Washington, Texas, on January 22, 1836.

The Birthplace of Texas has been a ghost town for more than a century. In the 1840s, it was a thriving cotton port, with steamers operating between Washington and the Gulf Coast, but in the 1850s, its residents decided they didn't need the railroad that proposed to come through town. Big mistake. Still, it's not a *deserted* ghost town, like Jonesboro or Lost Prairie, because it's part of a beautiful Texas historic site complete with a star-shaped museum, a living history farm, and a reconstruction of the building in which Texians finally declared independence on March 2, 1836. It also has a visitor center that sells coonskin caps and copies of Crockett's autobiography, not to mention David Crockett dolls whose tags sum up his story in verse ("David was uncontainable and quite an impetuous child / He lived his life precariously and was often rather wild").

The best part of the Washington-on-the-Brazos State Historic Site, however, was the reception I got when I walked in the visitor center door.

Mary Borgstedte was behind the register, but she came out to ask how she could help.

I explained.

"Oh, Reba's our Davy person," she said, making a quick phone call and leaving a message.

A few minutes later—Reba Corley, apparently, had been trying to have a quiet lunch—two grown women in park uniforms were serenading me:

> *Born on a mountaintop in Tennessee*
> *Greenest state in the land of the free*

They finished the verse; chanted, "Second verse! Same as the first!"; and cracked up.

"He was just looking for Davy Crockett, but I told him that you were his biggest fan," Borgstedte said.

"He's a *perrrsonal* friend of mine," Corley said, flipping open her cell to display an image from a painting of Crockett that hangs in the state capitol in Austin.

Borgstedte and Corley introduced me to a couple of their colleagues, historical interpreters Janice Campbell and Scott McMahon. Campbell, who wore a white coonskin cap when she was a girl, showed me a lovely small display she'd put together as a teaser for an appearance by a Crockett reenactor. She had filled it with books, images, and quotations, most of which I'd already seen by now, and had thrown in one Crockett relic I definitely hadn't.

"Oh, and that bark right there? He grinned that bark right off the tree," she said. More laughter ensued, followed by the real explanation: "I was looking for a visual."

Turning serious, Campbell mentioned that when kids on one of her tours get antsy and she wants them to listen up, "all I have to say is 'David Crockett.' It's amazing." She once watched Stephen Hardin do the same thing with some of his students. "He was walking along in his very nonchalant way and he says, 'And Crockett came and he was like a rock star.' And when he said that, he got those kids' attention—even though they were college kids."

We know very little, however, about the rock star's 1836 appearance in Washington.

"He stopped over and stabled his horses here with Mr. Lott," McMahon said, referring to an early settler who "had a tavern-inn type thing and a stables as well." Crockett signed a receipt committing the Texas government to pay John Lott $7.50 for accommodations for himself, four other volunteers, and their horses—the last hard evidence of David's movements before he rode into Béxar.

A dark-haired young man sporting a pair of impressive sideburns, McMahon had worked at the historic site for four years, but his connection to the area went back far longer. "My family settled just across the river in 1828," he said. He'd had a history-centered childhood—"I mean, family vacations, some people would go to SeaWorld and we'd go to the Alamo"—and had been participating in reenactments since he was fourteen. When he set off to lead a tour of Independence Hall, I tagged along to hear the story of what happened there in March 1836, five weeks after Crockett passed through town.

Finally, *finally*, it seemed that Texas was getting its revolutionary act together.

In December, the General Council had adopted a resolution calling for another statewide gathering, to be known as the Convention. (Henry Smith vetoed it, naturally, but couldn't make the veto stick.) Local elections produced delegates who were to deal with the independence question and replace the provisional government with something more functional. They met in Washington, McMahon said, because funds were short and the town offered a meeting hall free of charge. By now our guide had shepherded us inside an elegant replica that helped us imagine the scene: fifty-nine delegates plus various hangers-on crammed into a spare, unfinished building, barn-shaped but way smaller than the average barn. Thin cloth hung in empty window frames was the only protection from a bitter wind.

On March 1, the Convention opened; the next day, independence was declared. "It only took an hour," McMahon said. Over the course of the next two weeks, the delegates wrote a constitution, picked a president and vice president, and reappointed delegate Sam Houston as commander in chief, finally having the sense to put him in charge of *everyone* fighting for Texas.

The full story of those two weeks is dense with complications that a quick tour can't be expected to parse. Convention delegates, for example, fought more bitterly over land policy than over anything else. "The label 'land speculator' was with varying degrees of accuracy widely applied to powerful or ambitious politicians," Lack notes, while politicians so accused "could with equal justice label their opponents as 'demagogues.'" Human property proved less controversial. Anglo Texas had always been slave territory—that was part of its quarrel with the Mexican government, which had tried to ban slaveholding there, then backed off—and the Convention carefully "wrote into the framework of government a long list of positive guarantees of slavery." A provision empowering the government to "compel the owners of slaves to treat them with humanity" didn't make the final draft.

Meanwhile, the delegates confronted a military situation whose direness was hard to exaggerate.

It, too, was complex, and the Convention didn't know all the details. The pathetic remnants of the Matamoros expedition had only recently been wiped out—in two lopsided engagements—by one of Santa Anna's lieutenants, and the largest remaining concentration of Texian volunteers had hunkered down in Goliad while their irresolute leader, James Fannin, tried to figure out what the heck to do. Yet there was an extremely simple way to understand the military crisis as well. A Mexican army was camping out 170 miles southwest of Washington, and the undermanned Texian garrison in the Alamo was in no shape to deal with it.

That, the delegates did know. Six days before they convened, the Alamo's latest commander had sent out one of the most famous pleas for help ever written.

"To the People of Texas & all Americans in the world—" it began. "I am besieged, by a thousand or more of the Mexicans under Santa Anna—I have sustained a continued Bombardment & cannonade for 24 hours & have not lost a man—The enemy has demanded a surrender at discretion, otherwise, the garrison are to be put to the sword, if the fort is taken—I have answered the demand with a cannon shot, & our flag still waves proudly from the walls—*I shall never surrender or retreat.*" Those words would make William Barret Travis immortal, though what came next was more to the point: "I call on you in the name of Liberty, of patriotism & every thing dear to the American character, to come to our aid, with all dispatch."

But the Convention was otherwise engaged.

"For the most part these men were politicians; they weren't military men," McMahon explained. "They didn't have supplies or weapons to send," and they decided to finish what they had come to Washington to do. On the morning of March 6, however, while the delegates were at breakfast, a courier rode in with yet another Travis plea. Somehow this one got their attention. So they told Sam Houston to put on his soldier hat, go to Gonzales, take charge of some troops who had been gathering there, and, by God, "relieve the siege of the Alamo."

Good idea. A bit late.

The Alamo had fallen before those delegates even sat down to eat.

Back at Independence Hall, I stuck around long enough to hear the revolutionary endgame. McMahon told how Houston had retreated eastward as fast as his "army" could go, with most of civilian Texas fleeing with him; how hundreds of Texians had been murdered at Goliad, victims of Fannin's incompetence and Santa Anna's brutality; and how, on April 21, a surprise attack on part of the divided Mexican army at San Jacinto turned the war around—it took just eighteen minutes—and transformed the much-maligned Houston into the greatest Texas hero who was still alive.

Then I went for a walk.

I headed down Ferry Street, reversing Crockett's route into town. Washington was built on a bluff above the Brazos, and by the time I reached the river, Independence Hall was no longer in sight. After staring for a while at the mud-red water, I found a nature trail and kept walking. There were no buffalo—just wildflowers and a single startled rabbit—but I kept thinking back to Honey Grove and the paradise David believed he had found.

★

Not long after the grim news from Béxar reached Nacogdoches, Charles Sterne would recall, "my father came home and told my mother of it." Eva Sterne began to weep. When her son asked why, she told him that "David Crockett, our friend, the man who had patted me on the head, was among the dead."

As an old man, Charles visited the Alamo to pay his respects. Removing his hat in front of a striking portrait he found there, he astonished the "veteran lady" in charge by calling it a "perfect likeness" of the man he had met in his parents' home. He was the first person she'd ever seen, the lady told him, who had known David Crockett alive.

Charles didn't identify the portrait, but it was probably the smaller of the two John Gadsby Chapmans, which had been purchased by the Daughters of the Republic of Texas in 1906.

I was eager to pay my respects at the Alamo, too—and, more than that, to really explore the place. What was left to see on the route by which Crockett came riding into San Antonio de Béxar in February 1836? How much remained at the old mission-fortress itself that would help me reconstruct the way the siege and battle had unfolded? What about the specific places where David Crockett might have fought and died?

So many questions. I couldn't wait to get started.

Except—I had to.

Because I also knew that San Antonio, more than any site I had visited so far, would bombard me with Mythic Davy images. They would come at me so thick and fast as to be inseparable from the man himself. Before I could even begin to sort them out, I would need to know a great deal more about who this very human rock star had become—and why—in the 175 years since the still un-solved mystery of his Alamo death.

Trekking through nearly two centuries of mythmaking was going to be a whole different kind of Davy tour.

❄ 9 ❄

"Crockett Goes A-head, Though Dead"

Word of Crockett's death traveled east at a rate that seems incomprehensibly slow today. A month after the fact, it still hadn't hit New York; the eastern papers had been filled instead with whimsical updates on his travels. They reported, among other things, that the colonel "had been a Coon hunting among the Rocky Mountains" and that he "makes the woods of Texas resound with his alligator voice." When East Coast readers finally learned the fate of the Alamo, the details were sparse and contradictory, and many questions remained. Had David fought ferociously to the bitter end? Had he been one of a handful of prisoners—as a correspondent for New York's *Courier and Enquirer* wrote from Texas in June— who had survived the battle only to be executed on Santa Anna's orders? What had those final, heroic Alamo days really been like?

A miraculous discovery answered some of them.

Crockett, it seemed, had started keeping a journal when he set out for Texas in the fall of 1835 and had continued to write in it until less than twenty-four hours before his death. A Mexican officer had found and preserved it, only to die himself at San Jacinto. Almost torn up for use as cartridge paper, the journal instead made its way to Philadelphia, where, in the summer of 1836, it was published as *Col. Crockett's Exploits and Adventures in Texas*. It climaxes with a vivid, day-by-day account of the siege. Here comes an early Mexican artillery bombardment, but "we haven't lost a single man." Here's Colonel Bowie, suddenly taken sick. Here's Crockett, wishing he could get Santa Anna in his sights: "For just one fair crack at that rascal, even at a hundred yards distance, I would bargain to break my Betsey, and never pull trigger again." Here he is picking off one enemy gunner after another, using loaded rifles a comrade hands him. And here he is on March 5, hastily scribbling a final entry: "Pop, pop, pop! Bom, bom, bom! throughout the day.—No time for memorandums now.—Go ahead!—Liberty and independence for ever!"

For decades people believed these words were David's. In fact, an unauthorized ghostwriter made them up.

Exploits was the brainchild of Crockett's regular publishers, Carey and Hart, though another firm gets the credit on the title page. As editor John Seelye explained in his introduction to the 2003 Penguin Classics edition—yes, you read that right; there is a Penguin Classics edition of a phony Crockett text—Carey and Hart had two goals: they hoped the hoax itself would sell, of course, but also that the attention it generated would help clear out an overstock of the previous year's Crockett product, the northeast tour book. So they hired a Philadelphia writer named Richard Penn Smith and told him to get cracking.

Smith had written sketches, short stories, poetry, a novel, and twenty plays, none of them now available from Penguin Classics. He proved a whiz on deadline, though. He threw in whatever fact-based material he could lay his hands on—descriptions of Arkansas and Texas landscapes, newspaper articles on the war, a pair of letters from Crockett to his publishers dating from the summer of 1835—and he cribbed so avidly from other writers' work that Seelye called the result "a tour de force of literary amalgamation."

But mostly he just wrote fiction. The Crockett of *Exploits* travels to Béxar with chance-met companions, a gambler called Thimblerig and a star-crossed lover known as "the Bee hunter." This David hunts buffalo, fights a giant cougar, and runs into fifty fierce-looking Comanches, who turn out to be sweethearts. Oh, and Smith's narrator is a poet, too. Before leaving Tennessee, he pens a lament called "Farewell to the Mountains," the last stanza of which goes like this:

> Farewell to my country!—I fought for thee well.
> When the savage rush'd forth like the demons from hell.
> In peace or in war I have stood by thy side—
> My country, for thee I have lived—would have died!
> But I am cast off—my career now is run,
> And I wander abroad like the prodigal son—
> Where the wild savage roves, and the broad prairies spread,
> The fallen—despised—will again go ahead!

The real David didn't talk or write in that stilted fashion, and anyone who had known him would have seen right away that *Exploits* was fake. Yet Smith wasn't outed as its author for nearly half a century, by which time his inventions were deeply embedded in the Crockett saga. The book was widely reprinted as part of a one-volume Crockett "autobiography" that also included the real thing and the abridged *Col. Crockett's Tour*. Biographers recycled various Smith fictions; anthologizers of American hero tales did, too. *Exploits* would play a role in Disney's "Davy Crockett at the Alamo," of which more later, and that "Pop, pop, pop! Bom, bom, bom!" quotation was still showing up in children's books as late as 1996.

Smith, however, turned out to be a piker when it came to faking Crockett lore for profit. Davy Crockett's biggest nineteenth-century venture into the unexplored territory of myth—from which the flesh-and-blood man was never fully to return—came courtesy of the authors and publishers of the Crockett almanacs: cheap, mass-marketed pamphlets that offered entertaining stories along with practical information on phases of the moon, times of sunrise and sunset, and so on. Almanacs were right up there with the Bible as standard reading material in American homes, and the market was crowded. One way to stand out was to exploit David's brand as—in the words of Crockettologist Michael Lofaro—"the wild, untamed comic spirit of the westering frontier."

Lofaro, who teaches at the University of Tennessee, knows as much about the Crockett almanacs as anyone else alive. His writings are filled with reminders that he's not talking about the real David but about a set of "fantastic tall tales" in which Crockett "assumed the character drawn for him by others." And lest anyone be misled by the benign-sounding phrase "comic spirit," Lofaro once issued a kind of surgeon general's warning to those about to experience Almanac Davy directly. "A face-to-face confrontation with the blatant racism, chauvinistic humor, and comic stereotypes that many nineteenth-century Americans found appealing," he cautioned, "is a disturbing experience for those who prefer to hide from history."

Richard Penn Smith wasn't available for interviews, but Mike Lofaro was. I had some scary reading to do before I went to see him, though.

The idea of the Crockett almanacs that I'd been carrying around had more to do with twentieth-century children's literature than with the real thing. In a favorite book of tall tales we'd read with Lizzie and Mona, Davy was an unambiguously likable fellow. He halted a charging bear just by staring at him, then spared the creature's life and turned him into a faithful companion. He sang duets with a friendly buffalo who had "a fine bass voice." He won the hand of the formidable Sally Ann Thunder Ann Whirlwind in a hellacious dance contest, then headed off to watch his pal Andy Jackson be sworn in as president. And in the middle of a ferociously cold winter, when the earth froze on its axis, he hiked up Daybreak Hill to the Peak o' Day and applied a ton of bear grease to the problem, strolling home with a piece of sunrise in his pocket.

All those stories had roots in the Crockett almanacs. But, as Lofaro had warned, the originals turned out to feel . . . different.

Take the "Speech of Colonel Crockett in Congress," published in the 1837 almanac, in which Davy introduces himself to his House colleagues. "Who—Who—Whoop—Bow—Wow—Wow—Yough," he begins, before summing up his qualifications for office: "In one word I'm a screamer, and have got the roughest racking horse, the prettiest sister, the surest rifle and the ugliest dog in the district. I'm a leetle the savagest crittur you ever *did see.* . . . I can run faster, dive deeper, stay longer under, and come out drier, than any *chap* this side the big *swamp.* I can outlook a panther and outstare a flash of lightning: tote a steamboat on my back and play at rough and tumble with a lion. . . . To sum up all in one word *I'm a horse.* . . . I can walk like an ox: run like a fox, swim like an eel, yell like an Indian, fight like a devil, and spout like an earthquake, make love like a mad bull, and swallow a nigger whole without choking if you butter his head and pin his ears back."

Yikes. It's not as though I wasn't familiar with this Crockett's rhetorical style—once again, he was sounding like Nicolas Cage on the Rabbit Ears CD, not to mention the protagonists of *Sketches* and *The Lion of the West*—but that last line was a shocker. Having Davy boast that he could swallow "a nigger" rather than "General Santy Anna" turned the brag's emotional meaning inside out.

Almanac Davy wasn't facing down death on an Alamo wall. He was just a racist blowhard, showing off.

The 1837 almanac wasn't all bad for David's image. It had him going down fighting with a heap of dead foes stacked around him, and it offered such harmless entertainments as "Colonel Crockett's Account of His Swimming the Mississippi," in which our hero wards off aquatic attacks by a wolf and a bear. But when I paged through the almanac for 1839, I found a Crockett who was impossible to like.

Where to start? Perhaps with the illustration showing an aggressive-looking Davy seated in a parlor while a bug-eyed, half-naked black man crouches at his feet with a spittoon. (The joke is that Crockett doesn't know what it's for and berates the unfortunate "sarvunt" while continuing to spit on the carpet.) Or perhaps with "A Scentiferous Fight with a Nigger," a charming tale in which descriptions of hair-pulling, head-butting, eye-gouging combat mingle with Davy's complaints about his opponent's "cussed strong smell" and his assertion that, had the black man not given up, "I would have made him so near-sighted that he couldn't have seen a whip till he felt it."

Another extreme low point of the 1839 almanac has nothing to do with race. It's about class, and it occurs when Crockett—who in real life, remember, called himself "the poor man's friend"—confronts a poor white squatter who has lied about his improvements on some land he hopes to buy cheaply. "You're a fool, and you can't dance, and your daddy's got no peach orchard, and I think it ar my duty to bring you to justice," Davy tells the squatter. He then points a gun at the man and forces him to choke down a fresh cow pie, spoonful by spoonful.

Believe it or not, there was worse to come.

Before moving on to later almanacs, though, I need to go back to the 1837 edition and mention the striking woodcut that adorns the cover. It shows an alert-looking frontiersman in a fringed jacket, clutching a rifle and wearing a wildcat on his head. This widely circulated image was a direct steal from an engraving of James Hackett playing the comically exaggerated Nimrod Wildfire in *The Lion of the West*—and, as Crockettologists have been pointing out for decades now, it's the main reason we picture Crockett in a fur hat with a tail attached.

Does this prove, as is sometimes claimed, that the real David *never* wore a coonskin cap? Nope. It's impossible to prove the negative here, and in any case, several people have testified that they saw him wearing one. Yet all that testimony, as with so many "facts" about Crockett, comes from stories told about him decades after he was dead. By that time, his furry image was well established. It has only gotten more so since.

"Folks who cut their Crockett teeth on the likes of Fess Parker and John Wayne," as Lofaro once gently observed, can be surprised to hear that the real David wasn't quite as tall as the actors who portrayed him and that "he seldom if ever wore a coonskin cap." That "seldom if ever" is a nice touch, the kind of hedge that even the most knowledgeable Crockettologist can't—or at least shouldn't—avoid.

I was looking forward to meeting the guy.

✦

Lofaro, it turned out, also has a story about his daughter and "The Ballad of Davy Crockett." It goes back to when she was two years old, he told me over lunch at a Knoxville seafood restaurant, which was a few years after he had edited his first Crockett anthology, *Davy Crockett: The Man, the Legend, the Legacy, 1786–1986*. One day he came home from teaching, "and she started humming, and

I said, 'What are you humming, El?' and then she started *singing.*
And I ran to my wife, saying 'Nancy, Nancy, it's genetic!'

"She said, 'No, I just got the Disney Channel on cable and they're
rerunning that stuff.'"

A friendly sixty-something man with a neatly trimmed beard,
Lofaro is the kind of academic who does his best to discuss complicated ideas without lapsing into jargon. He joined the University
of Tennessee's Department of English right out of graduate school
and never left, though an umbrella label such as "American studies"
might better reflect the range of his interests. A childhood fan of
Disney Davy himself—"I've still got my Davy Crockett wallet that
I got at the movie theater, with the little fake fur hat on it"—he
goes so far as to credit Fess Parker with helping launch his academic
career.

That isn't because Parker played Crockett, however. It's because
he also played Daniel Boone.

Lofaro wrote his dissertation on the ways Boone's image got re-
invented in the eighteenth and nineteenth centuries, and he's been
fascinated ever since by how American culture manipulates the
legends of famous frontiersmen. In the 1980s, that led him to the
Crockett almanacs. Tracking down rare copies of the flimsy originals, he explored the gap between the Davy who tames bears and
unfreezes the earth and the one who forces squatters to eat shit.

A key to understanding the almanacs, he reminded me, is
that while they're undoubtedly important cultural documents,
they're "cultural documents of the power elite in the *East.*" They
offer a "popular interpretation of the western hero" created not by
frontiersmen but by hack writers working for publishers in Boston,
Philadelphia, and New York. What kind of interpretation? Well,
you can read into the almanacs pretty much whatever you want.
Almanac Davy is a "trickster-transformer," Lofaro said, who can
shift his shape at will.

Here's another way to look at the shape-shifter those easterners created. Western expansion was remaking Americans' world at a shocking rate, and Almanac Davy embodied both the impulse to glorify this expansion and the cultural anxiety it generated. The extreme violence of the Crockett myth, as another almanac scholar, Carroll Smith-Rosenberg, once put it, can be explained by the need to incorporate "the power and fury of the disorder inherent in the process of massive social-structural change."

Jargon or not, that made sense to me.

The Crockett almanacs had a remarkable two-decade run, allowing their hero to shift his shape many times. But by the 1850s, Lofaro said, their publishers had started to think that Davy was getting tired. More recent frontier figures such as Kit Carson were auditioned for Crockett's role, but "nobody really hit it big" and the series ended in 1856.

Almanac Davy didn't die, however. As Lofaro put it, "he hibernated." Seven decades later, he woke up to find himself a key figure in the history of American folklore. His chief scholarly cheerleader was the folklorist Richard Dorson, who in 1939 published a cautiously edited selection from the almanacs. Because the originals were so hard to track down, *Davy Crockett: American Comic Legend* became the main source for anyone writing about them, and Dorson's collection spawned numerous other works, including many for children.

There were a couple of problems, though.

One was that Dorson and his fellow folklorists didn't understand, at first, where Almanac Davy had come from. They assumed that the Crockett stories had grown out of genuine folk tradition, sometimes uniquely American, sometimes paralleling European myths. Later, Dorson would correct that false impression, coining the term "fakelore" for commercial products, such as the almanacs, that "misled and gulled the public" into thinking they were "authentic oral tradition."

The second problem was what Dorson's book left out. And that is where Lofaro's research came in.

"It's an attractive, general-audience book, and so it's sanitized," he said, summing up the conclusion he reached after he'd compared the full texts of the first seven almanacs to what Dorson had selected. "It's the plain-vanilla Davy, suitable for consumption by, you know, most people. And then you start looking at the stuff that Dorson omitted. That changes things."

Like what?

Well, Dorson tended to ignore stories in which Davy gets naked, whether during a fight with a "monstratious great Cat-Fish" or a brawl sparked by an adulterous affair. He skipped most tales that don't end with Crockett triumphant, including those in which Davy—as Lofaro has written—is "saved by his wife, chased by a snake, shamed by an elk, scared by an owl, and duped by a peddler." And although he did include stories featuring offensive acts and language, Dorson's presentation deemphasized their offensiveness. He changed the title of "A Scentiferous Fight with a Nigger" to "A Black Affair," for example, and he deep-sixed the most racist woodcuts.

To fully grasp the primitive Crockett the almanacs were peddling, however, you have to consider all of them, not just the first few. In Lofaro's anthology, Catherine Albanese took up the task. She showed that Almanac Davy—who got more and more jingoistic in the late 1840s as the Mexican war and the dispute with the British over Oregon unfolded—is at his horrifying worst when dealing with the people he invariably calls "red niggers."

A few examples: Once some Indians tried to steal Davy's hay. He took up his scythe to defend "a decent white critter's property" and "made their heads and legs fly about" so that "the red niggers' sap both watered and manured my field." Once Davy's pet bear "showed simtums of a bowel complaint." Davy shot an Indian and boiled him in a pot filled with "toads, lizards, a crocodile's tail, and other spurious vegetables" to make the bear a medicinal broth. Another time, after Davy had killed a couple of Indian chiefs, he realized he was starving. He turned one into gravy, poured the gravy onto the other, and produced a "superlicious" dinner for himself and his dog.

But remember—please!—that we're not talking about the real David here.

Yes, there was plenty of extreme racist behavior directed at nonwhites in what was then the American Southwest. But Almanac Davy's racism, Lofaro said, was "racism from the *East*, put through the mouth of a southwestern character. So they're not liable for it, okay? They can say the things they wouldn't say in polite company, and Crockett gets tarred with it."

My lunch with Lofaro was long and informative, and I'm happy to report that we got off the subject of cannibalism pretty fast. We moved on to discuss, among other things, the "riproarious shemales" who inhabit the Crockett almanacs—"hugely active" women who, like Davy, "go out and kill bears, but they kill them with knitting needles." Lofaro thinks those satirical portraits were conceived as attacks on women but served instead to liberate them from passive stereotypes. We also talked about how myth trumps historical reality ("always, always; ask John Wayne") and how Daniel Boone's longevity may have worked against him, mythologically speaking. Late in life, Boone moved from Kentucky to Missouri. When the War of 1812 came along, he tried to volunteer. Why not? He was only seventy-eight. Imagine how it would have added to his legend if he had gone down fighting the British or the Creeks.

Instead, Lofaro said, America's number one frontiersman died in near anonymity at eighty-five, "probably of heart failure brought on by indigestion"—setting up the Hero of the Alamo to take his place.

"Crockett Goes A-head, though Dead," one almanac proclaimed—and for the next century or so, Mythic Davy kept doing just that. Beyond his star turn in the almanacs, he appeared onstage and on marble monuments; in biographies and poems; in the names of towns, counties, steamboats, clipper ships, and locomotives; and in dramatic paintings of the fall of the Alamo. After motion pictures were invented, he showed up on-screen, too.

And sometimes, like Elvis, he came back to life.

In 1840 came a report from Mexico, published in an Austin newspaper, that David had survived the Alamo and was laboring as a prisoner in a Mexican mine. David's son John Wesley took this seriously enough to ask the U.S. secretary of state to investigate, but nothing came of it—except that the 1841 almanac had a field day. Announcing Davy's resurrection under the headline "Latest from the Mines," it printed a letter in which "Kurnill Crockett" expressed his desire to be rescued ASAP.

"I ar very fond of posthumorous fame," he wrote, "but why don't you send sum won to git me out of these infarnal green skin varmints' hands, for it's very diffrnnt from being in Kongress?" Crockett sightings would continue at least until David's ninety-ninth birthday, when someone supposedly made a drawing of him.

John Wesley Crockett, it's worth noting, had gotten himself elected to David's old seat in Congress, where he outdid his father by actually getting a land bill passed. (It looked a lot like the compromise David had pushed in 1830.) By that time, Andrew Jackson had retired to the Hermitage, his Tennessee mansion, leaving David's bête noire Martin Van Buren in the White House. In 1844, James K. Polk—yet another David Crockett enemy—won the presidency on a platform favoring the annexation of Texas. Polk sealed the deal the following year, ending the Lone Star State's brief run as an independent nation.

Meanwhile, the Alamo was not—as one might assume—immediately converted into a shrine.

After the battle ended, Santa Anna had ordered the defenders' bodies burned; it was 1837 before the Texians got around to burying the ashes. A few years later, wagonloads of stones from the Alamo complex were selling for $5 as building material. A man who played there as a boy would remember that "no doors or windows shut out the sunshine or storm; millions of bats inhabited the crevices in the walls and flat dirt roofs." A romantic watercolor, painted in 1847, made the place look like a Roman ruin. Then the U.S. Army moved in and changed its shape forever.

The army took over the Alamo during the Mexican-American War and decided to clean it up. In the process, contractors capped the front wall of the church with what the offended watercolorist called "a ridiculous scroll" that gave it "the appearance of the headboard of a bedstead." Much later, an equally offended observer would write that the Alamo had been "Taco-Belled." Control of the church eventually passed to the state of Texas, though by that time the rest of the Alamo complex was in private or city hands. The outer walls were gone. The wing known as the Long Barracks, where many desperate defenders had made their last stand, had been converted into a garish retail establishment selling "Groceries, Provisions, Dry Goods, Queensware, Glassware, Boots, Shoes, Whiskeys, Wines, Beer, Cigars, Tobacco, and Country Produce."

But though the physical Alamo was left to decay or worse, the story of the Alamo turned legendary from the start. Texians immediately began comparing it to the battle of Thermopylae, in which a small force of Greeks, led by a king of Sparta, died trying to hold a mountain pass against a vastly superior force of invading Persians. "Thermopylae is no longer without a parallel," the citizens of Nacogdoches proclaimed just three weeks after the battle, "and when time shall consecrate the dead of the Alamo, Travis and his companions will be named in rivalry with Leonidas and his Spartan band." A more famous version wound up on an early Alamo monument. "Thermopylae had her messenger of defeat—the Alamo had none," it read.

There are problems with this analogy, not least the fact that Santa Anna didn't *have* to eliminate the Texians in the Alamo. Unlike Xerxes, his Persian counterpart, he could have marched around the negligible force opposing him and gotten on with his campaign. Also problematic is the haze of myth that clouds our understanding of what actually happened in 480 B.C. Someday I hope to learn more about the hundreds of forgotten men from Thespia who died fighting beside the Spartans—but not now! I've got more than enough Alamo mythology to worry about.

The Thermopylae comparison reframed the whole Alamo picture. What could easily be seen as a bungled waste of valiant lives became, instead, an epic of deliberate sacrifice in which Travis, Bowie, Crockett, and the rest *chose* to die so their country might live. Then along came a glowing visual metaphor for this choice. Thirty-seven years after the Alamo fell, William Zuber—who had been a teenage volunteer during the Texas Revolution but hadn't seen much action—published an astonishing story that he credited to a man named Moses Rose, said to have been part of the Alamo garrison until its final days. Rose had told his story to Zuber's parents, Zuber claimed, but no one had ever written it down.

In the event that you haven't heard the tale, here it is, greatly abridged from Zuber's 1873 version.

On March 3, 1836, Colonel Travis gathered the men of the Alamo and informed them that there was no longer any hope of reinforcements. He said that he himself planned "to stay in this fort, and die for my country, fighting as long as breath shall remain in my body" but that anyone who wished to attempt escape was free to do so. Then he drew his sword and "traced a line upon the ground," asking those who would stay and die with him to step across it. All but one Alamo defender—including the gravely ill Jim Bowie, who had to be carried—crossed over.

The exception was Rose.

"You may as well conclude to die with us, old man, for escape is impossible," Zuber quotes David Crockett as telling Rose. Instead, Rose scaled a wall, jumped down into "a puddle of blood," and "walked rapidly away."

Shockingly, some skeptics doubted Zuber. But gosh, why *wouldn't* a man sit on a hot story about the most dramatic event of his era for thirty-seven years, bringing it to light only after experiencing "a phenomenal refreshment" of his memory? And why *wouldn't* he choose to turn a fourthhand story—remember, we're talking about Zuber's recollection of what his parents said that Rose said that Travis said—into an exact quotation more than a thousand words long?

"Having been somewhat personally acquainted with Travis, & having read printed copies of most of his dispatches from the Alamo," Zuber explained later, "I thought myself able to put it in Travis's own style; & I am not without a confidence, that, to a considerable extent, I succeeded in doing so."

Case closed?

Far from it.

Zuber's story had fallen into enough disrepute by 1908 that it was dropped from a standard textbook called "History for Texas Schools." But in 1939, documents unearthed in Nacogdoches revealed that there actually had been a man named Rose—real first name: Louis or Lewis—who said he had left the Alamo on March 3, 1836. He had testified to his presence there several times, in reference to land claims filed by heirs of Alamo defenders, and had been believed. Rose's brief testimony included nothing about a thousand-word Travis speech or a dramatic line in the dirt of the Alamo courtyard. Still, its discovery encouraged those who wanted to believe.

And really, they didn't need much encouragement.

In an essay published soon after the Rose documents emerged, the Texas folklorist J. Frank Dobie quoted a reworked version of the story in which Crockett "lifted Rose up and helped him out of one of the windows," then summed up the unequal contest between mythic and historical truth. "[N]obody forgets the line. It is drawn too deep and straight," Dobie wrote. "Reading the documented historians, you'd think nothing could be so unless it happened." Two decades later, in a popular narrative history of the Alamo called *A Time to Stand*, Walter Lord made the same point. "If Zuber was hiding a gentle fabrication," Lord declared, "he was also protecting a shining legend—and what harm in a legend that only serves to perpetuate the memory of valor and sacrifice?"

Dobie and Lord are right: this "gentle fabrication," if that's what it was, immortalized every Alamo defender. We can *see* those men crossing that line.

Mythic Davy, as an individual, got a huge boost from another extremely sticky visual—a 1903 painting called *Fall of the Alamo* by San Antonio's Robert J. Onderdonk. It put Crockett smack dab in the center of the action, arms raised above his head, swinging his rifle like a club. Onderdonk's painting, as Eric von Schmidt wrote in *Smithsonian* magazine in 1986, went on to acquire "quasi-official status" as a depiction of "David Crockett's Last Stand," which was its original title. And not only was Crockett's pose dramatic, there was something "most intriguing" about how familiar it seemed.

Von Schmidt's explanation is worth quoting in full. "In 1895, the Anheuser-Busch Brewing Association began to swamp the country with a wildly popular and delightfully inaccurate lithograph by Otto Becker called 'Custer's Last Fight,'" he wrote. "If you rev erse the mythically potent Custer over the figure of Crockett in Onderdonk's 'Alamo,' you have a near-perfect fit. Both are complete with legendary yellow-tinted buckskins, legendary red bandannas, and even their legendary trademarks at full brandish: George's saber, Davy's long rifle."

Von Schmidt (who died in 2007) had one of the great job descriptions of all time: "singer-songwriter-painter." He was the only man who could claim both to have influenced the young Bob Dylan *and* to have produced an epic 10-by-23-foot Alamo painting that ended up in a university library in San Antonio. In his version, Crockett appears in the background, gesturing for some hard-pressed defenders to fall back to the church. David wears neither buckskins nor coonskin cap because, as von Schmidt explained, he didn't want to put "the mythical 'Davy'" into what he was trying to make "a true painting of the battle."

From what I can tell, he came as close as anyone to reaching that goal. Still, there wasn't a chance in hell that his Crockett—or anybody else's—would replace that intense buckskinned fellow waving a gun over his head.

One picture, worth more than a thousand words. Still, even after *Exploits* and the almanacs, hundreds of thousands of words continued to be written about David.

Take the popular minstrel tune "Pompey Smash," in which a black, Almanac Davy–like "Skreamer" holds his own in an encounter with the legendary colonel. "Now I'll tell you 'bout a fite I had wid Davy Crockett / Dat haff hoss, haff kune, and haff sky rocket," one verse begins. Five verses later, the fight ends in a draw, each combatant having bitten the other's head off.

Or take "Davy Crockett's Electioneering Tour," an 1867 article in *Harper's,* in which the pseudonymous author recalls paying a call on Representative Crockett in Washington City, decades earlier, and being told a morally uplifting story about the meaning of the Constitution. The story consists mainly of a single quotation that goes on for pages, but here's a short version: It seems that Crockett once voted to appropriate $20,000 to help some families made homeless by a fire. Back in Tennessee, he encountered an influential constituent by the name of Horatio Bunce, who told him that because of that vote, he could no longer back Crockett for reelection. Where in the Constitution, Bunce demanded, do you find "any authority to give away the public money in charity?" The chastened Crockett promised never to cast such a sinful vote again.

Great stuff, but it's about as real as Pompey Smash biting off Davy's head. *David Crockett in Congress* coauthor Jim Boylston once took the trouble to check it out. The pseudonymous *Harper's* writer turned out to be a dime novelist named Edward Ellis, who later recycled his invented anecdote in a quickie Crockett biography. Ellis couldn't have talked to Crockett, as he claimed, because David had been dead for four years when Ellis was born.

True or not, more words followed.

William "Buffalo Bill" Cody celebrated Crockett in a book called *Story of the Wild West and Camp-Fire Chats,* crediting Davy with an "abundant supply of motherwit" and "a heart that was absolutely fearless as it was honest, open, generous and sympathetic." Teddy Roosevelt included him in *Hero Tales from American History,* calling Davy "the most famous rifle-shot in all the United States." Less famous writers churned out books with titles such as *David Crockett: Scout, Small Boy, Pilgrim, Mountaineer, Soldier, Bear-Hunter, and Congressman, Defender of the Alamo* and wrote dialogue like this exchange from a collection called *Pioneer Heroes:*

"Not Texas, Davy!" cried Mrs. Crockett in dismay. "You've done enough fightin' anyhow. Time you took a little rest."

"Rest? While good Americans are bein' killed by Santa Anna's Greasers? No, I reckon I must be goin'."

Onstage, meanwhile, the Crockett story was getting both hilarious and weird. The playwright Frank Murdock and the actor Frank Mayo appropriated Davy's name and motto for an 1872 collaboration they called *Davy Crockett; Or, Be Sure You're Right, Then Go Ahead*. Like Nimrod Wildfire, this Davy had wandered into a classic nineteenth-century melodrama, but, unlike Nimrod, he had been cast as the romantic lead.

Richard Boyd Hauck offers a plot summary. "When the curtain rises," he reports, we see the hero "as a bachelor living in a mountain cabin with his mother, Dame(!) Crockett, his nephew Little Bob, and his niece, Little Sally. Soon we are introduced to Davy's childhood sweetheart Eleanor, whose rich father took her away long ago for travel and education." Dad having died, Eleanor has returned, accompanied by "a wimpy fiancé, and a wicked villain." For some reason, she starts reading Davy "Lochinvar," by Sir Walter Scott. During a blizzard in a lonely cabin, Davy saves her from a pack of ravenous wolves "by barring the door with his arm."

"This is getting kind of monotonous, this business is," he says, still fending off the wolves as Act II turns into Act III.

You might not think this was a formula for success—but you would be wrong. Mayo played Davy for twenty-four years, despite having acquired, by 1886, what one journalist described as "a most extraordinary aversion" to the role. The play's run ended only with the actor's death in 1896, but then Hollywood made a movie of it. Four times!

In three of the four films, Davy shows up at the very last minute, like Lochinvar himself or Dustin Hoffman in *The Graduate*,

Colonel Crockett, 1839, engraved by C. Stuart from the original 1834 portrait
by John Gadsby Chapman. Courtesy of Library of Congress Prints and
Photographs Division.

David Crockett outfitted for bear hunting, in a pose the
congressman himself suggested to the artist.

David Crockett, engraved by Asher Brown Durand from the original watercolor portrait by Anthony Lewis DeRose. Courtesy of Library of Congress Prints and Photographs Division.

David Crockett, 1831, watercolor on paper by James Hamilton Shegogue. Courtesy of National Portrait Gallery, Smithsonian Institution, gift of Algernon Sidney Holderness, NPG.84.231.

David Crockett, 1810, oil portrait by John Nava, detail. Courtesy of John Nava. From the collection of David Zucker.

Surviving portraits of Crockett date from the time of his service in the House of Representatives, when he was in his forties. John Nava's late twentieth-century painting portrays him as an unknown twenty-four-year-old frontiersman.

Davy Crockett's Almanack, 1837. Courtesy of Dolph Briscoe Center for American History, University of Texas at Austin.

The 1837 Crockett almanac borrowed its cover image from an engraving of actor James Hackett playing Nimrod Wildfire in *The Lion of the West*. Fess Parker, Jr.— shown visiting Crockett's birthplace in 1955—helped make Walt Disney's Davy the coolest guy in American history.

Courtesy of *Look* magazine Photograph Collection, Library of Congress Prints and Photographs Division. LC-L9-55-3998-KK frame 24. Photograph by *Look* staff photographer Maurice Terrell.

Mythic Davy in action: Crockett plays a fiddle to entertain his fellow Alamo defenders, as shown in a modern drawing by Gary Zaboly, and swings his rifle in the thick of the fighting, as pictured in a Crockett almanac from 1848.

CROCKETT AT THE ALAMO.

Courtesy of Library of Congress Rare Book and Special Collections Division.

Courtesy of Gary Zaboly. From the collection of James R. Boylston.

to prevent his honey from marrying the fiancé. But my favorite, at least judging from Hauck's summaries—none of the four films has survived—is a 1915 slapstick version called *Davy Crockett Up-to-Date*. In it, the attacking wolves are replaced by Indians, who are driven off "by hardtack biscuits thrown at their heads."

Another Crockett-related film was released in 1915, and, thanks to a print rescued from someone's basement, this one is now watchable on YouTube. Anxious to get a firsthand glimpse of Silent Cinema Davy, I sat down at the computer one afternoon and clicked on part one of *The Martyrs of the Alamo, or, The Birth of Texas*.

Not without some trepidation, however. I had concerns about the company Davy was keeping.

Martyrs came out of a studio run by D. W. Griffith, the director of *The Birth of a Nation*. Griffith hadn't directed the Alamo film himself, but I knew it echoed the racism of his inflammatory masterwork. As the film historian Frank Thompson (no relation of mine) has written, it "presents the Texas Revolution as a conflict of skin colors" in which the chief threat posed by Santa Anna and his swarthy troops is "their disrespect for white men and mindless lust for white women."

If anything, this warning turned out to be understated. But the good news, I found, was that the more I watched of *Martyrs*, the more its Davy—played by the scraggly-haired, youthful A. D. Sears—seemed to rise above his toxic context.

For starters, he's physically taller than anyone else—a good thing, because just about every Anglo character except Jim Bowie wears a coonskin cap, making them hard to tell apart. (The filmmakers eventually threw in the towel and gave Crockett a distinctive checked shirt.) But more important, Davy's gentle charisma tugs at heartstrings in ways the most emphatic emoting cannot. Whether he's joking with Bowie about the relative merits of knives and rifles or cheerfully picking off enemy gunners from an Alamo wall, he steals the show from characters with more central roles in the racialized plot. His quiet presence is especially noticeable in the line-drawing scene. At first, just one man steps across to join Travis. The others all hesitate—until Davy flashes a smile and saunters across, too.

Crockett's image continued to have its ups and downs—but mostly, it had ups. An otherwise forgettable 1926 movie called *Davy Crockett at the Fall of the Alamo,* for example, gave him what Thompson described as "a nice scene with genuinely mythic overtones," in which the defeated politician "changes from his top hat and tailcoat—his Congress clothes—into his buckskin suit and coonskin cap, his legend clothes." It's true that in 1927, the historian Vernon Parrington dismissed David as "the biggest frog in a very small puddle, first among the Smart Alecks of the canebrakes," whose vanity had made him easily exploitable by the Whigs. But Parrington's influence paled compared to that of a student of American humor and folklore named Constance Rourke, who, in 1934, published a peculiar but popular book called simply *Davy Crockett.*

Rourke's work is most often described as a biography, but it's really an uncategorizable mashing together of fact, legend, and invention. When it's time for her Davy to cross the Red River, she digs up the story of Isabella Clark warning him about Comanches but then, without missing a beat, starts borrowing from *Col. Crockett's Exploits and Adventures in Texas.* Rourke knows that *Exploits* is fiction, but never mind. "A pattern of evidence may yet be woven," she wrote, "to prove that it had a basis in fact." Before you know it, she's reworking benign Almanac Davy tales, as if writing for ten-year-olds.

Yet as the middle of the twentieth century approached, there were signs that Crockett—however mythic the keepers of his flame might make him—was in danger of fading from public view.

"If, seventy-five years ago, anyone had suggested that Davy

Crockett was somebody you had to look up in a book, he would have been looked upon as insane and un-American," wrote the Harvard cultural historian Howard Mumford Jones in 1939. "Davy Crockett was a living reality like George Washington, Napoleon, and Satan."

No more. "Wasteful of our literary inheritance as we have been of our natural resources," Jones lamented, "we have forgotten Crockett and what he stood for."

Fifteen years later, a Crockett fan named Marion Michael Null published a biography lauding Davy as "a self-made, mature, honest man—a man who could weep—a man devoted to the common people—a statesman—a soldier." But Null, too, had observed a trend that troubled him. The Americans of 1954, he wrote, no longer "appreciate the hardships" that heroes such as Crockett endured to make their country great.

He called his book *The Forgotten Pioneer.*

✦

One of the main things that interferes with our ability to understand the past is hindsight. We can't imagine David Crockett without his Disney incarnation, especially if we're old enough to have worn the coonskin ourselves, and so we don't. But if it's a mistake for us to push our favorite what-ifs beyond the knowable—hey there, Ben Milam—it's equally a mistake to assume that what really happened *had* to happen.

Disney Davy is a case in point.

Did the fifty-two-year-old pop culture maestro Walt Disney, for instance, have to decide in 1953 that he needed a weekly television show to help him get his massive, not-yet-completely-funded Anaheim theme park off the ground?

No, he didn't.

Did Disney have to order up a three-episode, history-based series in order to promote the Frontierland section of his theme park?

Of course not.

And when the members of the Disneyland team put together a short list of historical characters who could be featured in that series—a list said to include Crockett, Boone, Johnny Appleseed, and William Alexander Anderson Wallace—did they have to pick Davy as the one to pitch to Uncle Walt?

Nope.

They could have gone for the six-foot, two-inch, 240-pound, Comanche-fighting Texas Ranger with the catchy nickname. And if they had, the song that would soon stick permanently in countless young American brains might have gone like this:

> *Bigfoot, Bigfoot Wallace,*
> *King of the wild frontier!*

But they didn't choose Bigfoot, of course. They chose Davy. And the rest was an explosion of television-fueled cultural history that no one—not Howard Mumford Jones, not Marion Michael Null, not even Walter Elias Disney himself—was yet equipped to understand.

⊰ 10 ⊱

"The Whole Country Came Unglued"

In an age when media frenzies collide like bumper cars in hyperspace, it's hard to convey how bonkers America went over Crockett in 1955. But let me start with a strange and wonderful story I heard late one afternoon in Winchester, Tennessee. It brought home the power of the Crockett craze in a way that even my generation's unwavering nostalgia for Disney Davy couldn't do.

It was the day after I'd visited David's well and Polly's grave, and I was back at the Franklin County Library going through files that Jerry Limbaugh, the county historian, had kindly pulled for me. In one, I found a somewhat startling document.

"There's an item I just noticed here on James Blevins?" I said, the question mark obvious in my voice.

"Oh, the Popcorn King! Yessir!" said Limbaugh, laughing, and he told me a bit of the backstory. But really, he said, I should talk to the guy who had dug it up. "You need to call Tom Ore. He's on Dinah Shore Boulevard. I'll give you the address."

I didn't call, I just drove.

Dinah Shore Boulevard, named after the Winchester-born singer and TV star, is a commercial strip running northeast from the town square, and number 1131, which housed Tom Ore's surveying and engineering business, turned out to be a nondescript building across the street from the Camino Real Mexican Restaurant. Ore's son and namesake, who goes by Thomas, was alone in the office when I arrived. He looked busy, but when I mentioned Davy, he invited me right in. His dad showed up a little later, and the two Ores—who seemed to have the kind of partnership any father-son team would envy—took turns telling me what Mr. Blevins was doing in that Crockett file.

A couple of years before, it seems, the elder Ore had been working for some people whose property abutted the Polly Crockett Cemetery. They wanted to split off a chunk of their land for some reason, and needed it surveyed. The parcel in question ran right up against the graves, Tom said, so he was trying to figure out if there was anything about the cemetery in the county records, "because if it's described, that will help me describe what's *not* in the cemetery." What he found, instead, was a document indicating that 3.1 acres of the property he was supposed to be surveying had already been sold—by previous owners, on June 4, 1955—to someone else.

Not only that: two days later, on June 6, 1955, the buyer—whose name was Forrest Larkin—had resold those 3.1 acres to an entity called Davy Crockett Frontier Lands, Inc.

And not only *that:* in that same June 6 deal, one of those 3.1 acres had been further subdivided—many times.

"Dad's eyes about came out of his head," Thomas Ore said, showing me a copy of the warranty deed in question. "Because it says, 'The one acre of land described hereinabove and hereby conveyed consists of 6,272,640 tracts of land each having an area of one square inch; the said tracts lying in tiers and being numbered consecutively from 1 through 6,272,640 . . .'

"Six million little pieces!"

The Ores had no luck, at first, figuring out what this was about. People at the county deeds office had "some faint remembrances of something screwy," Tom said, and they thought it involved a giveaway by Cracker Jack, the snack company famous for its boxed prizes. Not true, said a Cracker Jack spokesman. The tax assessor then found a document offering further clues. It was a copy of a deed of land for an inch-square parcel "on DAVY CROCKETT MOUNTAIN overlooking the Polly Crockett grave," and it identified Davy Crockett Frontier Lands as having "its principal office at Popcorn Village, near the Tennessee Capital."

Popcorn Village. Okay, getting warm.

Eventually, with the help of the Internet and a phone call to the elderly Forrest Larkin—the man who'd bought and sold those 3.1 acres over two days in 1955—things started to become clear. Larkin was a lawyer and a Franklin County native, he told Tom, and at the time, "I was working for Jim Blevins up in Nashville." Blevins was the founder of the Blevins Popcorn Company, and he liked to call himself the Popcorn King. One day, it seems, the Popcorn King stuck his head into Larkin's office and said, "Hey, we've got to get on top of this Davy Crockett thing. You know those people down in Franklin County. I want you to go down, buy three acres around where Davy was—and we'll go from there."

This would have been sometime in the late spring of 1955. The three-part Disney series had kicked off on December 15, 1954, and concluded on February 23, 1955. More than 40 million Americans, one quarter of the population, had tuned in, and by my informal count, every single child in the United States except me was now wearing a coonskin cap. ("I've got a *picture* of me in a coonskin cap, me and my brother," Tom told me. "I was five years old.") In May, a movie version of the combined TV shows opened in theaters nationwide.

Davy Crockett. Movie theaters. Popcorn.

Bingo!

Blevins was competing for the theater concession business,

Tom explained, at a time when movie popcorn wasn't yet as universal as it would become. "The way he did that was he made the supply available, and he invented a machine that would pop it for 'em, and the buttery thing—he invented all that." He also bought up a worthless outcrop of mountain rock; carved it into 6,272,640 square-inch pieces; printed cute deeds decorated with long rifles and powder horns; put up signs in movie theaters saying something like "Own a piece of the Davy Crockett Homestead"; and gave those deeds away to anyone who shelled out for a large popcorn.

What could be more all-American than using Davy Crockett to establish one's product as the nation's movie snack of choice? Not much, I thought admiringly. Then I made a joking reference to land fraud—another traditional American pursuit, and one the real David had tried hard to fight—because, of course, "Davy Crockett Mountain" was just as much a made-up name as "Popcorn Village," and not one of those 6,272,640 square inches had anything to do with an actual Crockett homestead.

"He didn't live there?" Tom Ore asked.

No, he didn't. Kentuck, I explained, had been over the hill, a mile or so west of the cemetery.

Tom started to laugh.

"Well, then, yeah, even better!" he said.

✳

If the real David Crockett had come back to life in the spring of 1955, he'd quickly have discovered—even if he didn't go to the movies and order a large popcorn—that he was more famous than he'd been when he died. For that, he had Walt Disney and Fess Parker, Jr., to thank.

Disney had toyed with the notion of putting Crockett on-screen years earlier. In 1946, the painter Thomas Hart Benton had done him a rough outline for an animated, *Fantasia*-like Crockett operetta. Not much is known about this brief collaboration, but the idea never got any traction. In the spring of 1954, however—obsessed with getting his theme park built—Disney cut a deal with the American Broadcasting Company. ABC would invest in Disneyland (and guarantee millions in loans) while Disney provided programming for an ABC TV show. Walt decided to build the show around the four "lands" he was planning for the park: Fantasyland, Tomorrowland, Adventureland, and Frontierland. His TV team persuaded him that Crockett, not Boone or Bigfoot Wallace or anyone else, was the man for the Frontierland job. Producer Bill Walsh would later call the choice of Davy "dumb luck."

Next question: Who would play him?

Many possible Crocketts were considered. Sterling Hayden and George Montgomery were among them, as was Buddy Ebsen, who wound up in an important role as Davy's sidekick, Georgie Russel. At one point the focus turned to a big-shouldered young actor named James Arness—best known today for his role as Marshal Matt Dillon on *Gunsmoke*—and Disney was persuaded to watch a few scenes of Arness playing an FBI agent in a 1954 science fiction hit called *Them!*

Here's some of what Disney saw:

Arness has been called in to investigate some horrific killings in the New Mexico desert. An old scientist and his beautiful scientist daughter help the G-Man finger the culprits: giant mutant ants, the unforeseen consequences of radiation from A-bomb tests. The investigators must track down the mutants before they can multiply and wipe out humanity. A story wired from Texas offers a clue: a small plane has crashed, and the pilot is blaming strange-shaped flying saucers. Arness and the beautiful scientist show up at the mental ward where the man is confined. She sits ramrod straight in one chair, white blouse looking freshly ironed; Arness slumps backward on another, hat in hand. Between them paces a tall, dark-haired fellow in a hospital robe, waving his arms and railing at the injustice of being disbelieved.

"I've *already* told those head-shrinkin' doctors four dozen times. I'm *sick* of tellin' it. I tell it, and I get laughed at or clucked over," he says. "You promise not to laugh at me?"

Arnett promises.

"Okay. I was flyin' south from Corpus Christi, headin' here, Brownsville. And I turned in from the gulf, headin' for the airport about forty miles out. And all of a sudden I see these, these flyin' saucers. Three of 'em. One big one and two little ones. I had to do some fancy flyin' or they'da run right *into* me. . . . I don't know what else to call 'em. They were shaped like—well, like ants. Well, I *know* that sounds crazy, but that's what they were *shaped* like. The big one was maybe fifteen feet long and had wings like a *fly* or somethin'. And the other two seemed to be chasin' the big one. And one here and two here and they were zoomin' around like regular kamikazes. Like to scared me out of my *pants*!"

Then he catches himself.

"Excuse me, ma'am," he says.

Studio legend has the excited Disney taking one look at the on-screen Fess Parker and exclaiming, "That's our Davy Crockett!" We'll never know exactly why. But if you ask me, that sincere and perfectly timed "Excuse me, ma'am" had to be part of it.

Parker was twenty-nine at the time, just one of thousands of Hollywood wannabes living from bit part to bit part. "I didn't miss a meal, and I didn't sleep in the rain," he told a video interviewer once, but he did live in a toolshed for thirteen months, and he couldn't afford a social life. When the offer of a day's work on *Them!* came along, he explained to Disney's biographer Michael

Barrier, he was "on location, making a film for the Navy medical department on battle fatigue." What if the casting guy hadn't tracked him down? Or what if Disney had been distracted at that screening?

"If Walt had taken a phone call or lit a cigarette or sneezed," Parker said, "I wouldn't be talking to you today."

Growing up in Texas, he had never gone hungry either. But he remembered his cattle-ranching grandmother working "unbelievably hard compared to women today," and he remembered his mother, a gentle woman with a "streak of iron," knocking on doors during the Depression to collect money owed to his father's Purina feed store. World War II interrupted Parker's education—he did a stint in the navy, seeing no action—but he wound up with a degree in American history from the University of Texas and a mysterious ambition to be an actor. Playing Mars, the god of war, in a campus production might have been part of it (at least it taught him to be careful when wearing a miniskirt onstage). Meeting the actor Adolphe Menjou through a professor gave him someone to call when he got to Hollywood. His most valuable asset, however, was the "formula" he said he carried with him throughout life. "Ignorance plus optimism," he called it.

After the *Them!* screening, Parker got a call from the Disney people and ended up interviewing with Walt, for whom he strummed a guitar on request. By September 1954, he was playing Davy on a Cherokee reservation in North Carolina, decked out in smelly buckskins and dodging rubber-tipped arrows loosed by the descendants of a band of Cherokees whom Andrew Jackson had somehow failed to remove. Most of the warriors he battled in "Davy Crockett, Indian Fighter" were played by "actual American Indians," Parker said with some pride.

It was as if he were talking about an endangered species—which is what, in David Crockett's time, their ancestors had become.

Disney couldn't have picked a more beautiful location in which to shoot his TV series or one that better evoked—though he probably didn't know this—the complex history of the Indians for whom Crockett had risked his political career.

A Cherokee creation myth explains that the dramatic blue-green landscape surrounding the town of Cherokee, North Carolina, was formed when Water Beetle dove to the bottom of the sea and brought back mud; Buzzard then flapped his wings over it, sculpting the peaks and valleys of the Great Smoky Mountains. Members of the Eastern Band of Cherokee Indians have a more modern creation myth as well. It explains how their ancestors were able to cling to these mountains while the rest of the tribe was forced west on the Trail of Tears.

A few had earlier acquired legal status (it's complicated) permitting them to stay in North Carolina. Others simply hid in the Smokies. Then an old Cherokee named Tsali and his sons got into a fight with federal troops, killing two soldiers and putting every Cherokee in the area at risk. Reminded of that by fellow tribesmen, Tsali surrendered and allowed himself to be executed so that the Cherokees could remain in their homeland. It's an irresistible story—a man dies so his people can survive—and it's embedded in Eastern Cherokee culture, despite a regrettable lack of evidence that Tsali really surrendered voluntarily. To question the legend, as John Finger discovered, was to draw a prompt rebuke from the tribe.

"We don't need outsiders coming in and attacking our heroes," the chief of the Eastern Band told the historian.

Sound familiar? It did to me. Texans say the same thing about David Crockett.

I spent two days on the Cherokee reservation tracking down traces, both architectural and human, of the 1954 Disney filming.

Like Fess Parker, who'd recently died at the age of eighty-five, most of the Cherokees who'd had roles in the Crockett production were gone. Still, I'd found several who'd been extras as boys, and one had pointed me toward the road I was on now, heading toward the remote hillside cabin that had served as Davy's on-screen home. As I remembered from the movie—I had yet to see the original TV shows—he rides up to the cabin after completing the first part of his Creek War service and is greeted by his two blond boys and his pretty brunette wife.

"Oh, Davy, you're back!" Polly says. She thinks he's home for good and a bit later says as much.

"Well, not prezackly," he explains.

Life on the reservation has changed a great deal in the past half century. Making my way up Big Cove Road, I drove past Cherokee Central Schools, the biggest batch of new public school buildings I'd ever seen. Over the past decade or so, the Eastern Band's share of the profits from Harrah's Cherokee casino has helped fund everything from this massive K–12 complex to improved diabetes care, a new water and sewer system, and efforts to preserve the Cherokee language. Casino money has also put a floor under individual Cherokee incomes.

Yet, as I drove toward Davy's cabin, I sometimes felt as though the 1950s had never ended.

I passed trailer parks and campgrounds (HI KIDS—SEE YOGI BEAR—TURN RIGHT AT BRIDGE) where families fished roadside pools. I saw a tiny, run-down building that housed the Big Cove Grocery, some old-fashioned wooden play structures, and a wooden bear carved from a hillside stump. Someone had told me that the Big Cove community hadn't gotten electric power until 1953, and I could believe it. Someone else, when giving me directions, had advised me to go "straight, *country* straight," by which he meant "never mind how much the road twists and turns." I tried, though I had to backtrack once. Finally I rounded a corner, and there was the cabin, just as I remembered it—except for the new siding, the chain-link fence, the three neatly aligned trash cans, and the telephone poles and wires that might cause problems for a film crew shooting there now.

No one seemed to be home, so I snapped a couple of photos and headed back to town.

Between interviews, I spent some time in a souvenir shop on Tsali Boulevard. Surrounded by teepees, totem poles, dream catchers, and cheap baskets from China, I was reminded of something else I'd learned about Cherokee survival. For a century after Tsali was shot, his people had scraped out hard livings through hunting and subsistence farming. Then tourists drawn to Cherokee by the newly created Great Smoky Mountain National Park had given them another employment option: they could impersonate "actual American Indians" for pay.

Those tourists, it soon became clear, were looking for the stereotyped "redskins" they'd seen in western movies. No problem: the town's merchants, many of whom were white, stocked up on Plains-style souvenirs. Meanwhile, the North Carolina Cherokees invented a survival tool called "chiefing." Donning the regalia of the Sioux or Cheyenne, they staked out positions on town sidewalks and cheerfully posed for visitors who wanted photos taken with the brand of Indians they knew.

"Davy Crockett, Indian Fighter" fit right into that cultural hodgepodge. Disney didn't make his Indians wear Sioux war bonnets, but still: playing members of another tribe (the Creeks) in a war that had taken place someplace else (Alabama and Florida) must have seemed as natural to the Cherokees as chiefing—and never mind that their ancestors had fought on Crockett's *side* in the real Creek War.

Ken Blankenship, the director of the Museum of the Cherokee Indian, was in seventh grade when a Disney casting crew came through his school. "I got marched up to the auditorium," he told me, "and they put on pants right there, and what we called clod-hoppers, and a three-pointed hat, and off we went." He was too young for the battle scenes, and the clothing was a tipoff that despite his ancestry, he would play a white boy, not an Indian: "I was in the scene where they had the shooting match for the cow—just walked up and looked at the target after they shot."

Ken's brother, Bob Blankenship, also got a few days' work. His Hollywood memories, however, revolve around the old Boundary Tree Lodge and Motel, where the Disney crew was staying and where he was working as a night clerk. Fess Parker sometimes got out his guitar in the evenings, and once he even tried to teach Bob to play: "He wrote me down some chords and I put them behind a picture frame, and I don't know what the hell ever happened to the chords he wrote down."

Tom Beck, another extra, recalled being paid $5 a day. "I worked two days and I got ten dollars," he said, "and I went and bought me a gun holster set with two guns with my money." Beck lived on the Oconaluftee River at the time, though his parents' house is gone now, and he remembers the riverbank tarted up to make it look like Florida, with "the moss hanging down, and the grapevines." One day he came home to find "this Indian laid out on our front porch, and he had his head split open."

How did that happen?

"Well, Davy Crockett throws a hatchet at him, if you remember the movie, and he didn't duck the first time." The Indian on Beck's porch was Pat Hogan, the actor playing Davy's main Creek opponent, Chief Red Stick. Eventually Red Stick got up to fight again.

Speaking of not ducking: one man I wished I could have talked to was Richard Crowe, a talented Cherokee craftsman and actor who died in 2002. I'd read that Crowe had once zapped Parker with a rubber-tipped arrow, but I wasn't sure about the reliability of the source. Someone told me that Crowe's daughter, Linda, worked "at the McDonald's down by the Food Lion," so I dropped by and she confirmed the Fess zapping. Linda didn't remember much else about the Disney shoot, she said, except that her dad had gotten shot off a rock and plunged into the river.

Later, I found an interview in which Parker elaborated on the story. Richard Crowe, he said, was "a real athlete and a local actor who has a big part every year in the wonderful Cherokee pageant called 'Unto These Hills.'" In the Disney production, he played "an Indian sentinel standing duty on a bank twenty feet above the river. The camera was shooting from behind my right shoulder and I was to spot the Indian and fire just as he drew a bead on me with his bow and arrow. Then, my bullet was supposed to hit him and knock him off the small cliff." But there were two flaws in this carefully planned scenario: Parker's gun produced enough smoke to cloud his vision, and Crowe's aim, as he fell and released his arrow, was true.

"It hit me smack in the forehead right above my left eye," Parker said, "and as things went black for a few seconds, I thought to my-self, 'Well, this is one Davy Crockett who's never going to get to the Alamo.'"

The actor had bigger problems in North Carolina than stray ar-rows, though. Ignorance and optimism may have gotten him there, but director Norman Foster—who had played no part in choosing him—couldn't stand his laid-back style. The director summed up his view of Fess in a quote Frank Thompson included in *Alamo Movies*: "I found if I didn't do something to get adrenaline into his system, he would get slower and slower," Foster said. "He seemed to lack vitality. I told him to take vitamin pills."

Parker, in turn, thought Foster was trying to get him fired and lying about it. "I'm relatively soft spoken, and I think he was afraid that I would not come off," he recalled. "I was so unhappy." At one point, he thought the best thing might be just to leave.

He didn't, and eventually things got better.

Disney and his wife showed up one day, terrifying Foster, who was behind schedule—but Walt's only complaint seems to have been that a zipper on a bear suit was visible in one scene. Paul Anderson told the story in his book *The Davy Crockett Craze*, and he mentioned another legend I was anxious to verify. The adult Cherokee extras, Anderson wrote, got a bit tired of losing battles to white folks. One day they decided "they were going to rewrite history—Davy and his buckskinned friends would not take the Indian village!" Chaos ensued.

No Cherokee I talked to had memories of that uprising, but they all laughed when I brought it up.

I had a good time cruising for movie locations, though I couldn't always pin them down. Where was it, exactly, that Tom Beck had said his house by the river was? I wasn't sure. Was this the field where the Disney crew had cut down sycamore trees and used them to disguise the telephone poles? I couldn't tell. The one location I was certain about, besides the hillside cabin, was a collection of historic buildings that had been relocated to the National Park and is known today as the Mountain Farm Museum.

Many of the Mountain Farm buildings have been moved since 1954. Still, it's recognizable as the west Tennessee town where Davy files a land claim; where his pal Georgie dances up a storm; and where, after Davy wins his first election, excited constituents hoist him onto their shoulders. A two-story farmhouse made of chestnut logs may seem especially familiar to Crockett fans. The Disney crew used it as the town's general store, and one end of its porch is where Georgie reads Davy a letter containing heart-wrenching news. While he's been out west, scouting for land and fighting villains, his wife has taken sick and died.

Poor Polly. She's never allowed to wander more than ten yards out of the house and doesn't even rate an on-screen death. The screenwriter, Tom Blackburn, didn't think she belonged in the Disney version at all, though he ended up being pleased with the scene in which her demise is announced. Fess Parker played that scene the way he did—turning away from the porch and walking slowly into the dark forest—because he was a Gary Cooper fan. At the time the connection was subconscious, but years later, Parker realized that he had based his performance on the way Cooper, playing Lou Gehrig, had walked away after his farewell speech in *The Pride of the Yankees.*

Parker and company finally finished shooting in North Carolina and moved on to Tennessee. Locations included Nashville, where the state capitol impersonates the U.S. House of Representatives, and the nearby Hermitage, where Davy drops in to talk politics with Andrew Jackson. I'd been wanting to see the Jackson shrine ever since Lizzie latched on to Andy as her favorite president, so I spent an afternoon on a Hermitage tour, despite the fact that the real Crockett never set foot in his enemy's stately home.

"Don't mention his name in here," a docent cracked after I told him why I'd come.

I didn't hear anyone mention Davy in the visitor center's introductory film, which does a pretty good job of balancing the fierce triumphs and unconscionable brutalities of Jackson's remarkable life. I don't recall any mention of the general's adopted Indian son, either, but I found Lincoyer's story on the wall of a small side museum before I got to the house itself. Reading it, I saw that the boy had died less than a year before his adoptive father became president and started pushing Indian removal. But what really hit me at the Hermitage was the width of the class divide between Andy and Davy. Both started life poor, but only one ended up living in a Greek Revival mansion where the wallpaper told the story of Odysseus's son, Telemachus; or riding in a carriage described as "the luxury limousine of its time"; or lording over more than a hundred slaves who managed his household, worked his fields, ran his cotton gin, endured his overseer's lash, and slept at the foot of his bed when he was old and sick.

After Tennessee, the Disney crew packed up and headed back to California. They did some outdoor shooting at the Janss Conejo Ranch near Los Angeles, a popular location for TV and movie westerns, but mostly it was time for studio work. Disney's Alamo consisted of a few walls on a Burbank sound stage combined with some painted backdrops, and there was nothing left for me to see.

If I wanted to follow the story of Disney Davy to its glorious end, I realized, I needed to break the seal on my copy of *Davy Crockett: The Complete Television Series* and immerse myself in the shiny new Crockett legend that debuted on December 15, 1954.

✦

Two minutes into "Davy Crockett, Indian Fighter," I know I'm dealing with something a lot more interesting than I remember from the movie version.

Here comes Georgie Russel, in a scene edited out of the movie, riding up to Davy's hillside cabin (no new siding, trash cans, or power lines visible). On the sound track, "The Ballad of Davy Crockett" has been setting up the narrative to come: it's taken Davy from Tennessee to Washington to Texas. Now the harmonizing chorale fades out and Georgie picks up the tune. He and Davy are off to fight the Creeks, and Georgie sings a verse about the yarns they'll make up as they ride.

Polly interrupts him. "If you don't stop makin' up those outlandish songs about Davy," she says, "there's no tellin' what'll happen to the Crockett name."

No telling, indeed! Meet Postmodern Davy, King of the Deconstructed Frontier. Disney characters, apparently, are going to stop in the middle of the action to let us know—wink, wink, nudge, nudge—that they're just part of a story they're helping to shape.

Georgie is a fictional creation (though his name is borrowed from Crockett's real Creek War comrade), and even before he starts singing, Disney and his team have made it clear that they will be mixing fiction with fact. Frontierland has been defined as "tall tales and true from the legendary past." Walt Disney himself, holding an obviously fake book called *Davy Crockett's Journal*, has underscored the point. "It's characteristic of American folklore," he says, "that most of our favorite legends and fables are based on the lives of real men like Davy Crockett of Tennessee."

Claiming that stories are "based on" something real can cover a multitude of sins. As the DVD continues, I'm fascinated to see that just about every aspect of Disney's Crockett really is based— in at least some small way—on either David's life or his legendary ghosts. "Davy Crockett, Indian Fighter," "Davy Crockett Goes to Congress," and "Davy Crockett at the Alamo" add up to a brilliant pillaging of the dubious source material available to Tom Blackburn in 1954. The result is nowhere near the truth, however hard truth is to define in Crockett's case. But Blackburn, who died in 1992, likely wouldn't have taken much offense if you'd told him that.

"It had to be a good story first!" the screenwriter's daughter once explained—and it is.

WHOOSH! A giant flaming arrow incinerates Fort Mims. Davy tells Polly that he's got to fight because "the Creeks massa-creed every man, woman and child" who was there. Yes, the real story is more complicated, but the shorthanding here is both commonplace and understandable.

GRRRRR! The bear Davy is hunting hasn't succumbed to his "grinning" technique. To bring back meat for Jackson's starving army, he must plunge into the bushes and kill the critter "the old-fashioned way," with a knife. The scene plays as slapstick today, but Crockett's supposed ability to grin down raccoons and such was part of his legend while he was still alive.

WHOO! WHOO! The clueless Major Norton, dispatched by Jackson on a scouting expedition, tries to imitate a hoot owl as part of a prearranged signal. Before long, Norton and his men find themselves pinned down on a riverbank by a band of Creeks, requiring Davy and Georgie to rescue them. And look, there's a handsome Indian poised high on a rock, and here comes a cloud of smoke from Davy's rifle, and down goes Richard Crowe—arrow presumably just released—plunging to his television death. I hit "pause" in time to catch Crowe in midair, stretched horizontally above the river, about to make a very big splash.

Whatever he was paid, it can't have been enough.

The scouting expedition was real, but the riverbank fight was not. David didn't fire at any Creeks until the massacre at Tallusahatchee, which Disney skips. The major battle filmed seems to be based on Talladega—Jackson's frustration when some Indians escape through his lines is the tipoff—but no women and children die on-screen and no warriors are roasted alive.

After the battle, Davy goes home for a few days. "I ain't goin' back till I get in a supply of meat for you and the young-uns," he tells Polly before heading off to chase Chief Red Stick around the moss-draped "Florida" that Tom Beck described. Georgie gets himself captured and tied to a tree. Davy challenges Red Stick to single combat and wins. "Turn my friend loose and lay down your arms. Join the other chiefs in a treaty. Do that, and I promise the government'll let you go back and live in peace on your own lands," he tells the chief.

"Promises no good. White government lie," says Red Stick, who appears to have spent some time in Realityland.

"Davy Crockett don't lie," Davy says, and that's that: the men shake hands to seal the deal.

Oh, my. Crockett really did go to Florida, where there really is moss on the trees, but that's the best I can do to find a basis for that particular scene. And I've left out Davy's unlikely sermon on the topic of "Thou Shalt Not Kill," which he delivers minutes after taking out one of Red Stick's warriors with a wickedly accurate knife throw.

"Davy Crockett Goes to Congress" is up next. Once again, Davy says good-bye to Polly, who appears to have survived his absences with her perkiness intact. (The actress playing her, Helene Stanley, had been the live-action model for Disney's animated *Cinderella*.)

"When you get back," she tells Georgie, "I suppose you'll have more outlandish songs about Davy."

"Feel one comin' on right now," Georgie says. That turns out to be a serious understatement.

Davy and Georgie are heading west to look for better land—as true a fact as any you can find about Crockett—but now here comes the line on the map that so annoyed the good people of Lawrenceburg. It sends Davy through The Town Walt Disney Forgot without so much as a pause to tip his furry cap, let alone build a mill complex or launch a political career, and it plunks him down in the Obion River country. There he rides into the plot of a classic western. The villain is a hulking brute named Bigfoot (wait, where have I heard that name?) who has been bullying friendly Indians off treaty-guaranteed land. Davy beats Bigfoot in a shooting match, the one where Ken Blankenship inspects the target afterward, and is promptly deputized to bring the bully to justice.

"Get this straight, Crockett. These yarns they tell about you don't scare me none," Bigfoot sneers. The fistfight that follows is straight out of *Shane,* only dirtier; the biting and eye gouging appear inspired by the Crockett almanacs.

Once more, the good guy wins.

Fellow settlers nominate him for the state legislature, and after Polly's death, he starts his campaign. We see him using a trick I've already mentioned—it's from the real David's autobiography—in which he invites voters to wet their whistles with him while his opponent blathers on. Now he's in Nashville, dolled up like Mr. Darcy in *Pride and Prejudice*, and now he's at the Hermitage, listening to Andy Jackson urge him to run for Congress. And what's this? Jackson is showing him a set of pamphlets with titles such as "Davy Crockett and the Monster of Reelfoot Lake" and "Exploits of Davy Crockett in the Rocky Mountains."

Georgie Russel strikes again.

Fast-forward to Washington, where Georgie shows up to hear his friend's first speech in the House. "Hey, I put up with your singin' them lies about me, but printin' em for everybody to read is goin' too fer," Davy tells him.

"Well, they helped put you here, didn't they?" Georgie says, and Davy doesn't dispute it.

"Now I gotta live *up* to 'em," he says.

Crockett's maiden speech turns out to be a toned-down version of Almanac Davy's, the one about having "the prettiest sister, the surest rifle, and the ugliest dog in the district." Blackburn has worked it in beautifully. His Davy plays on his own image for laughs, then puts his colleagues on notice that beneath his funky buckskins—which he's gotten out of mothballs for the occasion— he's a serious person. "The next time I get up before you," he tells them, "I'll have somethin' to say worth sayin'."

Yes, he will. The next Crockett speech is Blackburn's masterpiece, but it takes a while to set it up.

By this time, the clueless Major Norton has morphed into a political operative for President Jackson. One day, Norton tells Davy that he's arranged for him to go "on a speaking tour of all the big eastern cities." Why? Because he's now "a national figure" and his adoring public wants to see him in person. And by the way, with Jackson in his second term, it will be time for a new president soon, "and some of us have been seriously considering *you*." So Davy heads to Boston and New York, and now he's in Philadelphia, accepting a gift of "the most beautiful rifle gun I ever hope to see," and now here comes Georgie to burst his celebrity bubble. The real reason Norton sent Davy on tour, it turns out, was so he'd be out of town when Jackson's Indian Removal bill came to a vote. The bill's opponents are stalling, but they won't be able to hold out much longer.

Davy was duped!

"I know where we can get fresh horses," he says, and off they gallop. Their route is an odd one, taking them through landscapes I recognize as North Carolina and California, but never mind. They make it to Capitol Hill in the nick of time, and Davy charges onto the floor of the House—pausing only to deck the evil Norton, who tries to stop him—and begins to speak.

He's not joking this time, he tells his colleagues, so "you can fold up your grins and put 'em away."

Yes, the United States has to expand, "but not at the expense of the things this country was founded to protect. The government's promise, as set out in the Indian treaties, is as sacred as your own word. Expansion ain't no excuse for persecutin' a whole part of our people because their skins is red and they're uneddicated to our ways."

Yes, a vote for this bill would make "rich men out of the land grabbers and speculators." But they wouldn't be the real culprits, because "their no-account lot's about as natural as flies around a molasses barrel." It will be "nobody's fault but our own" if Indian Removal is passed.

Passionate, outraged, and utterly sincere, Davy has the House mesmerized. Now he's ready to wrap up. "We got a responsibility to this strappin', fun-lovin', britches-bustin' young b'ar cub of a country," he says. "We got a responsibility to help it grow into the kind of nation the good Lord meant it to be. If we rared up and showed we were the kind of men our friends and neighbors figured we was when they sent us here, a bill like this would never live long enough to even get on our desks, let alone come to a vote." The desk thing isn't a metaphor. Every congressman has an actual printed bill in front of him.

Davy rips his copy in half and walks out. His colleagues give him a standing ovation. And that's how tens of millions of Americans, glued to their TV sets on January 26, 1955, learned that Davy Crockett had single-handedly defeated Indian Removal and prevented the Trail of Tears.

To be fair, the Disney version only implies that Crockett stopped the Indian bill. And hey, David really did tour the Northeast and he really did give an anti-Removal speech in the House; never mind that those actions came in reverse order and four years apart.

Alamo, here we come.

"Well there she is: Texas," Davy says, gazing at a starkly beautiful chunk of landscape that a Disney map has placed just south of the Red River. "A man keeps movin' around all his life lookin' for his own particular paradise, and I reckon I've found mine."

One of his companions begs to differ. "A desolate, desiccated desert untouched by the hand of man and God alike," Thimblerig says.

That's right: Thimblerig. Davy and Georgie have joined forces with the fictional gambler invented by Richard Penn Smith in 1836 and incorporated by Constance Rourke into her twentieth-century mythobiography. He's a fantastic character, but his presence in Blackburn's screenplay tells you everything you need to know about the "lives of real men" on which this part of "Davy Crockett at the Alamo" is based. I notice only two hints of truth in Disney Davy's whole trek across Texas to Béxar: his belief that he has found an earthly paradise and the part where someone warns him about Comanches.

Alas, Isabella Clark is nowhere in sight. The warning comes from a goofy Comanche outcast called Bustedluck, who's just as fictional as Thimblerig and who also comes along for the ride. Their route takes them, apparently, straight across the most dangerous, unsettled part of Texas—no Nacogdoches, no San Augustine, no Washington-on-the-Brazos—and has them hightailing it into the Alamo with the Mexican army in hot pursuit. All this despite the fact that the real Crockett and his real companions rode quietly into town before Santa Anna even showed up.

Once they're inside the walls, things get a bit more real, with most elements of the traditional Alamo story in place.

Santa Anna demands unconditional surrender and is answered with a cannon shot. Jim Bowie gets sick, and William Barret Travis takes sole command. Davy draws a bead on an enemy cannoneer. The gallant James Butler Bonham rides off to seek help. Oops, it's Georgie Russel this time, not Bonham, but the outcome is the same: Georgie rides back a couple of days later to say no help is coming. Travis draws his line and everyone crosses, though Thimblerig hesitates so long that he makes me think of Moses Rose. Mexican soldiers swarm the walls. Now here's Davy, standing tall, swinging his rifle in those final, immortal frames before the camera cuts to flag and sky and the credits roll.

And here comes Walt Disney to preview next week's show. Cartoon fables! The good old tortoise and hare! But I'm not ready for Fantasyland right now.

I need to process what I've just seen.

To begin with, I have to mourn. Fess Parker's Davy has grown on me—a lot—since I first saw him in the movie version, and I'm extremely sad to see him go.

That first time through was different. I was so put off by Crockett's sitcom family, the hokey Indian scenes, and the shameless historical rewrites that Parker's quiet charisma barely registered. This time, I saw that his Davy is so relaxed and self-deprecating—not to mention tall and handsome—that he rises above his on-screen surroundings. He's too good to be true, of course, but somehow he persuades viewers otherwise. When he preaches to Red Stick, I still don't buy it, but when he gets the news about Polly and when he gives that angry speech in Congress, I do. I'm amazed that he can pull off singing "Farewell to the Mountains" the night before the battle, but he does. And there's another Alamo scene that startles me, because it shows an emotional range I didn't know Parker had.

Georgie has gone to Goliad for help, and now he's back, reporting his failure to Travis. In rushes Davy, wild-eyed and more out of control than he's ever been.

"You 'tarnal idiot!" he rages. "You was safe! In the clear! What'd you come back fer?"

This is a man who knows death is coming and briefly, very humanly, lets it get to him.

Score one for Walt Disney, who did the right thing when he plucked an unknown actor out of a film about mutant ants. Fess's Davy is not *David*, of course. The real man was louder, poorer, funnier, shorter, and far more thin-skinned, among other differences. Still, after 1954, it would get really, really hard to tell them apart.

What about the Alamo scenario as a whole? Every retelling of the defenders' story is questionable, for obvious reasons, so I'm not inclined to spend much time picking fights with Blackburn's. I also agree with Frank Thompson that—however unhistoric the details of Disney's Alamo may be—it gives a surprisingly good feel for "the tense, desperate conditions" during the siege. When it comes to Crockett specifically, any Alamo story must deal with two central questions. The first is how he lived, and here Blackburn sticks with the traditional role assigned to Alamo Davy: a respected, morale-boosting leader, never formally in command but invaluable to those who were. The second question, of course, is how he died. I'll be getting to that soon.

But enough about Texas for now. Nearly six decades after their debut, the Disney shows remain the only significant screen treatment of the rest of Crockett's life. Admittedly, they skip more than half of it—David's first twenty-six years are nowhere to be found, and there's no hint of his rough, adventurous childhood—but they still leave an amateur Crockettologist plenty to think about.

I've suggested this already, but I think the creation of Georgie as Davy's unofficial publicist is an inspired touch. The details may be invented, but the basic idea of the legend's creation rings true. Beyond that, the Disney version—which for the most part portrays Crockett as a flawless hero—at least hints at how he got above his raisin'. Those *Pride and Prejudice* clothes! That susceptibility to flattery! Those presidential ambitions! Georgie sees through all that, but it takes Davy way too long to understand what's going on.

The hardest part of Disney's Crockett to defend is the absurd overhyping of his Indian Removal vote. It ignores his true political priority, trying to help poor white settlers in west Tennessee, and it gives him a vastly bigger role in the Indian debate than he actually played or wanted to play. Perhaps most egregiously, it wimps out on criticizing the Great Man whose face now graces our $20 bills. Jackson's Indian policy isn't really his fault, Davy says: "I've known General Jackson for half of my born life, and I'm sure he's got nothing but the good of the country at heart."

Oh, please. We're talking about a man who used the Creek War as an excuse to steal millions of acres from Indians who *fought on his side*.

I'd give a lot to be able to ask Blackburn about all this. How much did he end up knowing about the real David's story? (Remember, the first serious Crockett biography wouldn't be published for two more years.) How much did he care? (After all, he made his living writing western fiction and screenplays, not history.) What marching orders did he have from Walt Disney?

But most of all, I'd want to hear him talk about the very first song he ever wrote.

A mock folk ballad wasn't part of anyone's original plan for the Crockett series. In *The Art of Walt Disney* by Christopher Finch, producer Bill Walsh explains how that changed: "[W]hen we got the film back to the Studio, we found we didn't have quite enough footage for three sixty-minute shows. So Walt said, 'Why don't you take some drawings and stick them all together and give an idea of what the show's going to be about.' So we put the drawings together, sketches of Davy's life, and Walt said, 'Well, that looks kind of dull. Maybe we can get a song to go with them.'"

Down the hall went Blackburn with George Bruns, an accomplished, veteran Disney composer also known to be able to play a trombone with his feet. Accounts vary on how long it took them to come back—it's commonly said to have been less than an hour, though such details have a whiff of the tall studio tale about them—but in any case, they got a start on what would eventually expand to comprise twenty stanzas of six lines each.

After listening uncounted times to the complete Riders in the

Sky version urged on me by Joe Bone at the David Crockett Cabin Museum, I feel qualified to summarize it here:

> Mountaintop!
> Creeks!
> Yarns!
> Andy Jackson!
> Florida!
> Becoming a legend!
> Justice for Indians!
> A swell dad!
> Restless!
> Knows he's right!
> Hunter's paradise!
> Sad about Polly!
> Politics!
> Living legend!
> Washington!
> Shaking hands!
> Speaking out!
> Heading west!
> Alamo!
> Dead legend!

I know, I know: the real song is a whole lot catchier than the condensed version makes it appear. Every stanza includes the unforgettable line "Davy, Davy Crockett," and you haven't lived until you've had the thing stuck in your head for a year.

"I thought it sounded pretty awful, but we didn't have time for anything else," Walsh said.

Disney didn't love it either. That didn't stop him, according to Paul Anderson's book, from underlining its significance in an editing meeting. "This particular story will hit the adults more," he explained, "but the lyrics will pick it up for the kids. It's what I call a comic book approach, and you know how many adults still read comic books! These lyrics are important. They help to keep the story moving in the minds of children and also in the minds of some adults who will be wondering what's happening."

Score another for Uncle Walt. Like plucking his leading man from a film about giant mutant ants, ordering up "The Ballad of Davy Crockett" seems to have been a stroke of pure, instinctive genius.

How big a stroke, even Disney had no clue.

Bruns and Blackburn's seat-of-the-pants ditty would soon get stuck in the heads of an entire nation. Recorded by more than twenty artists and selling something like seven million copies over the first six months of its existence, it was what has been described—aptly, I think, despite unfortunate connotations of rats and bubonic plague—as the "carrying agent" of the Davy Crockett craze.

✴

I have no memory of the Crockett craze. I was certainly old enough—I turned five in 1955, an age at which plenty of my contemporaries recall being inseparable from their coonskin caps—but as I've said, my father refused to have a TV in the house. My older brother found a way around that problem, though. When I asked if he had Crockett memories, he surprised me with a story I'd never heard. He'd had a paper route that year, he reminded me, and he'd had some especially friendly customers who used to invite him in to watch *their* television when he rang the doorbell once a week to collect their subscription money.

When the Crockett shows aired, he made sure to ring that bell in time for *Disneyland*.

I like this story because it reminds me what a radical change widespread TV viewing had made by 1955 and because that transitional media moment, in turn, explains the difference between Disney's Crockett and, say, *Star Wars* or J. K. Rowling's Harry Potter series. All three were hugely successful, mass-culture phenomena that appealed to both children and adults—but only one coincided with the emergence of TV as a dominant social, cultural, and economic force.

As the Crockett scholar Margaret King has written, the craze demonstrated the behavior-shaping power of the tube in a variety of ways and "with an intensity previously and since unmatched by any fad of its kind and brief duration." It showed "the ability of a popularizer such as Disney to mold and manipulate public concepts of history" by, for example, substituting "a minor American frontiersman" such as Crockett for "the traditional time-tested symbol" of westward expansion, Daniel Boone. More important, at least for those who didn't care about the history, it sparked the discovery and exploitation of "a fabulous new lode in American commercial life: the child market."

To put it more bluntly: Disney Davy taught advertisers how to sell to baby boomers. America would never be the same.

Nobody knows how many different products came to be associated with Crockett's name. A very partial list would include accordions, Alamo play sets, baby shoes, bath towels, bicycles, blocks, bow-and-arrow sets, bubblegum cards, canteens, caps, coffee, coloring books, comics, cuff links, dart games, dolls, grills, guitars, ice cream, imitation buckskins, kiddie pools, lamps, lunch boxes, moccasins, pajamas, panties, plastic Indians, play telephones, rifles, six-shooters, sleds, soap, tool kits, TV trays, ukuleles, wallets, wagons, and whistling peace pipes. Crockett rapidly became a "$300 million industry," King wrote, though I've seen higher figures as well.

In today's dollars, $300 million would be $2.5 billion or so. Pretty good for a fad created by three hours of television.

The ballad took off faster than anything else. At 8:30 A.M. on December 16, 1954, the morning after "Davy Crockett, Indian Fighter" aired, the proprietor of a fledgling company called Cadence Records telephoned a singing actor named Bill Hayes and asked him about recording the show's theme song. Hayes made it into the studio that night. As he told *Crockett Craze* author Anderson, he did the (abridged) song in one take; the Cadence guy tested it on a teenage daughter, who "jumped up and down" with enthusiasm; and the company ordered 750,000 copies the next day. Eddy Arnold, Tex Ritter, Mitch Miller, Fred Waring, Burl Ives, the Sons of the Pioneers, and Fess Parker himself, among others, would follow Hayes's lead.

The song was the craze's carrying agent, but the coonskin cap was its icon. Kids *had* to have them. The demand for raccoon pelts drove up the price from 25 cents to $6 a pound. There's no record of how many raccoons died for Davy, but it's known that raccoon coats from the 1920s were soon being sacrificed, along with a stash of old wolfskins at a fur company in Seattle. Meanwhile, as my North Carolina informants told me, a local manufacturer of Indian souvenirs had gotten into the act. It employed numerous Eastern Band members, and to this day, at Crockett sites around the country, you can buy coonskin caps with labels that say "Made in America by Native Americans."

Ah, the power of TV. Ah, the genius of Disney.

Except . . .

If Walt Disney had known that those things would happen, he'd have cornered the market on coonskins in advance. And he'd surely have ordered the script rewritten—if not history itself—so that he didn't have to kill off his star in the third episode. According to producer Walsh, as quoted in Anderson's book, there was a comic moment in which Disney contemplated rescuing Crockett anyway.

"We went on the air with this whole schmear and the whole country came unglued," Walsh recalled. "Walt calls me in and says, 'What's happening? I'm getting these . . . round robin letters from kids, who say, "Don't kill Davy! Don't kill Davy!" . . . Do we kill him? What are we doing—gonna kill him? We just invented him.'"

Walsh gave his boss the bad news: "Walt, he's gotta die, everybody dies at the Alamo. Everybody."

Fess Parker did his best to keep Davy alive, embarking on a forty-two-day, twenty-two-city American promotional tour. (He would hit fourteen foreign countries as well.) Though game, he was entirely unprepared for his new role as pitchman. Oklahoma City was the first stop. As Parker recalled in an interview for the Archive of American Television, he got off the plane in costume, climbed into a limo, and followed six motorcycle policemen to a packed arena where a rodeo was going on. "What do you want me to do?" he asked. "Here's a horse," he was told. "Go in and ride around," then find the band and sing "Davy Crockett." At a department store the next day, he found hundreds of kids waiting but "no one to figure out how to deal with this."

Why not line them up in a hallway, he suggested, so he could shake their hands without being mobbed?

In Detroit, "they let all the children out of school" and he spoke to them from a balcony at the giant J. L. Hudson department store, as if he were the pope. Seated on a dais in Washington, D.C., at a retirement ceremony for a deputy secretary of defense, he had to shoo away adults in formal attire who lined up for autographs while the speeches were still going on. Buddy Ebsen, who joined the Crockett tour partway through, said decades later that he could still hear the screaming that broke out whenever he introduced the King of the Wild Frontier.

"Different versions of terror would come along," Parker recalled. Take the time he and Ebsen were whisked away from an appearance without warning and told they were going to address the Texas Legislature. Not knowing what else to do—he tried to think up something to say on the spur of the moment, but it didn't work out—Parker ended up singing "The Ballad of Davy Crockett" a cappella, "and when I got to the chorus, Buddy joined in. And if we weren't friends before, we were friends forever after that."

By that time, Disney had conjured up a couple of ways to extend Davy's run. The movie cobbled together from the original shows was already in theaters, and shooting was about to begin on what we would now call "prequels": "Davy Crockett's Keelboat Race" and "Davy Crockett and the River Pirates." Like the almanacs a century before, they had little to do with the real David. Their job was simply to keep the brand alive.

The historical Crockett, however, was popping up all over the place in 1955.

In Boston, the Museum of Fine Arts displayed an authentic Crockett portrait beside a cardboard cutout of Disney Davy, just in case visitors missed the connection. In east Tennessee, a rumor spread that an old log building was Crockett's birthplace; souvenir hunters began slicing it to bits, and the owner had to beg the Tennessee Historical Commission to say it wasn't so. On Decca Records, Red River Dave McEnery sang "When Davy Crockett Met the San Antonio Rose," using what Decca claimed was "the original authentic Davy Crockett fiddle." In Lawrenceburg, Crockett boosters published a pamphlet containing a splendid, if unsourced, variation on the "gentleman from the cane" story. In it, David rushes his antagonist on the floor of the legislature like an enraged batter charging the pitcher's mound. He grabs the man's collar, pulls "the entire false front of his shirt" loose, and carries his "token of victory back with him to his seat."

Newspapers ginned up innumerable stories about David. "Four Loves Had Davy Crockett" proclaimed the Hearst Sunday supplement, headlining some overheated prose by the novelist Irving Stone. "Historian Says It Was Foxskin Cap Davy Wore" insisted the *Knoxville Journal,* which undermined its credibility by reporting that the last words in David's diary read "Pop, pop, boom, boom, boom, throughout the day. No time for memorandium."

The Crockett resurrected by the media was, for the most part, colorful and heroic. But the credulity and sheer volume of the coverage made a few journalists cranky.

The *New York Post's* Murray Kempton wrote that the real David was "a fellow purchasable for no more than a drink." Crockett fans picketed the *Post's* office carrying signs reading "Who you gonna expose next!—Santa Claus" and "Davy killed a b'ar at 3—What did Murray Kempton ever shoot—except the bull???" *Harper's* editor John Fischer charged that "infant brainwashees have been bedazzled into worshipping a Crockett who never was—a myth as phony as the Russian legend about Kind Papa Stalin." The real Davy, Fischer wrote, was "a juvenile delinquent who ran away from home at the age of thirteen, to dodge a well-deserved licking," and he "never was king of anything, except maybe the Tennessee Tall Tales and Bourbon Samplers' Association." Oh, and by the way, the Alamo was "the worst military blooper in American history, short of Pearl Harbor." Fischer concluded his tirade—which, like Kempton's, outraged Davy loyalists—with an indisputable observation about human nature: "Maybe real history always has two strikes against it. Ever since the fall of Troy, the mythical heroes and comforting legends have always seemed to find a more eager audience than the workaday fact."

The anti-Disney backlash has amused Crockettologists ever

since, but it did nothing to slow the rebirth of Crockett's legend. All over Tennessee, in particular, fans were inspired to memorialize him. Craze-inspired efforts would produce two state parks, at the birthplace and in Lawrenceburg, along with Morristown's Crockett Tavern and Rutherford's Crockett Cabin. Even Polly got a bit of reflected glory: 141 years after her death, she finally got a gravestone with her name on it.

Elizabeth didn't get much attention; she'd been edited out of the Disney version, after all. Then again, she already had a monument in Texas, where she'd gone to live in 1853 after being granted some land by the state. I had a bit of trouble finding her grave—it's in Acton, an hour southwest of Dallas/Fort Worth—but once there, I admired the marble statue, perched atop a tall column, that showed an erect pioneer woman gazing into the setting sun.

Back to the craze, though.

One of the great stories I ran into from 1955—it's right up there with those inch-square parcels doled out by the Popcorn King—was about another woman in David Crockett's life: the one we know almost nothing about, except that she raised nine children with a drunken tavern keeper and, alone among her family, went to church; the one who surely played some part in shaping David's character and soul; the one who, even more than Elizabeth, had become a missing person as her son's legend grew.

Rebecca Hawkins Crockett, as I learned from Rutherford's Joe Bone, had made her way to west Tennessee in her old age, settling a few miles out of town, not with David but with one of his sisters and a brother-in-law. Bone showed me where they had lived, stopping his truck and pointing to a line of trees on a low rise at the edge of someone's field. He said that Rebecca had been buried a bit farther up the hill.

He also explained why she wasn't there anymore.

It seems that a Mrs. Grover Reid, a historically minded woman from nearby Trenton, had taken an interest in Rebecca Crockett's neglected grave site. In June 1955, Mrs. Reid was in California visiting her own son when, somehow, she ended up as a contestant on *Queen for a Day*. As readers of a certain age may recall, this was a radio and TV show on which women vied with each other to tell the most pathetic tales of woe. Whoever got the loudest applause became queen and got a wish she had stated in advance, which might be for anything from medical care to a new washing machine.

Mrs. Reid's wish was a bit unusual. She wanted "a tombstone for Davy Crockett's mother's grave."

She didn't win.

But as Bone told me, a Catholic priest in Fall River, Massachusetts, by the name of Father John J. Casey had tuned in to the show, and he had been moved to telephone *Queen for a Day*.

"You tell that nice lady that I will provide the money for Mrs. Crockett," he said.

That is how Davy's mom came to be reinterred in the yard of the reconstructed Crockett Cabin, with a beautiful marble marker revealing that we don't know when she was born or when she died. And it's why the portrait of a silver-haired man in a clerical collar is one of the first things visitors see—it's on the back wall, right next to the bearskin—when they walk through the cabin door.

People thought the Crockett craze might last forever, or at least until Christmas. It didn't.

"By fall of 1955," Margaret King reported, "the craze went into a sudden tailspin that left retailers in the lurch. One manufacturer summarized for the rest the rule of crazes: 'When they die, they die a horrible death.'"

Why did this one die? King—whose 1976 dissertation, along with a much-quoted essay that Lofaro included in his anthology, made her the Queen of Craze Studies—seemed to favor the explanation offered by a "motivational researcher" whose argument she summarized. The craze's end was "the result of the 'downward mobility' factor of trends in general," she wrote. In Davy's case, that meant that "older children, who adopted the fad first," abandoned their obsession as "younger children, 'an age class they no longer wish to be identified with,' took it up."

Sounds good. But here's a simpler version: *It was a fad.*

Disney Davy may have been far bigger than Hopalong Cassidy or hula hoops; he may have demonstrated the superpowers of television, rewritten a chunk of American history, and lodged himself with ridiculous tenacity in the collective psyche of a generation—but he wasn't going to stay King of the Wild Fads forever.

Fess Parker, however, was always going to be Davy Crockett, whether he wanted to or not. Parker had ambitions to be a movie actor, not just a TV star, but he had made the mistake of signing a personal services contract with Walt Disney, which meant that Walt could veto any role he wanted to take.

"I am returning your copy of *Bus Stop.* Personally, I do not think that this is a good part for you," Disney wrote Parker early in 1956. So much for starring opposite Marilyn Monroe. And Walt didn't even bother to tell Fess that the great John Ford had wanted him to act alongside John Wayne in *The Searchers.* He could have played Wayne's adoptive nephew Martin Pawley, a major role that ended up going to Jeffrey Hunter, in what's often called the best western film ever made.

"This is my interpretation of my career," Parker said much later. "Two chances to break out of my Disney mold. *Searchers. Bus Stop.* Didn't happen."

He and Uncle Walt finally parted ways. In 1964, Parker reprised his buckskinned-frontiersman number, this time playing Daniel

Boone in an NBC series that lasted six years. Even there, however, Disney had blocked his way: Fess had wanted simply to revive his Crockett character, but Disney had said no.

Eventually Parker gave up acting and went into the hotel and wine business in Santa Barbara County—but not before he and the Walt Disney Company had one last Crockett go-around. In the 1980s, long after Walt himself was gone, the company made an attempt to revive Davy as a TV character and asked Parker to participate. He read the script and hated it. "It wasn't right," he told his Archive of American Television interviewer. "What it was like was a romance novel they put Crockett in." He thought Davy II would be ignored, and he was correct: it was gone after five episodes.

Meanwhile, Parker said, he'd come up with his own idea for bringing Davy back to life—and he'd written a screenplay laying it out.

Part of his inspiration, weirdly enough, was the controversy raging around José Enrique de la Peña, a Mexican officer whose memoir of the Texas Revolution was first published in English in 1975. The de la Peña narrative—or the "alleged" de la Peña narrative, as detractors were soon calling it—has Crockett surviving the assault on the Alamo, only to be executed, with six other defenders, on Santa Anna's orders.

Parker said he had taken the survival part and run with it.

What if Santa Anna, having captured the famous frontiersman, had realized that "there might be some value in hostages"? What if Davy and Georgie had ended up in a Mexico City prison and escaped twenty-five years later? What if they had "made their way back to the Alamo, because they felt it was unfinished business," and ended up in San Antonio on March 6, 1861, to find that citizens were celebrating the battle's anniversary "and there were speeches and they were reading off the names of the defenders"?

What if, indeed!

But the nice thing about being a screenwriter and not a historian—even if your movie never gets made—is that you get to *answer* the what-if questions.

"Davy and Georgie look at each other, and Georgie says, 'I know, we're heroes—and we gotta get out of here,'" Parker said, breaking into a laugh. "And with that, we just ride out over the hill."

⊰ 11 ⊱

Soldiers in the Crockett Wars

The man who inspired Fess Parker to write an alternative ending for Davy Crockett was not yet thirty years old when he played a relatively small part in the Alamo fight. His most notable contribution, according to his wounded battalion commander, was to brave "the cannon fire, the rifle and gunfire that was happening all along the front" to report the commander's wounding and the need for a replacement.

Nearly 140 years later, thanks to the Disney-enhanced power of Crockett's legend, de la Peña's memoir made him a famous man—though hardly in the way he had hoped.

Published in English as *With Santa Anna in Texas: A Personal Narrative of the Revolution,* the memoir devoted a full chapter to the Alamo—but it was just one chapter out of sixteen. The author's intent was to set down a detailed account of the whole Texas campaign, he wrote, because "events are being distorted to the point that we who actually witnessed them will soon fail to recognize them."

Mexico in the late 1830s was filled with "Who lost Texas?" finger-pointing, and de la Peña could point fingers with the best. The attack on the Alamo, he argued, had been premature and needlessly bloody: Why not have waited a couple of days for the bigger cannons to arrive, then smashed the old mission's frail walls? Wounded men had suffered and died because their commander, careless of his soldiers' lives, hadn't bothered to bring a medical corps. Santa Anna's insistence on executing prisoners at the Alamo and, on a far larger scale, at Goliad, had been barbaric and counterproductive. "So many and such cold-blooded murders tarnished our glory," de la Peña wrote, and they "provoked the enemy."

Two years after slogging home in defeat, de la Peña joined a federalist rebellion that landed him in a Mexico City prison. He struggled to complete his memoir but died, in 1840, before he could do so. The manuscript somehow survived, and in 1955 it was published in Mexico in the original Spanish.

Few people noticed. And when the English translation appeared two decades later and de la Peña finally got some attention, all anyone seemed to care about—never mind the sweep of his narrative or his passionate condemnation of the conduct of the campaign—was a single paragraph about the capture and execution of David Crockett.

By that time, there had been more than a century's worth of questionable reports, gossip, speculation, flat-out lies, and fiction about the final minutes of the Alamo defenders. The mythmaking began on March 11, when Sam Houston rode into Gonzales—remember, he was supposed to be relieving the siege—to discover that he was five days too late.

Two Tejanos, as native Mexican residents of Texas became known, delivered the evil tidings from Béxar, though neither had actually witnessed the March 6 onslaught. They reported that all the defenders had been killed; Travis had committed suicide; an artillery officer, Almeron Dickinson, had lashed his infant child to his back and leaped to his (and the child's) death from a rooftop; and seven unnamed defenders had surrendered, only to be executed by order of Santa Anna.

Before long there was more testimony, this time from a couple of noncombatants who had survived the battle. One was Travis's slave Joe, and the other was Dickinson's young wife, Susanna. (At least ten Tejano women and children also survived, but they were not much noticed at the time.) Susanna's mere appearance disproved the story about her husband's leap, because Angelina, their only child, was alive and accompanied her. Joe contradicted the Travis suicide report, saying he had seen his master shot and mortally wounded early in the fight. According to one of the men who heard him tell his story on March 20, Joe also reported that "Crockett and a few of his friends were found together, with twenty-four of the enemy dead around them."

Four days later, dropping a "t" from David's name, a Texas newspaper elaborated:

> The end of David Crocket of Tennessee, the great hunter of the west, was as glorious as his career through life had been useful. He and his companions were found surrounded by piles of assailants, whom they had immolated on the altar of Texas liberties. The countenance of Crocket was unchanged: he had in death that freshness of hue, which his exercise of pursuing the beasts of the forest and the prairie had imparted to him.

Newspapers all over the country recycled the image of David surrounded by heaps of dead Mexicans. Frequently, he was said to have gone down "fighting like a tiger." One report suggested that he had "fortified himself with sixteen guns well charged" before his last stand. Yet there were significant variations as well. In one, Crockett and several defenders tried to surrender "but were told there was no mercy for them," so they continued fighting until killed.

In another—119 years before the publication of de la Peña's memoir—David was captured and executed.

The execution story surfaced in a June 9, 1836, letter to New York's *Courier and Enquirer*, whose anonymous correspondent said he'd gotten it from an equally anonymous Mexican army eyewitness in a Texas prison camp. The letter told of a general named Manuel Fernández Castrillón who had accepted the surrender of Crockett and five other defenders, promising them protection, and marched them over to Santa Anna. David was said to have looked the Mexican commander "steadfastly in the face" as Castrillón asked what should be done with the captives. "Have I not told you before how to dispose of them?" Santa Anna asked angrily. His officers then "plunged their swords into the bosoms of their defenseless prisoners."

Richard Penn Smith, on deadline for his fake Crockett book, picked up the story.

Exploits included a postscript—supposedly by the man who had acquired Crockett's journal—that offered a description of David at the time of his surrender to Castrillón. "He stood alone in an angle of the fort," Smith wrote, "the barrel of his shattered rifle in his right hand, in his left his huge Bowie knife dripping blood. There was a frightful gash across his forehead, while around him there was a complete barrier of about twenty Mexicans, lying pell-mell, dead, and dying." Moving on to Santa Anna's execution order, Smith gave David a hero's exit: "Colonel Crockett, seeing the set of treachery, instantly sprang like a tiger at the ruffian chief, but before he could reach him a dozen swords were sheathed in his indomitable heart; and he fell, and died without a groan, a frown on his brow, and a smile of scorn and defiance on his lips."

Reprinted for decades, that scene made its way into numerous other works on Crockett, including popular biographies by John Abbott and Edward Ellis, who has the defiant captive being shot down rather than stabbed. As with the "Pop, pop, pop! Bom, bom, bom!" quote, it never quite went away, even after *Exploits* was exposed as a hoax.

But it didn't end up stuck in people's heads, either.

The went-down-fighting scenario, absent any hint of surrender, proved the most durable version of David's end. Recorded in newspapers, songs, histories, adventure stories, paintings, and films, it appeared too many times to count between 1836 and 1955, so I'll content myself with citing a personal favorite. It's from a 1908 novel for young people called *In Texas with Davy Crockett*, and in it, the last living Alamo defender tries to fight off the Mexican army by himself. Susanna Dickinson witnesses Crockett's death—never mind that in reality she was huddled with her daughter inside the Alamo church—and she tells Sam Houston what she saw:

> For a dread moment the fighting ceased. The cowardly jackals paused in awe of the terrible prowess of the king lion. I heard Colonel Almonte shout, 'Surrender!' I heard Crockett answer, 'Never!' I heard another officer yell, 'At him! At him!' And then the fight began again—a hundred, all that could get within striking distance, against one man.

Is it any wonder that Fess Parker never gave up? Or that, five years later, the Duke would go down fighting, too?

"Crockett! North wall!" yells a desperate, wounded defender. Davy hears him, but there's not much he can do. The scaling ladders are already up; Travis is already down; Mexican soldiers are already pouring over that wall on the other side of the compound; and the end is near for the most memorable Crockett impersonator besides Parker ever to ride into the Alamo—or, in this case, into *The Alamo*, the epic 1960 picture produced by, directed by, and starring John Wayne. Duke's Davy retreats, fighting, toward the church, where a Mexican lancer runs him through. But he's carrying a flaming torch, and he has one last mission to fulfill. He staggers toward the powder magazine and flings the torch.

Ka-boom!

It's quite a different exit from Disney Davy's, and, for that matter, from anything we know about how the real David Crockett might have died. But that's not the point. The point is that this Davy fights to his last breath for the idea of liberty embodied in the Republic of Texas—and there's not the slightest hint that he might have allowed himself to be captured and executed.

John Wayne simply wouldn't do that.

Wayne had boundless ambitions for his Alamo movie, which he spent more than a decade trying to get made. Personally and artistically, he wanted to break out of his cowboy mold and to prove—by directing the film himself—that he was more than just an unusually charismatic star. Politically, he saw *The Alamo* as a Cold War rallying point. "These are perilous times," he told a Hollywood columnist. "The eyes of the world are on us. We must sell America to countries threatened with Communist domination. Our picture is also important to Americans who should appreciate the struggle our ancestors made for the precious freedom which we now enjoy."

He put everything he had into it. "Few filmmakers have ever fought so long and hard," as Frank Thompson wrote, "to put a personal vision on the screen." Failing to get his project off the ground at Republic Pictures, Wayne started his own production company. He put his reputation and much of his personal fortune at risk— and it wasn't because he had his heart set on playing the lead. His interest was in the whole heroic Alamo tale, not just Crockett, and he was going to have his hands full producing and directing. He thought it might be better to play Sam Houston, who gets just a few minutes of screen time.

Not an option. If he'd tried it, his investors would have pulled their money and gone home.

But what would happen when one American legend merged with another on-screen?

The legend-playing-a-legend notion appeals strongly to some Crockettologists. John Wayne was a man used to wrestling his own outsized image, the argument goes, so he knew instinctively how Davy should be played. As I sat down with a DVD of *The Alamo* to contemplate the legend-melding question, I had an endorsement by Richard Boyd Hauck in mind. "Wayne captures Crockett's sense of humor, his clumsy gallantry and sentimentality, his impatience and his egotism," Hauck wrote. "He displays Crockett's moral flexibility, his harmless streak of trickiness, and his lusty bragging. He shows us Crockett's moderate love of flirting, rowdy horseplay, and whiskey." All this sounded like the David I knew, or thought I knew.

Unfortunately, it bore little relation to what I actually saw.

Take the scene where Crockett and Travis meet. David and his Tennessee followers, newly arrived in Béxar, are whooping it up in a local cantina. The Alamo commander drops by to talk, but the two are interrupted by some rowdy horseplay. Travis takes offense and starts to leave. "Step down off your high horse, mister," Crockett tells him, suddenly all business. He then demonstrates that he knows as much about revolutionary Texas as Travis does and delivers a famous monologue about how hearing the word "republic" warms his heart and makes him feel like a man watching his baby take its first steps.

Travis is impressed. "You're not the illiterate country bumpkin you would have people believe," he says.

What's wrong with this picture? Well, it's true that the real David was smarter than he sometimes let on and that he cared a good deal about small-"r" republican principles. But not even someone as blind to the nuances of human relations as this movie's William Barret Travis could look at Wayne's character, at any point, and see him as a country bumpkin. And to judge from Crockett's autobiography—

the closest thing we have to his authentic voice—he didn't sound one little bit like the man Wayne and his screenwriter invented.

Whatever David had to say on the subject of republics would have been a lot less sappy, and it would have employed the pungent vernacular of the true frontier.

Does Wayne's character have a sense of humor? Yes, and a subtle one at that—but it's not Crockett's. Does he display "clumsy gallantry" in his weirdly chaste fictional romance? I didn't see it as clumsy. Is he impatient? To the contrary: he shows great patience while manipulating his Tennessee followers into deciding, supposedly for themselves, to stay at the Alamo and fight. Can you really call that manipulation "harmless," given the consequences? I'm not so sure. Duke's Davy has plenty of ego, but he keeps it better hidden than David did. He never comes close to tossing out a classic Crockett brag. And though he certainly drinks and indulges in horseplay, he is always, always in control.

Why wouldn't he be?

He's John Wayne!

And that, of course, is the real issue here. By the time Wayne played Crockett, he had been trading on his John Wayne–ness for decades. I couldn't take my eyes off him—but I never for one minute saw him as anyone else.

There is a lot more to be said about Wayne's movie, which opened in San Antonio on October 24, 1960, and did far less well, critically and commercially, than its producer-director-star had hoped. If I were focused on the Alamo story as a whole, for example, I would need to deal at length with the script's astonishing disregard for historical reality. Thompson, who's a fan of the film—he called it "John Wayne's crowning achievement"—has summed this point up nicely. "*The Alamo* was made to celebrate heroism, not history," he wrote. "In fact, there isn't an instant in the film that corresponds to the historical event of 1836 in any way, except coincidentally."

Not an instant? Surely he's exaggerating.

Afraid not.

I can't swear the movie doesn't contain a few instants of truth. Still, I don't think that Houston rode into Béxar before the fight and told Travis that the fate of Texas "rests in your hands now." I'm pretty sure that the Alamo defenders didn't sally blithely forth during the siege to blow up a Mexican cannon the size of a Minuteman missile or to steal a herd of lowing longhorns from under Santa Anna's nose. And I'm absolutely certain that David Crockett didn't die tossing a torch into a powder magazine, blowing half the Alamo to kingdom come.

But facts are facts and images are images, and it was the heroic image of Davy Crockett—as personified by Fess Parker and John Wayne—that most Americans had in mind, a decade and a half later, when another flaming torch was flung into history's powder magazine.

The year was 1975. The torch flinger was José Enrique de la Peña, from more than a century beyond the grave. And the woman who lit the match was a former Daughters of the Republic of Texas librarian named Carmen Perry, whose English translation of de la Peña's memoir—often referred to as the Mexican officer's "diary"—included this passage about the Alamo aftermath:

> Some seven men had survived the general carnage and, under the protection of General Castrillón, they were brought before Santa Anna. Among them was one of great stature, well proportioned, with regular features, in whose face there was the imprint of adversity, but in whom one also noticed a degree of resignation and nobility that did him honor. He was the naturalist David Crockett, well known in North America for his unusual adventures, who had undertaken to explore the country and who, finding

himself in Béjar at the very moment of surprise, had taken refuge in the Alamo, fearing that his status as a foreigner might not be respected. Santa Anna answered Castrillón's intervention in Crockett's behalf with a gesture of indignation and, addressing himself to the sappers, the troops closest to him, ordered his execution. The commanders and officers were outraged at this action and did not support the order, hoping that once the fury of the moment had blown over these men would be spared; but several officers who were around the president and who, perhaps, had not been present during the moment of danger, became noteworthy by an infamous deed, surpassing the soldiers in cruelty. They thrust themselves forward, in order to flatter their commander, and with swords in hand, fell upon these unfortunate, defenseless men just as a tiger leaps upon his prey. Though tortured before they were killed, these unfortunates died without complaining and without humiliating themselves before their torturers. It was rumored that General Sesma was one of them; I will not bear witness to this, for though present, I turned away horrified in order not to witness such a barbarous scene. Do you remember, comrades, that fierce moment which struck us all with dread, which made our souls tremble, thirsting for vengeance just a few moments before? Are your resolute hearts not stirred and still full of indignation against those who so ignobly dishonored their swords with blood? As for me, I confess that the very memory of it makes me tremble and that my ear can still hear the penetrating, doleful sound of the victims.

Ka-BOOM!

Crockett fans were not happy *at all*. It wasn't just that de la

Peña's Davy was captured and executed, though that idea was news to most people in 1975. No, it was much worse. It appeared that this Crockett had tried to save his skin by claiming he had ended up inside the Alamo—the Shrine of Texas Liberty, consecrated by the blood of the martyrs who had willingly crossed Travis's line—*by accident*.

And here was the press, doing what the press always seems to do with such news: gloating about it.

"Students of American history and John Wayne fans take note. The legendary story of the Alamo may need revision" was one of the milder journalistic reactions. "Has the King of the Wild Frontier been relieved of his coonskin crown?" was another, with the reporter going on to note how tough it would be to get the Disney generation "to accept the mental image of a cowardly Crockett groveling in the Alamo corner." Meanwhile, *People* magazine took the prize for the stupidest, most inaccurate de la Peña headline. "Did Crockett die at the Alamo? Historian Carmen Perry says no," it read. Small wonder that Perry got what a colleague later described as "vituperative phone calls, at her home, in the middle of the night, accusing her of being a traitor to Texas and to the whole of history."

Three years after Perry's translation came out, Dan Kilgore, a recent president of the Texas State Historical Association, published a short book called *How Did Davy Die?* in which he weighed the available evidence, including a number of other execution accounts of varying reliability, and came down on de la Peña's side of the argument.

Kilgore's reception made Perry's look mild. As a nonacademic historian who made his living as an accountant, he could perhaps laugh when denounced as "a mealy-mouthed intellectual." As a political conservative, he might shrug off charges that he was part of a Communist plot "to degrade our heroes." But the press, once again, made matters worse—no, Kilgore did not write that Crockett was "a flop and a fink and maybe a coward to boot"—and some of the hate mail he got was so disturbing he wouldn't talk about it.

No amount of public outcry, however, could stop a critical mass of professional historians from declaring the case closed. The University of New Mexico's Paul Andrew Hutton, who collected most of the headlines cited above, was himself severely abused for what he has called a "hopelessly hero-worshipful" piece on David that included the execution story, but he didn't change his mind. "There really is very little room for doubt that Crockett was captured and executed at the Alamo," Hutton wrote a few years later. "It is in fact rather surprising just how much detail we have on this incident."

But that was before a New York City fireman with a background in arson investigation flung another explosive torch into the Crockett War. His name was William Groneman III, and in 1994 he published a book in which he argued that *With Santa Anna in Texas* couldn't possibly be the last word on David Crockett's death.

The reason Groneman gave was stunning: he thought the de la Peña memoir had been forged.

✴

Sixteen contentious years later, Bill Groneman still hadn't changed his mind about the Crockett execution question, and I was back in Knoxville to hear him talk about it.

The occasion was the annual convention of the Western Writers of America, which was hosting a Crockett panel at the East Tennessee Historical Society's museum, just yards from where Joe Swann's rifle was on display. Swann was among the panelists, and Hutton, who was chairing, introduced him as a consummate "grassroots historian." I hadn't heard the term, but it seemed perfect for Joe and for a lot of the other people I'd met while walking where Crockett walked. It certainly fit Jim Claborn, my guide to David's Morristown, who was on the Knoxville panel as well.

It also fit the neatly mustached, silver-haired gentleman seated a few chairs down from Swann and Claborn.

"Bill, of course, is a retired captain of the New York City Fire Department," Hutton said, introducing Groneman. "He hates me when I say this, but he is a hero of 9/11." After the applause, Hutton went on to describe Groneman as someone with whom he shares a "love and passion for Davy Crockett," despite his having "written a whole series of books attacking me and everything that I believe."

Crockett's life, not his end, dominated the conversation. Swann spoke about David's three years with the Quaker family, from whom he learned how important it was "to have a good name." Claborn talked about Crockett's mother, who bore a child roughly every two years for twenty years and "sacrificed her whole life for her children." The panel's most unusual expert, David Zucker—who for nearly two decades had been trying to make a Crockett movie based on a screenplay on which he and Hutton had collaborated—said that Crockett's brags reminded him of those of the young Muhammad Ali. Knoxville's own Michael Lofaro pointed out that Crockett's venture to Texas allowed history to keep seeing him as a westerner, unlike Jackson, who had become "essentially a southerner" by the time he died.

Finally, Hutton asked the panelists to spend "just a moment" talking about David's death.

One by one, they ducked the question.

"I tend to avoid this issue as much as possible," said Lofaro, joking that he'd had "coonskin caps burned on my lawn" when his Crockett anthology was published.

"It's just like scratching a sore—just causes it to bleed again," said Claborn.

"There was this famous publicist in Hollywood who, upon hearing the news that Elvis Presley had died, simply commented, 'Great career move,'" said Zucker.

Then it was Groneman's turn.

"Okay, somebody send out for pizza," he said. "We're gonna be here for a while." When the laughter died down, he launched into the argument he's been making ever since 1994. "The alpha and the omega of the thing about Crockett being executed," he said, "is the alleged de la Peña diary. It would take about two days for us to sit here and explain the whole thing, but I'll give you the short version."

As it happened, I had met Groneman the night before at the Western Writers' annual auction. He had donated a manuscript of a then-unpublished 9/11 memoir, which went for $90. Over breakfast, between questions about Crockett, I took the opportunity to ask him about it.

He'd written the memoir, he said, because "I wanted to remember everything I witnessed." Off duty that day, he'd gone for a run at Jones Beach. He saw a cloud of smoke on the horizon but didn't know what it was. Then he saw some surfers clustered around a radio—that was odd, because "the surf was really good"—by which time he'd already started thinking "I've got to get back." From another radio he heard five words: "disaster Mayor Giuliani thousands dead." Stopping to collect five men from his Queens firehouse, he made it downtown "about an hour and a half after the second tower collapsed; we were there for the next twelve hours." Late in the evening, they joined an effort to rescue some trapped Port Authority cops. A line "like a bucket brigade" passed equipment into the pit, including fire extinguishers someone had taken from a McDonald's and given to Groneman's men. Sometime after the rescued men were handed up the line on stretchers, Groneman got "a little incoherent" and noticed he was having trouble breathing. "You have carbon monoxide poisoning," a doctor told him. "Don't go back on the pile."

Groneman said he got interested in Crockett through Disney "like everybody else my age," though he was a bit too young to catch the original broadcasts. He was eight when Wayne's movie came out, and "that was a must-see." In the mid-1970s, he started going to San Antonio—"I just wanted to actually *see* the Alamo, after reading about it for years"—where he met some like-minded people and started writing for tiny Alamo·newsletters. "It was real amateur stuff," he said, but he was hooked. In a newsletter piece I later tracked down, he called the tale of Travis's line "worthy of Greek mythology" but noted a small problem: "I find it difficult to believe this event really happened."

He found de la Peña's description of Crockett's death hard to believe as well.

"It didn't ring true to me," he said. "One of my main questions was: How would this Mexican officer have known Davy Crockett?"

He tracked the brouhaha over Perry's translation, and he deplored the downward spiral of David's reputation that came with it. "The view of Crockett was turning into 'He didn't die fighting, he was executed. So if he was executed, that meant he surrendered. Oh, he surrendered? Then he was a coward. Then he was a groveling coward.' And I didn't like the way things were going. And finally, when Jeff Long's book came out—did you read Jeff Long's book?"

Long's *Duel of Eagles*, published in 1990, is a popular history of the Texas Revolution, and its gloss on the de la Peña execution story exemplifies its amped-up style. "David Crockett made a choice," Long wrote. "The Go Ahead man quit. He did more than quit. He lied. He dodged. He denied his role in the fighting."

"I read this and I said, 'Enough,'" Groneman recalled. "'What do we even *know* about this thing?'"

Not much, it turned out.

The de la Peña manuscript had been edited and self-published in 1955 by a Mexican antiquities dealer named Jesús Sánchez Garza. In the early 1970s, it had been purchased from Sánchez Garza's widow by John Peace, a Texas lawyer-politician closely connected to the University of Texas at San Antonio, where Carmen Perry had translated it into English and where, at the time, it still resided. But no one, as far as Groneman could tell, had ever seriously examined whether it was real.

Some of his questions: Why couldn't anyone say where the manuscript had been between the 1830s and 1955? Why did historians seem so eager to proclaim it the most reliable source on the Alamo and Crockett's death? What about problems such as de la Peña's vivid description of Travis's death late in the battle, which contradicted eyewitness testimony (from Joe) that he was one of the first to go down? Why hadn't anyone done forensic tests or a handwriting analysis? Why did people insist on calling de la Peña's book a diary when the published version had obviously been completed after the campaign and fleshed out with material from other sources?

Oh, and by the way: Why did anyone who publicly doubted the manuscript's authenticity risk being lumped in with the crazies who had harassed Perry and Kilgore or condemned as a racist or mocked as a Davy-worshipper with a "fragile psyche" who couldn't handle the idea that his childhood hero hadn't gone down swinging?

"I have to see this thing itself, the original," Groneman decided. So he headed for San Antonio.

He had assumed that he would find a single, coherent document. No such luck. "When I got down there, it was three stacks—tied with ribbons—of loose pages." Two of those stacks, as Groneman would eventually learn, are key to understanding the manuscript that became the de la Peña memoir. One is "the papers which Carmen Perry's book was published from, and Jesús Sánchez Garza's twenty years earlier in Mexico." That one has "all the juicy information"—including Crockett's execution—yet "there are a number of different handwritings in it." The other stack, in which the handwriting is uniform, "has none of the exciting stuff in the published account." In that version, Crockett is not mentioned.

What the hell was going on?

It was an excellent question, and it's one that Groneman was the first to raise. His most troubling finding, however, was an apparent anachronism he had discovered earlier while reading Perry's translation. Perry's preface had suggested—and what looked like a title page had appeared to confirm—that de la Peña had published the memoir in Mexico in September 1836, though no copies of an 1836 edition had ever been found. But Groneman noticed that de la Peña made reference to another Mexican account of the Texas campaign that had not been published until 1838.

Whoa. Anachronisms are a key indicator of forgery, and that one looked to Groneman like a smoking gun.

He soon began work on the book that became *Defense of a Legend: Crockett and the de la Peña Diary*. In it he not only laid out his argument that the published "diary" was a twentieth-century fake, but he named the likely forger: John Laflin, a peripatetic rogue who'd spent decades peddling fake documents. Groneman even included a renowned handwriting expert's endorsement of his hypothesis.

In March 1994, with his book newly published by the Republic of Texas Press, Groneman returned to San Antonio to promote it. One day he walked into the Daughters of the Republic of Texas Library, on the Alamo grounds, and ran into another researcher who had been digging into a questionable account of an incident from the Texas Revolution. His name was James E. Crisp, and he had just published an article showing that a racist speech allegedly given by Sam Houston had actually been put into Houston's mouth by someone else.

The two had not met before, but Groneman had read Crisp's article and Crisp had heard excited talk about what Groneman had been up to. They talked, and Groneman showed Crisp a copy of his book.

"And *that* was a mistake, obviously," he said.

Why? Because despite all Groneman's friendly sparring with Hutton, Jim Crisp turned out to be the academic historian who really took him on. The resulting Crisp-Groneman confrontation over the de la Peña memoir and the manner of David's death had never been less than heated. Crockettologists and Alamo historians alike had rushed to take sides, though some, as the Knoxville panel showed, had by now wearied of the fight.

Crisp taught history at North Carolina State University in Raleigh, 360 miles over the Appalachians from Knoxville. Raleigh would be my next stop.

Forty-eight hours later, I was sitting in Crisp's living room, a few minutes' drive from campus, listening to him describe what it was like to grow up immersed in Texas history in the tiny town of Henrietta, 135 miles west of Honey Grove.

"One of the earliest memories I have is that this was a different *country*," he said. The Republic of Texas had "its own borders and currency and diplomats in Europe, and that was just fascinating to me." Reminders of that history were everywhere: "I would ride my bike down Crockett Street to get to the swimming pool."

Not surprisingly, when the Crockett craze came along, the nine-year-old future historian dived right in.

In Crisp's 2005 book *Sleuthing the Alamo*, a first-person account of his engagement with the question of Davy's death and related historical mysteries, he wrote that he had been "mesmerized" by Fess Parker's rifle-swinging last stand. He took to flipping a backyard picnic table on its side to create a fort, allowing him to re-enact the scene "a thousand times." Viewers of the Disney series, of course, never got to see Parker actually go down, and Crisp took his cue from that.

"I don't remember dying, either," he recalled. "Like Davy, I just kept on killing Mexicans."

Flash forward forty years to his encounter with Bill Groneman at the DRT Library.

What was Crisp doing there? Well, he was researching an Alamo defender—but not for the usual reasons.

John W. Smith had survived the siege because he had been sent as a messenger to the Convention at Washington. He had "married into a Hispanic family," Crisp said, "and become the first Anglo mayor of San Antonio." Crisp had long been drawn to the subject of Anglo-Hispanic relations in revolutionary Texas; he thought ethnic friction had been overplayed as a cause of the revolt by historians projecting racial antagonism from their own time onto the past. He had also learned that a great deal of what had been written about the Texas Revolution could not be trusted. So he was prepared to believe that Groneman had produced a breakthrough book.

Then he read it.

Crisp had agreed to review *Defense of a Legend* for the *Southwestern Historical Quarterly,* and he had not been thinking that the task would take him long. But he soon realized that although "Bill had raised a lot of *really* interesting and valid points, he hadn't closed the argument of forgery."

Meaning?

"You know, the logic wasn't there, and the evidence wasn't there."

So much for doing a quickie review. Crisp ended up reading first the Perry translation, then the Spanish version published in Mexico, and finally, those same stacks of de la Peña documents, tied with ribbons, that Groneman had puzzled over. By the time he was done, he had made the alleged anachronism disappear.

That's because de la Peña's memoir, contrary to Perry's assumption, was *not* originally published in 1836.

The details of Crisp's historical detective work are, to say the least, complicated. But as he wrote in *Sleuthing,* he discovered that a preamble to the 1955 Mexican edition had noted that de la Peña "spent more than a year revising his manuscript, but was unable to publish it during his lifetime." A serendipitous discovery soon confirmed that. Crisp was checking a small fact in a bibliographic listing when he saw a mention of another work by de la Peña: a sixteen-page pamphlet published in 1839. Tracking down the only known copy, he learned that it had been composed in Mexico City's Inquisition Prison, where de la Peña's participation in the federalist rebellion had landed him. "In good time," the prisoner had written, "I will expose the causes which have prevented me from publishing my diary and the observations which I have almost completed."

If de la Peña was still writing in 1839, his use of material from 1838 was no anachronism.

Still, what about those stacks of documents in different handwritings that Groneman had seen?

More complications. Bear with me, we're almost there.

To start with, de la Peña's actual campaign diary is not to be found among his papers. The stack of document pages in *uniform* handwriting, which would prove to be de la Peña's own, is a rewritten version. It begins with the author noting that in July 1836, "I began to put my diary in clean form." The stack of document pages in *several* handwritings is what was eventually published. It was a work in progress that had been greatly expanded and included

material from other sources—and according to Crisp, de la Peña
had help with it. He was in jail, after all, and chronically ill. That
would explain the handwriting shifts.

"Let's face it," Crisp said. "If you're going to forge a document, do
you get four different handwritings in it?"

The *Southwestern Historical Quarterly* published Crisp's defense
of the de la Peña memoir in October 1994. "Once the charge of
anachronism is eliminated," he wrote, the case for fraud becomes
"a very thin case indeed." He agreed that the documents should
undergo further analysis, including forensic testing, but found the
alleged similarities to Laflin forgeries highly unpersuasive. Among
other things, Groneman's handwriting expert had never laid eyes
on an original de la Peña document: he had dashed off an opinion
based on a few pages copied in Perry's translation.

Crisp's "book review" had turned out to be almost forty pages
long. He figured it would put the de la Peña question to rest.

No way. As he should have better understood by then, the idea
that Davy Crockett went down fighting was *important* to people.
Kevin Young, a historical interpreter and researcher immensely
knowledgeable about all things Alamo, clued the newcomer in.

"Well, you've really stepped in it now," Young said.

When the Texas State Historical Association met in San Antonio in March 1995, a scheduled talk by Groneman turned into
what the startled author of *Defense of a Legend* described as "the
biggest session that they had had in a hundred years," drawing some
three hundred people into two merged hotel conference rooms.
Groneman gave a nod to Crisp's dismissal of the 1838 anachronism
but firmly restated his opinion that the de la Peña account was "a
modern-day hoax." Its "main selling point is this one passage about
Crockett," he said, and everyone should please stop treating it as
the gospel truth.

Meanwhile, Crisp, as he wrote in *Sleuthing*, had been fending off "media types from both sides of the Atlantic looking for a sound bite (which I wasn't going to give them) to the effect that 'Crockett was a coward!'" Invited to give his own talk in San Antonio on the same day as Groneman's, he heard "morbid jokes about my need for a bulletproof vest." The next day, a woman recognized him as he walked by the Alamo. "She blurted out, 'I know who you are—and if I had my Bowie knife I'd gut you right now, because hanging would be too good for you!'"

He managed to calm down that particular Crockett enthusiast, and they later became friends. But the intensity of Crisp's hate mail—which came, like Dan Kilgore's, with virulent anti-Mexican overtones—told him that more was involved here than some people's straightforward love for a heroic Crockett. He was sure "that the stubborn old issue of race was bound up with questions of myth and collective identity in the story of the Alamo and Davy's death."

Crisp made it clear, when he brought up the question of racial attitudes and the Alamo, that he was not talking about the kind of passionate historical arguments made by people such as Bill Groneman. He was talking about a different phenomenon, rooted in a complex cultural past.

Contemporary scholars are often accused of "injecting multiculturalism into history," Crisp said, but that is not what has been going on with the story of the Texas Revolution. Yes, there has been some recent emphasis on Tejano rebels such as the Alamo defender and messenger Juan Seguin and the Texas Declaration of Independence signer José Antonio Navarro. But to make Tejanos part of the story is hardly some kind of politically correct distortion, because the true history of Texas in the 1830s "is multiculturalism in spades. What happened is *not* that we have injected multiculturalism—it's that all that got whitewashed *out* in the late nineteenth and early twentieth centuries." Historians from that era painted the revolution as "a race war with only one color on each side and nothing in between." Yet "the real story, the dramatic story, of these Tejanos is that they were being pulled apart—I mean, their *souls* were being pulled apart"—because they were forced to choose between their Mexican homeland and an independent Texas.

Why did that story disappear?

"What happened in Texas over time," Crisp said, is that whites "came to use the Mexicans as a negative image" and to view themselves "as the mirror image of the Mexicans. They were defining themselves. And I think that sense of self-definition through history is a thousand percent stronger in Texans than it is in Americans generally."

As the Alamo became a touchstone for Texan identity, "Crockett's death became a symbol for many people, and different people used it in different ways. But it became a way of talking about other things that are more difficult to talk about. It became a way of talking about race; it became a way of talking about heroism; it became a way of people defining who they were through their myths."

And if all that made it something too big for a single, memoir-writing Mexican officer to take on, well, why should anyone be surprised?

Crisp never used the term "culture war" as we talked about the uproar over de la Peña, but I couldn't help thinking about it. A hopelessly broad and poorly defined concept, it has long served (among other meanings) as a crude shorthand for the clashing worldviews of academic historians and proponents of what's often called traditional history. For decades now, academics have been trying to bring out the stories of people once ignored by the traditional narrative, while traditionalists have been complaining that their heroes—Davy Crockett among them—were being shunted aside.

Yet one reason I find Crockett so fascinating is that his life is illuminating whichever historical frame you put on it. Want traditional history? Think of David as a classic pioneer pushing bravely west in search of land and prosperity—then add a heroic ending. Want to think outside the traditional box? Remember his dirt-poor constituents and his futile, largely forgotten struggle to secure their inclusion in the American dream.

I resisted the urge to float this notion to Crisp, however. I'd come to talk about Crockett's death, not the Tennessee Vacant Land Bill, and we had a lot more ground to cover. Not long before Crisp had to head toward campus, in fact, he threw me a serious curveball.

De la Peña, he said, "is not the best evidence we have about how Crockett died."

Wait, wait, wait.

"It's the Dolson letter by far," Crisp said.

That is how I learned that the leading academic expert on the controversial memoir of José Enrique de la Peña—the professor who had spent fifteen years arguing that the memoir is genuine—doesn't think it's even close to the last word on the execution debate.

*

Actually, I knew about the Dolson letter. I just hadn't had time to sort through all the details. But before plunging into this exciting new briar patch, I decided to see what another well-known Crockettologist, Billy Bob Thornton, had to offer on the subject.

Thornton is the actor who played Crockett in the 2004 Touchstone film *The Alamo* (not to be confused with Wayne's film of the same name). It was a massive commercial and critical flop, but that wasn't what interested me. For one thing, I'd been told that Billy Bob had made an intriguing Davy. What's more, I knew that the filmmakers had decided—nearly half a century after the de la Peña memoir's first publication—that they had to take the execution story into account.

Which, in their weird Hollywood way, they did.

Near the end of the battle, David rushes toward the Mexicans and what looks like certain death, empty rifle raised ever so briefly in the classic Fess Parker pose. Cut! A minute later he's kneeling—bloody-faced, exhausted, hands tied behind his back—in the Alamo courtyard, surrounded by Mexican soldiers.

How did this happen? We're offered no clue.

"If you wish to beg for your life, this would be the proper time," says the smirking Mexican commander, in Spanish, with subtitles.

"Are you Santa Anna?" David asks, almost under his breath. "I thought he'd be taller." The Mexican interpreter doesn't pass this on, which explains why the general doesn't order Crockett's execution immediately.

After a long pause, David starts to talk.

It's the opposite of begging.

"You tell the general that I'm willin' to discuss the terms of surrender," he says. "You tell him, if he'll tell his men to lay their weapons down and assemble peacefully, I promise to take you all to General Houston and I'll try my best to save most of your lives. That said, Sam's a might prickly—so no promises.

"Tell him," he repeats.

The interpreter remains silent.

"TELL HIM!"

And now here come David's last words, a deliberate, ironic nod to his half-alligator, half-horse legend. "I want to warn you all: I'm a screamer," he says, and sure enough, as his killers rush toward him, he lets out a death-defying "Aghhhhhhhhh!"

I'd call that pretty damn heroic. But it's not helpful if you're trying to figure out what actually happened.

The rest of Thornton's performance as Crockett reminded me, strangely, of John Wayne's, not because the two are the least bit alike but because neither bears much resemblance to the David I thought I'd come to know. Billy Bob's Crockett plays the fiddle like a concert violinist, and in general, he is far too somber and angst-ridden. Yes, David knew that his "Davy" persona wasn't his real self—just think back to the "They came to see a bar" scene that John Gadsby Chapman described—but he didn't agonize over it. He was too busy going ahead, or at least scrambling to survive, and being the life of the party while he was at it.

File Thornton's effort under "Trying Too Hard."

But back to that Dolson letter. How persuasive *is* it? Might those who think it clinches the execution scenario be trying too hard as well?

Written in July 1836 by Texian army sergeant George Dolson and sent to his brother in Michigan, the letter showed up in a Detroit newspaper two months later. It would not come to the attention of modern historians until 1960, however, when a graduate student who had run across the newspaper version published an article about it. In the letter, Dolson—who was fluent in Spanish—told the story of an interview with a Mexican officer at a Texas prisoner-of-war camp for which he had served as interpreter.

Here is part of what Dolson wrote:

> [T]he following may be relied on, being from an individual who was an eye witness to the whole proceedings. . . . He states that on the morning the Alamo was captured, between the hours of five and six o'clock, General Castrillón, who fell at the battle of San Jacinto, entered the back room of the Alamo, and there found Crockett and five other Americans, who had defended it until defense was useless. . . . [T]he humane General ordered his men to keep out, and, placing his hand on one breast, said, "here is a hand and a heart to protect you; come with me to the General-in-Chief, and you shall be saved." . . . The brave but unfortunate men were marched to the tent of Santa

Anna. Colonel Crockett was in the rear, had his arms folded, and appeared bold as the lion as he passed my informant (Almonte). Santa Anna's interpreter knew Colonel Crockett, and said to my informant, "the one behind is the famous Crockett." When brought in the presence of Santa Anna, Castrillón said to him, "Santa Anna, the august, I deliver up to you six brave prisoners of war." Santa Anna replied, "who has given you orders to take prisoners, I do not want to see these men living—shoot them." As the monster uttered these words each officer turned his face the other way, and the hell-hounds of the tyrant despatched the six in his presence, and within six feet of his person.

Sounds kind of like the de la Peña version, right?

Well, yes and no.

In both accounts, Castrillón takes the prisoners to Santa Anna; Crockett is among them; and Santa Anna orders them killed, outraging some of his officers. Yet Dolson did not suggest that Crockett offered any kind of alibi. Nor, for that matter, did the anonymous author of another significant execution account, published earlier in the *Courier and Enquirer,* who said he had interviewed a Mexican officer in the same prison camp. That was the version adapted by Richard Penn Smith at the end of his fake Crockett autobiography.

Jim Crisp and Bill Groneman, as you will no doubt be astonished to learn, have strongly differing views about how much the Dolson letter is to be trusted.

The most vehement anti-Dolson arguments, however, came from the late Thomas Ricks Lindley, a close friend of Groneman who is widely acknowledged as the most relentless Alamo researcher ever. Lindley and Crisp exchanged views in six *Alamo Journal* articles in 1995 and 1996. They featured page after page of dense debate over such things as a possible, crucial mistranslation of the Spanish word *pabellon* (which might refer to either a tent or a flag) and a possible, equally crucial typesetting error (which made Santa Anna's aide-de-camp appear, wrongly, to have been Dolson's source). Lindley put forth a conspiracy theory worthy of the Kennedy assassination to explain why Dolson's letter to his brother might have been intended as anti–Santa Anna propaganda. All this is impossible to summarize. You can read it for yourself—googling "The Lindley-Crisp Debate" should bring it up—or you can take my word for it that the exchange is both substantive and a little insane.

Okay, just one example. I can't resist.

In his opening salvo, Lindley presents an elaborate comparison of three execution accounts, including de la Peña's and Dolson's, in which he charts how many times they "agree" or "disagree." Here's part of Crisp's response:

> Imagine that you have the deposition of three witnesses, all of which are now deceased and beyond cross-examination. The first says: "Jack and Jill went up the hill to fetch a pail of water." The second witness recalls that: "I saw Jack going up the hill with Jill to get some water. He had an empty pail with him, and she was wearing a yellow skirt." The third witness says: "I saw Jill yesterday wearing a knock-out yellow dress. She was with Jack, and the two of them were going up a hill to fill their pail with water." Incredibly, Tom Lindley would see more disagreement here than agreement!

What I see is two ferociously competitive people wrestling on a slope of slippery facts.

I'm leaving out far more than just the details of the Lindley-Crisp smackdown here. There's a pile of additional execution evidence to weigh, all of it at least partially tainted. After months of digging through it, I still needed a scorecard to keep the players straight.

Which Mexican officer was it who said that he had seen "Castrion" try but fail to save "a venerable looking old man" called "Coket"? What was the name of the loquacious sergeant, described by Kilgore as "probably the least reliable Alamo eyewitness," who claimed that Travis and Crockett had been executed together? And how about that champion fabulist William Zuber, the man who gave us Travis's speech and the line in the sand? What did Zuber think he was doing when—in 1904! nearly seventy years after the Alamo fell!—he offered for the first time a thirdhand story about David's execution; immediately denounced it as "a gross falsehood"; then claimed, bizarrely, that it nonetheless "shows what Santa Anna would have done if it were true"?

You can't make this stuff up.

Or can you?

The de la Peña papers were put up for auction in November 1998 by the heirs of John Peace, the man who had brought them back from Mexico. The *New York Times* quoted a representative of a Los Angeles auction house as saying he and his colleagues had been "stunned" by how much interest they had generated. "It's the weirdest thing I've ever seen," he said. "We're sitting out here in California scratching our heads going, what the heck?"

The papers ended up going for $350,000 to a couple of rich Texans, who turned around and donated them to the University of Texas at Austin. The university decided to do some forensic testing and in April 2000 released its verdict on the forgery charge: not guilty. The man responsible for the testing, David Gracy, later published an article in the *Southwestern Historical Quarterly* laying out what had been done.

If you think de la Peña nonbelievers threw in the towel at this point, you haven't been paying attention. The complaint that no one had tested the papers now became: no one but the self-interested University of Texas has tested the papers.

But I don't think it's necessary to go down that road.

When I started out to track down David Crockett's ghosts, I promised myself that I would decide the question of his death—not definitively, but to my own satisfaction—and it's time for me to try. As I hope I've made clear, I can't possibly go point by point through all the evidence. What I *can* do is say what I've come to believe.

Yes, a number of Alamo defenders were executed after the battle. The evidence on that point is so strong that both sides of the Crockett debate agree on it.

No, the de la Peña memoir is not a forgery. There's always a chance that someone will turn up a smoking-gun anachronism and everything will change. But even disregarding all the arguments cited above, it's very hard to read the almost two hundred pages of *With Santa Anna in Texas*—in which the Alamo executions take up one page—and imagine why a forger would do the vast amount of work required to create it. De la Peña was a complete unknown, not Adolf Hitler or Howard Hughes, so how much profit could his memoir be reasonably expected to generate? If the material on Crockett was really the point, why not forge a three-page letter instead?

The forgery question, in fact, has been a major distraction. Crisp and Groneman have both said that the debate has had positive results, by which they mean that we now know a great deal more about de la Peña's memoir than we did before. That is true. But the clash also had a serious unintended consequence: obsession with the memoir's authenticity created a widespread impression that settling that question would also settle the question of Crockett's possible execution. That is *not* true. The sheer volume of the forgery debate has drowned out the essential point, also made by both sides, that authenticity is not the same as accuracy. Even if we assume that the manuscript is genuine, it doesn't prove de la Peña's story about David right.

This, of course, is why the Dolson letter becomes vital to the argument.

Which brings me to a crucial point I think has been underemphasized: the "naturalist" passage makes de la Peña's Crockett radically different from Dolson's. Without so much as hinting at a source, de la Peña described David as an innocent trapped in the Alamo by circumstances. To those who know better, the clear inference—as we've seen—is that he was trying to talk his way out of death by denying the cause for which he fought. Having never been in combat, much less faced imminent execution, I am not about to pass judgment on this. Yet it's easy to see why the scenario became such a flash point for Crockett admirers: it's a shocking violation of the traditional narrative of deliberate, heroic sacrifice.

Had de la Peña merely echoed Dolson's version—with David simply fighting "until defense was useless," then falling victim to a brutal tyrant—I doubt that the outrage would have reached the same level.

William C. Davis has written that "when it comes to Davy's death, hypothesis is really *all* we have." That said, the author of *Three Roads to the Alamo* has put forth an intriguing argument about how the execution version might have come to be.

In a 1997 article called "How Davy Probably *Didn't* Die," Davis suggested that the whole thing might have started with the report of seven unnamed Texians being executed that reached Sam Houston five days after the battle. Houston passed the story along, and variations of it soon spread across the United States. By April, it was showing up in Mexican newspapers, presumably as a result of sea trade between New Orleans and the Mexican port of Vera Cruz. By May, copies of those Mexican papers could have carried Spanish versions of the story back to New Orleans and on to the prison camps in Texas where Mexican troops were being held. And it was a month after that, Davis noted, that the first known Crockett execution report emerged from the prison camp on Galveston Island.

There are at least a couple of reasons why Mexican prisoners might have attached Crockett's name to the execution story. The camp would have been a rumor mill, and the rumor that David and several defenders had tried to surrender "but were told there was no mercy for them" was already out there. The Texians, in the meantime, were most likely asking the prisoners what had *happened* to the most famous man at the Alamo. And those prisoners—anxious about their own fates, aware that their captors loathed Santa Anna, and eager to please—might have thought it helpful to pin Crockett's death directly on El Presidente.

Is that a clinching argument? Not at all. Davis is careful not to overstate what's provable, hence all the "might have"s and "most likely"s in my summary.

Still, I'm drawn to his theory for reasons beyond its considerable internal logic.

After more than a year on Crockett's trail, I was used to seeing David's name linked to false or unprovable stories. Did he righteously face down Andrew Jackson during the Creek War? No, he didn't. Did he win an election by tricking a farmer into thinking a peg-legged political opponent was trying to bed the farmer's daughter? I don't think so. Did he carve his initials on a Honey Grove stump? Trek across Texas with a suave gambler named Thimblerig? Climb the Alleghenies to wring the tail off Halley's Comet? Well, it's always possible that he carved those initials. As previously noted, however, Jim Boylston *has* proved that the poor man's friend never harangued a writer for *Harper's* magazine about why it was unconstitutional for the government to help actual poor people. A pseudonymous dime novelist made that up! But if you google Crockett and "Not Yours to Give," you'll get tens of thousands of hits, most of them treating that fable as fact.

Why would we assume that *anything* people say about David's death is true?

Speaking more broadly: we live in a media universe that is

drowning in false stories (both positive and negative) about famous people. As a journalist, I spent decades watching mutant versions of the truth take root, whether by design or accident. But it's a mistake to see this as a recent phenomenon. Within a few years of his arrival in the nation's capital, Crockett had become perhaps the first pure American celebrity, a man famous less for his real accomplishments than for the backwoods "screamer" image that he and his political and media collaborators had created. By the time he rode into San Antonio de Béxar, his life story had long since passed into the public domain.

In the early days of my pursuit of David, I figured I knew what my answer to the execution question would turn out to be. Among other things, I'd been greatly impressed by Crisp's *Sleuthing the Alamo*. The book, I thought, was a terrific evocation of the multi-layered complexities and uncertainties behind historical narratives.

I still think so.

But I no longer think that Crockett was captured and executed with those other men.

I think his name got attached to that story *because he was Davy Crockett*. For precisely the same reason, I don't believe he went down surrounded by huge piles of Mexican soldiers whom he had single-handedly slain.

I don't think we know how David died, and I don't think we ever will. But we make sense of the world by telling stories, as Crockett himself understood so very well, and we're simply not willing to let the mystery be.

I tried. For a while, it seemed I'd put the whole execution firefight in my rearview mirror. But then I thought: I need to be in Austin anyway. Why not go see the de la Peña papers for myself? Which is how I ended up at the Dolph Briscoe Center for American History, on the east side of the University of Texas campus, staring at an acid-free document box filled with the same loose pages Groneman and Crisp had examined almost two decades before.

They weren't tied with ribbons anymore, though the ribbons had been carefully preserved.

It would be more accurate to describe the manuscript pages I saw as "unbound folios." Most of the folios had been created by folding sheets of paper in half, giving each four pages, or "faces." Everything specifically to do with Crockett, however, appeared on folio 35, an unfolded sheet with just two faces. To my untrained eye, the handwriting seemed to change partway down the last face of the previous folio and again at the beginning of the one that followed, which picks up the execution description shortly after Santa Anna orders the captives killed.

"Untrained eye" is an understatement. Still, what I observed seemed consistent with the idea that de la Peña—sick, imprisoned, and needing help—had revised his first-person narrative by adding Crockett material from unspecified, and thus unverifiable, outside sources.

What most struck me, however, were a few specific words—or their absence—in two short passages.

"I had one minor quibble here," said veteran Center for American History translator John Wheat, who had agreed to walk me through the manuscript. Carmen Perry's translation described the executed captives as having "died without complaining," Wheat said, but what the Spanish text actually says is "*murieron quejándose*—died protesting—which is a different thing. She's trying to say that they were just stoically silent, and they were anything but. They were protesting loudly that this was murder."

That's more than a quibble, I'd say.

Even more revealing, however, was a mistranslation that Crisp had been the first to notice. "Santa Anna answered Castrillón's intervention *in Crockett's behalf* with a gesture of indignation," Perry's version reads, and then "ordered *his* execution" (italics mine). Yet the Spanish text I was looking at doesn't mention Crockett in this sentence, and it has Santa Anna ordering the execution of the captives as a group. The translator's change, clearly deliberate, seemed to echo the distorting impulse I've been talking about: we always want the famous guy to be at the center of things.

David never made it to what is now Austin; the closest he probably came was Bastrop, some thirty miles to the southeast. The city is nonetheless full of destinations for a Crockett tourist: there are paintings, an Alamo memorial, a Texas history museum, and knowledgeable people with whom to talk. One such person is University of Texas anthropologist Richard Flores, now an academic dean with an office in the shadow of the university's landmark tower.

Flores is the author of *Remembering the Alamo: Memory, Modernity, and the Master Symbol.* The book begins with a personal story, which I asked to hear again. He was in third grade, he said, which in San Antonio was the year your class got to go to the Alamo on a field trip. His father, a pharmacist, "used to work at a place catty-corner from the Alamo, on Alamo Plaza," but Flores had never been inside the Alamo church, which was (and still is) known simply as "the shrine." He found himself awed by the mystique of it all, amazed to be standing in the place where Bowie, Travis, and Crockett had given their lives for Texas. Back outside, after the tour had ended, his best friend nudged him and whispered in his ear.

"You killed them! You and the other 'Mes'kins'!" the boy said.

The adult Flores began his Alamo research while the debate over de la Peña's memoir was still white hot. He found it astonishing. "Everybody was so concerned about how Crockett died," he said, "but no one was asking why was it even *important*." His answer became part of his book's overall thesis, which is that economic changes in Texas in the late nineteenth century—"the closing of the range, the introduction of the railroad, and the beginning of commercial farming"—led to social stratification in which Mexican Americans became far more segregated from whites, and that around the same time, not coincidentally, the Alamo emerged as a symbol of triumph over the Mexican "other." Crockett, as the preeminent Alamo hero, became strongly associated with that triumph.

Which meant he had to go down fighting, of course. Surrender was not an option.

I knew that one of the classic going-down-fighting images, Henry McArdle's 1905 painting *Dawn at the Alamo*, was on display somewhere inside the pink granite Texas Capitol, so one afternoon I headed over to take a look. What I didn't know was that a very different Crockett would greet me just inside the main door. There he stood, alone in the forest, buckskinned brown shading into green, in a painting by William Henry Huddle from 1889. Serious, straight-backed, and alert, he made me think of the Elvis-like fellow in the poster for Zucker's unmade movie, though Huddle's David looked a bit older and less slick.

The Crockett I found upstairs in the Senate Chamber was another story, one more easily connected to the dark cultural history Flores had explored.

Dawn at the Alamo depicts a chaotic, nightmarish scene that's been compared to the hellish work of Hieronymus Bosch. Travis and Crockett are focal points, with Travis standing proud atop a high wall (though about to be bayoneted from behind) while below him, a white-shirted Davy fends off an attacker with his left hand while swinging a broken rifle barrel with his right.

As for the Mexicans they were fighting—well, I'll let Senate messenger Garrett Nicholas pick up the description. The only person in the chamber when I got there, Nicholas had spent many hours contemplating McArdle's work. "If you look at the Mexican soldiers, they are gorillas and monsters," he said. "There's even a demonic chihuahua here at the bottom."

Really? A chihuahua?

"Yeah!"

Sure enough, I spotted a vicious, ratlike creature snarling at a defender. McArdle's human demons, however, were far more disturbing. The soldier closest to Crockett had especially gorillalike features, and Travis's assailant had the creepy leer and crouching body language of a comic-strip villain.

Much has changed since 1905, thank God. At the Bob Bullock Texas State History Museum, a few blocks north of the Capitol, I took in a Texas Revolution video narrated by Tejano Alamo defender Juan Seguin, who had been sent out as a messenger and lived to fight at San Jacinto. I still had the sour taste of *Dawn at the Alamo* in my mouth, however, when Stephen Harrigan picked me up outside the Bullock and whisked me off for lunch at Curra's Grill, a crowded restaurant off South Congress Avenue that calls itself "the Mother of all Mex."

Harrigan is a journalist, novelist, and screenwriter who showed up in Austin in the 1960s to go to college and never left. He is best known for *The Gates of the Alamo,* a justly praised historical novel that tells the Alamo story through five invented characters and casts David Crockett in a major supporting role. I was looking forward to talking Davy with him because I thought his challenge must have been similar to mine: How do you take a remarkable life, filled with the normal human gaps and contradictions, and decide who the guy who lived it really was?

First we had to talk Fess Parker, though.

"I have all sorts of theories about why the Disney movie was so overpowering to kids my age," Harrigan told me. "One is, he was just such a cool guy, Davy Crockett. He had great outfits, and he was at home in the wilderness. There was a Peter Pan quality to him that was intoxicating. And then, you know, it's a three-hour movie, more or less, and you're following this guy all the way through, and you're seven years old, it's 1955, every movie has a happy ending. And all of a sudden the coolest guy you've ever seen on-screen gets *killed*. And not only does he get killed, but we don't *see* it. It's offscreen."

The mysterious aura of Davy Crockett and the Alamo, he said, "completely and utterly changed my life."

He started *The Gates of the Alamo* in the early 1990s. It took him eight years. When he began, he said, he was "a cocky revisionist," but over time "I became much more humble about what I could know and how much I could judge these people"—referring not just to historical figures such as Travis and Bowie but to "the people who *created* this Alamo myth. Because it's an organic, authentic thing, whatever you want to say about it."

He revised his picture of David Crockett, too.

"I didn't know at first how I was going to portray him," he said. "I assumed that when you looked critically at Crockett's life, you would find a guy who, you know, was out for himself and who was insincere and kind of a one-dimensional politician. And the story just got more interesting than that." He ended up seeing Crockett as the most engaging of the major Alamo figures.

Why?

"As corny as this sounds, I think he is the embodiment of a lot that is great about America. I think he's a restless soul. He's a great fund of humor and goodwill toward other people; a relatively simple guy who wants to live his own life and prosper, and wants his friends to prosper; and a little naive, not cut out for the complexities and vicissitudes of politics as much as he thought he was."

Bearing all this in mind—along with David's age, fame, and legendary skill with a rifle—the novelist made his Crockett the most popular man in the Alamo.

"He had a soft heart, it seemed, and he took an interest where another man might not," Harrigan wrote shortly after introducing David. "Joe liked him, and all the other men at the post did too, though some of them still couldn't believe he was standing there in front of them in flesh and blood. . . . Even the people of Béxar, Tejanos who spoke not a word of English and had no notion of the distant politics of the States, glanced with interest as Crockett walked by, and he in turn gave them all an easy smile and waved as if he were in a parade all his own." Later in the book, this one-man parade—knowing his likely fate—moves from weary man to weary man along the Alamo walls, greeting and bantering briefly with each.

How could you *not* like him?

Good question—but Harrigan anticipated it.

One of his most compelling characters is the fictional Mary Mott, the mother of a young Alamo defender, who ends up trapped in the old mission as well. At one point, Mary gets a chance to ask David what he's doing there.

"Why, because I am a wayward, wandering soul, Mrs. Mott," he jokes, then gets more serious. "I lost an election, you see, and it hurt my sensibilities to have such a quantity of people say they could no longer stand the thought of me. And the only cure that's ever worked for me when I'm feeling hollow like that is to move on to a new country."

Mary Mott is not buying this.

"She could not see Crockett's eyes in the darkness and shadows of the church, but she supposed them to be bright with self-delusion—a shattered fifty-year-old man still hostage to his boyhood dreams of flight and renewal."

Harsh? Perceptive?

Maybe both. "I intended it to be the way a woman would see this guy," Harrigan said.

Speaking of points of view: two of Harrigan's main characters are Mexican soldiers, and the depth and care with which he draws them helps humanize the sad, brutal, heroic story. And he has filled his battle scenes with shocking bursts of realism that make the Alamo far harder to romanticize. His Crockett dies fighting and, like Billy Bob Thornton, screams defiantly as he goes down. But it's not a Hollywood ending, and it takes a single short paragraph to describe.

Lunch was over too soon, though it probably lasted longer than the climactic Alamo assault. I told Harrigan I was driving to San Antonio that afternoon. "I wish I could go down there with you," he said, and I got excited at the thought. He would have made a fabulous guide. But he had a deadline to meet, and as I headed south on I-35, I realized that it was better this way.

I had been traveling with David Crockett for a long time. I wanted my first impression of the place where he fought and died to be my own.

☆ 12 ☆

The Ghosts of Davy Crockett

David Crockett rode into San Antonio de Béxar early in February 1836, in the company of maybe a dozen men. They materialized at the Campo Santo, a graveyard on the west edge of town, where Jim Bowie and a Béxar resident named Antonio Menchaca soon came to meet them and guide them in—assuming, of course, that the account Menchaca gave many decades later is to believed.

Then, standing on a packing crate in one of Béxar's two central plazas, David gave a speech.

"Frequent applause greeted him, as he related in his own peculiar style, some of those jolly anecdotes with which he often regaled his friends," reported another eyewitness, Dr. John Sutherland. "He alluded frequently to his past career, and during the course of his remarks stated, that, not long since he had been a candidate for Congress in his native State, and, that during the canvass he told his constituents that 'if they did not elect him, they might all go to —— and he would go to Texas.'" Wrapping up, Crockett told his listeners why he was there: "I have come to aid you all that I can in your noble cause. I shall identify myself with your interests, and all the honor that I desire is that of defending, as a high private, in common with my fellow-citizens, the liberties of our common country."

Sutherland's testimony wasn't written down until 1860 at the earliest, and it comes to us in the form of various manuscripts and manuscript fragments, most of them altered by others. De la Peña comparisons, anyone? Still, the incidents he reported witnessing have been accepted as true by most Alamo scholars, and they certainly bring the beginning of the siege to life.

Here is some of what Sutherland tells us:

On February 20, bad news arrived in Béxar. A Tejano scout reported to Juan Seguin that Santa Anna's army had been observed crossing the Rio Grande, far ahead of the schedule that the Texian leaders had assumed. Travis convened a council of war to consider what action they should take in response, but many argued that "it was only the report of a Mexican," and the council broke up without deciding whether they needed to heed the warning or not. Two uneventful days passed. On February 23, however, the sharp-eyed Texians observed that many of Béxar's Tejanos were packing their belongings and leaving town.

Gosh, why were they doing that?

A friendly townsman clued Travis in: it seemed that the Mexican cavalry was eight miles away. Still Travis took no serious action, though he did order a sentry posted atop San Fernando Church, which fronted the plaza where Crockett had given his speech. Church and plaza sat in the center of Béxar, across the San Antonio River and half a mile or so down Potrero Street (now Commerce) from the decrepit old Spanish mission on the outskirts of town. The Texians had been working hard to shore up the Alamo's defenses, but had not yet moved all their meager force inside its walls. The sentry had orders to ring the church's bell if he spotted the enemy.

Clang! Clang! Clang!

Up climbed some other Texians, who didn't see what the sentry had seen and declared that "the whole tale was a lie."

Finally, Sutherland and John W. Smith rode out of Béxar to

look around. The sight of "fifteen hundred men, well mounted and equipped" left no room for further doubt, and the pair galloped back in such frantic haste that Sutherland's horse slipped and fell on the muddy road. Sutherland scrambled up and made it back to the plaza, where Crockett informed him that Travis had ordered a retreat into the Alamo.

The phrase "not a minute too soon" seems, in this case, entirely appropriate.

When I arrived in San Antonio for my first visit, ten months before the 175th anniversary of the battle, I decided to start my Alamo tour by walking the route of that Texian retreat. Not yet knowing where David had come into town, I parked, by sheer coincidence, near a giant mural of an angel, a boy, and a dove; it turned out to be on Santa Rosa Children's Hospital, which now occupies the site of the old Campo Santo. In a city park across the street, I noticed a more belligerent image, the statue of a man with a rifle raised triumphantly over his head.

WHO WILL FOLLOW OLD BEN MILAM INTO SAN ANTONIO read the inscription on a memorial nearby.

Sorry, Ben. I was following Old Davy.

San Fernando Cathedral, a few blocks away, had been upgraded from a mere church and heavily remodeled since Crockett's time. Twin gothic towers made it look more like Notre Dame de Paris than the modest edifice he would have seen. Barefoot children waded through fountains in the plaza, which, a historical marker informed me, had been the communal heart of old Béxar, filled with "the noise of merchants and shoppers haggling and gossiping, of people dancing and mules braying." But on February 23, 1836, the scene would have been a good deal less festive.

Heading down East Commerce, I tried to imagine the street crammed not with cars and sidewalk-hogging Segways but with dusty, sweaty Texians carrying long rifles. Some rode, some walked, some drove a small herd of longhorns that they had acquired on short notice. "Poor fellows you will all be killed, what shall we do?" the women of Béxar cried out, according to Juan Seguin, as the men headed for the lone footbridge that spanned the San Antonio River.

Bridge to the past!

What must David Crockett have been thinking, I wondered, as he approached it?

The bridge's modern replacement, near the corner of East Commerce and Losoya, offered no hint. Gazing down, I saw only San Antonio's famous River Walk, thick with pricey restaurants and strolling tourists. Besides, as rereading Sutherland's account would remind me, Crockett didn't even cross the bridge that day.

Too crowded. The two chose a nearby ford instead.

Tracking down Travis in his Alamo quarters, they found him scratching out the first of many eloquent calls for help. He asked Sutherland to carry it to Gonzales. Before Sutherland left, he heard Crockett say, "Colonel, here am I, assign me a position, and I and my twelve boys will try to defend it." Travis assigned him to a gap between the church and the south wall that had been plugged with what Sutherland called a "picket wall." Commonly known as the palisade, it consisted of wooden stakes and packed earth.

I reached the Alamo myself in the early evening and stood across the street for a while, just trying to take it in. Sunlight warmed the facade of the church, silhouetting its trademark hump against the darkening sky. Once again, I did my best to bridge the chasm between then and now.

And once again, I couldn't make it across.

Tourist schlock—the Tomb Rider 3D Adventure Ride; Louis Tussaud's Plaza Wax Museum—mocked the memory of vanished mission walls. Hotels and their loud signage dwarfed the Shrine of Texas Liberty. I loved the funky green neon on the roof of the

Crockett Hotel, not to mention the name itself, but it was definitely distracting.

And what was this? A mob of screaming teenagers, trampling the sacred ground where heroes died?

The mob turned out to be a high school band, and the kids were actually quite sweet: they lined up for a giant group photo, then split into smaller groups for more. One batch of exuberant young women, who reminded me of my daughters at that age, linked arms and started dancing in a circle, chanting something I couldn't make out.

Still, it was clear that if I wanted to go on Davy Crockett's Alamo Adventure Ride, I would have to climb aboard somewhere else.

"I'm sure that some of you are a little confused by what you see," the voice with the startling British accent was saying. "Some people may even leave San Antonio thinking that the church *was* the Alamo, because that's become the iconic image. . . . It's hard to imagine what it really looked like, when you're standing out there in the plaza, because so much of this glorious place is gone now."

No worries, though. Phil Collins, Alamo-obsessed international rock star, was here to resurrect it.

It was the morning after my first Alamo experience, and I had made my way to a little storefront just across East Houston Street from the grounds. The History Shop sold antique weapons and maps, but, more important, it offered $3 tours of what it called "the largest and most historically accurate diorama of the Alamo to date." The diorama is the work of Alamo-obsessed Georgia artist Mark Lemon, who researched and built it (in his garage) for his book *The Illustrated Alamo 1836: A Photographic Journey.* Collins, the longtime lead singer and drummer for Genesis—who got hooked on the Alamo by watching Fess Parker play Davy—bought Lemon's diorama and put it on display in San Antonio in 2008, adding a few flashing lights and a narration he recorded himself.

Why not? Wasn't Crockett a rock star, too?

Who better to describe the unlikely stage on which he would spend the last thirteen days of his life?

Stark and nearly empty of human figures, the diorama filled most of the small, dark space that housed it. Collins's recorded tour took his audience clockwise around the walls. He mentioned Bowie's sickroom on the south wall; Travis's command post on the west wall; a partially ruined portion of the north wall that was "the fort's weakest point"; and the Long Barracks, east of the courtyard, the first floor of which is the only part of the Alamo besides the church still standing today. He talked about the inner rooms of the mostly roofless church, where women and children sought sanctuary, and about the palisade "defended by Davy Crockett and his Tennessee volunteers."

The most important thing the diorama does, however, is to let Alamo visitors grasp just how big the converted mission was and what a nightmare that created for its defenders. "Even today, no one can agree on how many defenders there actually were," Collins said. "Numbers range from 185 to over 200." Whatever the total, there weren't enough. They couldn't "properly man all the cannons they had," let alone defend nearly five hundred yards of walls against thousands of determined attackers.

Drumbeats on the sound track.

Here they came.

The Mexicans attacked in four columns, Collins said. Three ended up concentrated against the north wall, where, after heavy losses and with help from the reserves, they "crawled over the bodies of their dead and wounded comrades and poured into the Alamo complex." The fourth column broke through from the south.

"Realizing that they had lost control of the quadrangle, the defenders took refuge in many of the buildings, including the Long Barracks." Vicious, hand-to-hand fighting ensued as the bayonet-wielding Mexicans—obeying Santa Anna's merciless order—"hunted down and killed every defender." Among the last areas to fall "was the palisade in front of the church," where "Crockett and his volunteers were overwhelmed. Crockett may well have died here, although this will be forever debated among historians."

Well, that last part is right for sure.

Those who believe that Crockett was executed think it would most likely have happened in the middle of the main courtyard, not in the corner by the church. Those who think he was killed fighting have their reasons for favoring the near-the-church location, but those reasons are not conclusive, and other possibilities get frequent mentions. I knew I was going to have to look at them all, but I wasn't ready to do that yet. I was still trying to focus on the time when Crockett was alive in the Alamo and on Mary Mott's still unanswered question: What was he doing here?

For that matter, what was everybody *else* doing here?

I figured Bruce Winders might know.

Winders was the historian and curator of the Alamo, a job he had held since 1996. I found him in an office just a few feet east of the History Shop. Not knowing much about him but thinking how tricky it must be to walk the line between history and myth while working with the Daughters of the Republic of Texas, I had been expecting someone cautious and, just possibly, a little slick. Wrong. Jeans and a scraggly beard made him look scruffy enough to impersonate an Alamo defender himself, and he was completely relaxed about the history-myth equation.

"One of the things we've been able to do here is we say, 'Okay, we're a shrine,'" he told me. "We're not going to stop being a shrine, because a lot of people *want* it to be a shrine, and that's our state

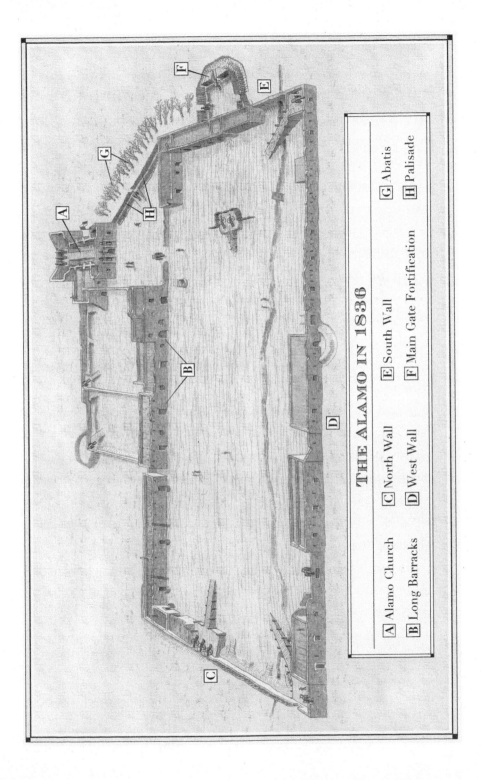

THE ALAMO IN 1836

A Alamo Church   C North Wall   E South Wall   G Abatis

B Long Barracks   D West Wall   F Main Gate Fortification   H Palisade

mandate. So we're going to be secure in our shrine-ness, and the story that goes with the shrine is the traditional story. It's part of Texas culture, American culture, and we're not telling you you're stupid if you like it." But what that's done is "free us to go, 'Okay, now we're going to tell a story—a *parallel* story—that's a story based on evidence.'"

I asked what the major changes had been, over his tenure, in the way the Alamo presents the battle.

"The big change," he said, "is that we've attached it to a context, instead of it just being, you know: 'There was a gladiator event called the Alamo.'" The context is that the Texas Revolution "occurs within an ongoing Mexican civil war"—and that war is about federalism versus centralism and what it means to be a citizen of a republic.

"What we've been able to do with Crockett," he added, "is plug him into this."

David was somebody "dirt poor" who, if he'd been born just a few years earlier, "would have been shut out of public life." In the Jacksonian era, however, he became "the person who best exemplifies the rise of the common man." America's newly democratized political culture gave him "the opportunity to rise up, and then to actually become something in his own *lifetime*," not just a hero glorified after his death.

So yes, it's true that most of the men in the Alamo—most definitely including Crockett—came to Texas for cheap land and a fresh start. But they were fighting for political principles, too.

I had more questions for Winders than he had time to answer. Some were about Crockett directly and some about the revolution he'd wound up in the middle of.

What about the question—much debated then and now—of whether the old mission-fort was worth defending?

"You know the Alamo is to the Texas Revolution as Crockett is to the Alamo. *It* becomes the celebrity," Winders said. But what was important was the town of San Antonio de Béxar. "Across from the Alamo you've got a community of two thousand or more people. In a frontier area where there isn't a lot of settlement, if you find a collection of two thousand people, where it's a political seat, a garrison, an economic crossroads, that becomes an important place."

What about the Matamoros fiasco that stripped Béxar of men and supplies? Wasn't that a giant what-if when it came to the garrison's, and Crockett's, fate?

"It's the key to everything that goes wrong. It's like, 'No, we probably shouldn't go off on spring break.'"

How about the comforting notion that the lives sacrificed at the Alamo bought Sam Houston time to build a Texian army?

Not true. The defenders were dead before Houston so much as started building an army. But "they did buy time for the Convention" to declare independence and craft a constitution.

Oh, and speaking of the Alamo as a shrine: What was the deal with all the Crockett relics on display?

In the church hangs a beaded buckskin vest identified as Crockett's. I had asked a woman at the information desk how we knew it was his. "It was given to him by some Indians," was all she could tell me. In the Long Barrack Museum stands a case labeled TOUCHED BY HEROES. Among other things, it holds a broken-handled knife said to have been "used by David Crockett while hunting bear" and a locket said to contain "a clipping of David Crockett's hair."

"We've got a lot of Crockett hair products," Winders said with a straight face. "We've got a hairbrush, we've got a razor of his— straight razor, supposedly he gave it to this person *right* before he came to Texas."

The provenance on them, alas, is not as strong as a museum curator might like.

David's death spawned a phenomenon "where people wanted

to be connected to him," often through physical objects—some of which, years later, ended up at the Alamo. They have a lot in common with a famous relic owned by another San Antonio museum, Winders said: "It's like the Crockett fiddle at the Witte. It has a little piece of paper on it that says 'Davy Crockett's fiddle.' It could have been put there at any time. And when the Witte got it, it was with an oral story that, you know, we got this from so and so who got it from Crockett.

"But have you ever seen anything where Crockett is playing the fiddle? Contemporary?"

I had not—just the reminiscences of an octogenarian Texas Ranger who told an anonymous chronicler that he'd seen "old Davy" play, one time, six decades earlier.

Before I left town, I went by the Witte to see its fiddle for myself. The museum's helpful registrar got it out of storage, along with some doubt-inducing letters connected to its 1930s acquisition. He did not appear to believe that the real David—as opposed to the mythic hero everyone wanted a piece of—had ever touched the thing.

Back in San Antonio the following March for the Alamo's 175th anniversary, I ran into Davy before I had time to put my suitcase down. There he was, high on a lobby wall at the Crockett Hotel, in the same computer-aided, Elvis-like image I had first seen at his birthplace but blown up far bigger this time. That was also the day I met David Preston Crockett in Alamo Plaza, playing Davy in his Walmart chamois cloth.

That evening, I was lucky enough to have an invitation to a Crockett-related party. Hosted annually by San Antonian Joan Headley, it draws people so devoted to the Alamo that many call the anniversary period "the High Holy Days." Reenactors, historians, novelists, filmmakers, Crockett impersonators, and Alamo Society members filled the white-walled courtyards of the old Spanish Governor's Palace, not far from where David rode into town. A band fronted by the historical balladeer K. R. Wood set up along a back wall. Wood wore a cowboy hat, but I noticed a coonskin cap hanging from a piece of band equipment as he launched into his first number:

> In the southern part of Texas near the town of San Antone
> There's a fortress all in ruins that the weeds have
> overgrown.

"Whooh!" went the crowd, instantly recognizing the song from John Wayne's movie.

Next he sang "Remember the Alamo" by the Texas songwriter Jane Bowers ("Brave Davy Crockett was singin' and laughin' / With gallantry fierce in his eye"). Then it was time to call for some backup singers. "Lila, c'mere. Suzie, c'mon up here," Wood urged, and up came—among other Crockett descendants—David's great-great-granddaughter Lila Beth Flowers Davis and his great-great-great-granddaughter Suzie Brooks.

We all knew what ballad was coming, and we sang loudly along.

As a Mythic Davy moment, it was hard to top. Still, I'd have to give the weekend's prize to a show put on the following morning by two Crockett obsessives from Australia.

The scene was Ballroom A of the Menger Hotel, the venerable establishment where Teddy Roosevelt recruited some of his Rough Riders in 1898 and where, or so one tour operator told me, Roy Rogers used to rent Trigger a room of his own. The occasion was the annual symposium of the Alamo Society, founded a quarter century before as a way for committed Alamo fans to connect. The Australia ιs were Dr. William Bor, a child psychologist, and Lial Heiser, the manager of a medical practice, and their lecture was listed in the program as "Portraits of David Crockett's Last Stand: Iconography and Symbolism of Heroics throughout Western Culture."

Forget that mouthful of a title, though. The great thing was that Bor and Heiser had dug up a zillion images of Crockett swinging his rifle at the Alamo, and now—mythic swing after mythic swing, thanks to the miracle of PowerPoint—those images were flashing before my eyes.

Here was a towering, ferocious Davy, outlined against black smoke and orange flames, lunging forward to bash the cluster of Mexicans cowering before him. Here he was, standing awkwardly straight this time, grasping his rifle at the very tip of its barrel. Then came an image in which a mustachioed enemy officer falls backward before Davy can even swing; one that made Davy look like a dark-bearded ruffian out of Dickens; and one in which the hero's face—intense, angry, framed by scraggly hair—made him look weirdly like Neil Young. I saw plenty of Davys I recognized, including the ones painted by McCardle and Onderdonk, but many more I'd never seen, among them a crudely evocative fellow in buckskins from a Classics Illustrated comic and a more recent close-up that let you look straight into its subject's wide-open eyes. Fess Parker and John Wayne were there, too, of course: Parker in that last, frozen TV frame and the Duke swinging his symbolic torch in a poster for *The Alamo*.

Time for the "throughout Western Culture" part of the presentation.

"I want to ask the question: Why that pose?" Bor said. Then he put up a slew of other last-stand images: Custer waving a cavalry saber at the Little Big Horn; Roland hoisting a medieval sword at Roncesvalles; Leonidas wielding both sword and spear at Thermopylae. But wait: we weren't just talking last stands. Here came Hercules battling the Hydra with a giant club and the biblical

David, poised to decapitate the fallen Goliath, and Zeus, portrayed in a famous statue, his right arm raised and extended in the act of hurling a thunderbolt. It's the raised arm that does it, Bor said, conveying a sense of "dignity, determination and domination" as it shows heroes through the ages in the act of "bringing down the monster, bringing down the oppressor and bringing down tyranny."

Zeus hurling a thunderbolt—wow. It's one thing to use a dirt-poor Tennessee boy to exemplify the rise of the common man and quite another to put him on Mount Olympus with the Father of the Gods. But with Crockett, we have somehow managed to do both.

Bor told me later that he'd come by his love of Davy in the usual way, despite being thousands of miles across the Pacific when the Crockett craze began. "I was in Fiji when it happened," he said. "I had a Crockett gown and everything in Fiji." He and Heiser, he added, had coauthored a paper called "Alamo Addiction" in which "we tried to talk about the baby boomers needing some sort of hero father figure."

He said it, I didn't. But there were certainly plenty of Alamo addicts of a certain age in Ballroom A.

Paul Hutton, Bill Groneman, Bruce Winders, Stephen Harrigan, David Zucker, and Alamo Society main man Bill Chemerka were all on the program in one capacity or another. Headley was there, along with what seemed like half the people I'd met at her party the night before. Of those I didn't yet know, one of the most interesting was Daniel Martinez, whose Alamo addiction story was more complicated than some.

Martinez is the chief National Park Service historian at Pearl Harbor. As a young man in the 1970s, he said, he visited the Alamo and found himself angered by the one-sidedness of its presentation. Male visitors were asked—as they still are—to remove their hats in the shrine, but Martinez marched up to a Daughters of the Republic of Texas attendant to protest.

"Where are the pictures of the *Mexican* heroes?" he asked. "Why should I take my hat off in here?"

He has the same question today—not about Winders's museum presentation, which he called "a huge advance," but about the overall message conveyed by the shrine. Alamo fans "talk about getting young people involved," he said, but young Hispanics must still deal with "what Native Americans used to face in the Custer story: they were always the faceless enemy."

So how did Dan Martinez, Alamo critic, get addicted to its story in the first place?

Surely you can guess by now.

"I got caught up in Walt Disney," he said. "I had my outfit— I still have my coonskin cap—and I had my rifle." To him and his brother, who was equally hooked, Fess Parker's Crockett "represented adventure; he represented kindness; he represented the great outdoors; he represented a hero; and he represented what friendship was about." Never mind Martinez's Mexican-American heritage and the fact that those were Mexican soldiers attacking the Alamo. "I couldn't identify with that. But I could identify with *him.*"

The symposium wrapped up in the early afternoon, but I was scarcely done with Davy images for the day.

Heading out, I stopped by a small Crockett exhibit in the Menger lobby. Middle-aged Crocketts in congressional duds stared out at me, as did the young David from that ubiquitous movie poster, and—in the famous woodcut derived from *The Lion of the West*— the wild man wearing the wildcat on his head. A live actor in a more modest coonskin cap was telling visitors about Joe Swann's Crockett rifle, which was on display as well. "He won a lot of shooting matches with that," the actor said.

Ah, but what about fiddling matches? Or fiddling and bagpiping matches, to be precise?

At an Alamo art show hosted by another hotel, I noticed a painting of David seated in front of the Alamo church, sawing away on a fiddle. Firelight casts his shadow onto the facade; a dozen or so defenders have gathered to listen; and, standing to Crockett's left, a tall Scot in a tam-o'-shanter is piping along.

"They did that a few times during the siege at night to boost morale," said the painter Richard Luce, who was there to answer questions about his work.

The story is a famous one. Crockett didn't just play along with John McGregor, it is said; the two used to "duel" for the amusement of the stressed-out defenders, competing to see who could play loudest and longest. As the skeptical Groneman has written, the dueling tale seems to have begun with something Susanna Dickinson's granddaughter told the important but not always accurate Alamo historian Amelia Williams, who included it in her 1931 dissertation.

Too good to check.

After Luce finished telling me about *Crockett and McGregor,* he gestured toward the image beside it. "That one's a print of one I did years ago," he said. "It shows the moment the battle began, at five A.M." Crockett stands behind the palisade, fur cap glowing in the early dawn light, smoking rifle in his hand. It looks as if he's about to swing it like a club, but in fact, he's handing it behind him for a companion to reload.

"So no one is dead yet, no one is shot yet," Luce said. "It's just the moment it began."

By midafternoon, my brain was crammed with mythic images. I'd also begun to think how strange it was to be immersed in swinging, fiddling Davys just yards from ground where the real David Crockett had walked.

Wanting to put the myth behind me, at least for a while, I headed back to the Alamo to walk that ground myself.

A tiny plaque near the southwest corner of the church reads ALAMO MISSION ORIGINAL PROPERTY LINE, but no one cares about that. What the subtle parallel lines in the flagstones really mark is the wooden palisade that Crockett was assigned to defend the day the Mexican army first showed up. To this day, the palisade remains the part of the site most strongly associated with him. The lines aren't easy to see if you're not looking for them, but that wasn't a problem this weekend: a replica palisade had been installed for the anniversary reenactments, with yellow police tape warning people off when it wasn't in use.

Many Alamo visitors, as I learned from one of the red-vested guides, have the impression that the defenders fought off Mexican attackers for twelve days straight before succumbing, finally, on the thirteenth. That is not quite right. The twelve days they held out were a siege, not a pitched battle. Santa Anna made one semiserious probe of the Alamo's defenses, on February 25, but he mostly contented himself with bombarding the fort, moving his artillery closer and closer to the fragile walls as Travis sent out message after message to his fellow Texians, pleading for help.

The defenders had enough to eat, for a while.

They had ammunition, though none to waste.

But the odds were ten to one against them and they knew they were doomed if help in serious numbers didn't come. It didn't. In the early hours of March 1, thirty-two brave men from Gonzales—among them Jonathan Lindley, whose relative, Dave Lindley, I had met at Crockett's birthplace—rode through lightning, hail, and the Mexican lines into the Alamo. It's possible that a few additional reinforcements made it in as well. But James Fannin decided to keep his larger force in Goliad, and Sam Houston, who as yet had no army of his own, seemed in no hurry to remedy that situation.

The bombardment continued.

Nobody got much sleep.

On March 3, Travis composed a final letter to the Convention at Washington. Unless help came soon, he wrote, he would have to fight Santa Anna "on his own terms." If it came down to it, he was sure his men's "desperate courage" would not fail and that, "although they may be sacrificed to the vengeance of a Gothic enemy, the victory will cost the enemy dear" and "be worse for him than defeat." That was the letter that arrived as the delegates were eating breakfast on March 6.

And what was David Crockett doing all that time?

Well, he wasn't writing letters himself—at least not any that have survived. The truth is, we know very little about what Crockett did during those thirteen days at the Alamo. But sticking to known facts is a whole lot easier said than done, because we're so driven to fill in the gaps.

The most authoritative description of Crockett during the siege comes from a letter from Travis to Houston dated February 25, the day Mexican troops tested the garrison's defenses. After praising his officers and men for their "firmness and bravery" and singling out six for special mention, Travis added, "The Hon. David Crockett was seen at all points, animating the men to do their duty." Crockettologists tend to read a lot into this sentence, but I'm not sure it tells us much. If you're the commander at the Alamo, desperately trying to get people to pay attention and send help, you'd be a fool not to call attention to the living legend in your midst.

The same is true, in a way, if you're a nonfiction writer trying to make your Alamo history compelling. Crockett is one of your centerpieces, and you want him in the thick of things. You don't have many details to work with, so you need to milk what you've got for whatever you can.

And sometimes, inevitably, you're going to squeeze those details just a little too hard.

In my knapsack I carried a worn paperback copy of Walter Lord's *A Time to Stand*, first published in 1961 but still widely hailed as the best Alamo book ever. I loved reading it, and I remembered how Lord had livened up Travis's description of Crockett during that Mexican probe. "The Tennessee 'boys' joined in with their squirrel rifles," he wrote, "and David Crockett was everywhere cheering them on. Cavalryman Cleland Simmons, other volunteers, rushed over to lend support. Who wouldn't want to fight beside Crockett today?"

Now, as I watched parents lift up their kids for pictures beside the replica palisade, I recalled Lord's explanation that it had been "the soft spot" in the Alamo's defenses—but that "it wouldn't be nearly as weak with the world's greatest hunters behind it."

Who wouldn't want to believe that David fought here?

I had some doubts, though.

Was Crockett actually at the palisade when the battle began? We don't know. Travis could have changed his mind any number of times between February 23 and March 6. For that matter, was the palisade really weak? Apparently not. It had a cannon in the middle of it and another, near the main gate, guarding a flank, and it was protected by an abatis, a formidable barrier of felled trees designed to slow down attackers so they could be picked off. For whatever reason, the Mexican column assigned to attack the south wall seems to have given this "soft spot" a wide berth.

Meanwhile, as I moved deeper into Lord's narrative, his Crockett sightings seemed to get even less reliable, and the modern landmarks got harder to find.

The Alamo's outer walls had disappeared soon after the battle, torn down first by retreating Mexican troops and then by locals hungry for building material. Across Alamo Street, near the point where the south and west walls once met, I did my best to imagine them—ignoring a sign for Ripley's Believe It or Not!—as I recalled Lord's description of an incident involving a Mexican engineer "reconnoitering across the river," maybe two hundred yards away.

"A man in buckskin climbed up on the southwest corner of the fort—a living monument against the bleak, gray sky—and coolly shot the Mexican dead," Lord wrote. "Of course everyone always said the Texan was Crockett."

Of course. There's also a tale that David nearly picked off Santa Anna himself, though Lord didn't bite on that one.

Next up was the fiddle-and-bagpipe story.

Lord did a lot of careful Alamo research, but he was not a Crockett scholar, and there's no reason he should have known about the scarcity of contemporary evidence that David had played the instrument. So he milked what he could from the detail he had. "Crockett turned on the tested charm that had never failed him yet," he wrote. "His favorite device during these dark days was to stage a musical duel between himself and John McGregor. The Colonel had found an old fiddle somewhere, and he would challenge McGregor to get out his bagpipes to see who could make the most noise. The two of them took turns, while the men laughed and whooped and forgot for a while the feeling of being alone."

Can't you just see them?

I could, even through a thick haze of doubt.

I could also hear David saying what Lord had him say a few pages later: "I think we had better march out and die in the open air. I don't like to be hemmed up." The source, again, was Susanna Dickinson, or, to be more precise, Susanna Dickinson as quoted in a history of Texas by James Morphis, published in 1874 and featuring details that didn't appear in her other statements and interviews.

Did Morphis embellish the story? It seems likely. Yet to me—and to many others who have written about Crockett—those words about dying in the open air ring true.

If you'd been there, wouldn't you have felt the same?

I walked north on Alamo Street, tracing the site of the vanished west wall, then turned right on East Houston and climbed the steps of the Hipolito F. Garcia Federal Building and United States Court-house. The classical-columned structure—which houses a post of-fice as well—rises above where the north wall once stood, and it made a perfect vantage point from which to contemplate the vast, indefensible space Mark Lemon's diorama had modeled and Phil Collins's narration had described. I couldn't even see the church, which was hidden behind the Long Barracks and some trees.

Somewhere in that space, or possibly just outside it, the remark-able life of David Crockett came to an end.

But where?

Could it have been just behind where I was sitting?

If you had walked into the Alamo church in the early 1980s, as I'd read in a newsletter put out by a precursor of the Alamo Society, inquiring how Davy died would have gotten you this reply: "He died of multiple gunshot wounds near what is now the out-of-state mail slot of the post office across the street." Asked and answered! Except that there was no mention of where the shrine's "veteran hostess-librarian" obtained this highly specific information.

That doesn't prove it wrong. The main attack came on the north wall, and Crockett could have rushed to be where the fighting was thickest. He could have died there, or he could have retreated to the Long Barracks with other defenders after the Mexicans came over that wall.

There are more likely possibilities, however.

Among those who don't think that Crockett was captured and executed, the most widely held view is that he went down fighting somewhere in front of the church, near the palisade to which he had originally been assigned. The evidence, naturally, is complex and incomplete, but Susanna Dickinson figures heavily again. In the same 1874 history mentioned above, Morphis quotes her as saying, "I recognized Col. Crockett lying dead and mutilated between the church and the two story barrack building, and even remember seeing his peculiar cap lying by his side." The reliability of this testimony has sparked endless arguments among the Alamo-addicted, but it offers a simple, vivid image that will never go away.

Lord offered an equally vivid image, based on still more controversial evidence. "Crockett's Tennesseans, at bay near the palisade, battled with a wild fury that awed even the attackers," he wrote, but the deeds of individual defenders "were lost forever in the seething mass of knives, pistols, fists and broken gunstocks." Or were they? In a nifty rhetorical move, Lord then put David right back in the center of things by quoting a Mexican sergeant's description of a man who, in Lord's words, "could stand for any of them, including Crockett himself." The man was tall and dark, the sergeant said, with a buckskin coat and a fox-skin hat, and he "'apparently had a charmed life. Of the many soldiers who took deliberate aim at him and fired, not one ever hit him. On the contrary, he never missed a shot. He killed at least eight of our men, besides wounding several others. This being observed by a lieutenant who had come in over the wall, he sprang at him and dealt him a deadly blow with his sword, just above the right eye, which felled him to the ground, and in an instant he was pierced by not less than twenty bayonets.'"

Or so eighty-four-year-old Felix Nuñez is said to have recalled more than half a century after the battle, in a newspaper article not given much credence by Alamo researchers these days.

Dickinson isn't the only eyewitness to report having seen Crockett's body. Her main competition in this department comes from

Francisco Ruiz, who was the alcalde (mayor) of Béxar at the time of the battle. In a statement published in 1860, Ruiz recalled being asked by Santa Anna to identify the bodies of Travis, Crockett, and Bowie. "Toward the west, and in the small fort opposite the city, we found the body of Col. Crockett," Ruiz said. That is most often taken to mean that David's body lay along the west wall, perhaps at an artillery position there.

Not necessarily, though. Later I would meet a grassroots historian named Rick Range who had a Ruiz-related theory I had never heard before.

What if "the small fort opposite the city" referred not to anything on the *west* wall but to a half-oval fortification built out from the *south* wall to protect the Alamo's main gate? It looked like a fort; its west side faced the city; and it was near the part of the wall that the Mexicans attacked. It was also close enough to the palisade, Range suggested, that if Crockett saw that his original post wasn't threatened, "he'd have been able to run real quick" to the area that needed defending.

I can see David making that run.

Then again, I can see him everywhere—including outside the Alamo walls.

In the late stages of the battle, with all hope of victory gone, a good number of defenders *did* break out into the open air, only to be run down by waiting lancers on horseback. Might Crockett have been one of them? Sure. In fact, according to an 1842 newspaper report, a man who had been on Houston's staff passed on the following "anecdote" about David's end. "He continued to cheer on his companions till they were reduced to seven," the Houston staffer said. "Being then called on to yield, he shouted forth defiance, leaped into the crowd below, and rushed toward the city. Being pursued by two soldiers, he kept both at bay for a time, until he was finally thrust through by a lance."

The scenario seems unlikely for many reasons. But if David Crockett did go over that wall, I say: good for him.

A man with nine lives, trying to cheat death one more time.

✬

March 6, 2011, dawned cold and beautiful, with a rich blue replacing the blackness above the floodlit church and the Crockett Hotel sign. Behind a rope line, a bit northwest of the palisade, I joined an Alamo Plaza crowd of perhaps two thousand to watch the San Antonio Living History Association mark the 175th anniversary with readings (a Travis letter and a bit of de la Peña's memoir among them); the lighting of a candle for each of the siege and battle's thirteen days; and musket volleys fired by reenactors representing both sides.

The ceremony was solemn and moving, despite an awkward moment or two (the bagpiping wasn't up to John McGregor standards). Just being there, shivering as the eastern sky gradually brightened, made it easier to conjure up that Sunday morning in 1836: anxious Mexican soldiers in the freezing dark, awaiting orders to attack; exhausted Texians jolted from deep sleep; then a brief, brutal struggle—estimates vary, but it seems to have lasted roughly an hour—in which, as Lord wrote, the deeds of individual defenders were forever lost.

We remembered them all anyway.

And some of us were thinking, in particular, about a certain Tennessee volunteer.

"Daniel Boone, I mean Davy Crockett, he had a raccoon cap," I heard a woman behind me say early on. Then, a bit later: "I don't see no raccoon cap."

The cap was there, all right; I finally spotted it after the Texians fired their volley. But the most visible Crockett-related artifact at the Alamo that morning conveyed a different image entirely. It was a copy of the 1834 Chester Harding portrait, showing David in formal attire, that's now in the National Portrait Gallery. Surrounded by artificial red carnations, he gazed out at the place of his unlikely death from the center of a memorial wreath presented by his descendants.

On that day they were rock stars, too—at least minor ones. Cameras followed the descendants as a dozen or so gathered by the wreath for a family photo, and fans pressed forward to bask in reflected glory. "Who's the patriarch or the matriarch of the Crockett family?" someone asked. He was carrying a beautiful wooden cross with David's name lettered in gold, and he wanted to give it to someone.

"Oh, it's a democracy, sorry!" said Suzie Brooks. "It's a republic!" Then she steered him to a member of the descendants' organization's board of directors.

Next came a man who introduced himself as Eddie. "I've been following David Crockett since I was ten years old," he said. He looked as though his tenth birthday had been quite a few decades ago.

"It's nice to meet you, Eddie. Thank you for your interest," Brooks said.

Not so fast. Eddie had questions. "Was he one of the last survivors? Was he taken—and then executed?" he asked. "Another question: They say he was up against that wall under that window. Is that accurate?" Eddie went on to discuss the import of the de la Peña memoir with a Crockett great-great-great-grandson, to wonder how Susanna Dickinson could have seen everything she is supposed to have seen, and to express grave doubts about Travis's line in the sand. "Since the age of ten, I ask questions," he said, "and I'm still asking questions."

"My new best friend," Brooks told me later, smiling like someone who's no stranger to the obsessive passion her great-great-great-grandfather's name can induce.

Brooks was eight during the Disney craze. Her mother said, "Well, you *know* that you're related to Davy Crockett," and she said, "No, I'm not!" and her mother said, "What's your Daddy's name?" and she said, "David—Crockett—Brooks," and finally got it. But she never said anything at school, "because nobody believed you." Two days before the dawn ceremony, she had been called up to sing "The Ballad of Davy Crockett" with the band at Headley's party, and this evening, she was to attend a more intimate ceremony in the shrine, where she would help call the roll of Alamo defenders and would listen as a Crockett impersonator read the letter her celebrated ancestor sent home from Texas, a few days before he rode out of Nacogdoches toward Béxar.

"Do not be uneasy about me," David wrote in January 1836. "I am with my friends."

And so he is, even today.

Probably.

Because the final resting place of the Alamo defenders, strangely, remains almost as much of a mystery as how David Crockett died.

After the battle, Santa Anna ordered the Texian dead gathered in piles, and cartloads of wood collected from the countryside. Alcalde Ruiz described how soldiers stacked the wood and bodies in alternate layers and, around 5:00 P.M., set them alight. Another Tejano—interviewed much later by a journalist who realized that the last eyewitnesses were about to die off—added grim details. Pablo Díaz described the "[f]ragments of flesh, bones and charred wood and ashes" that remained after the burning, along with a sickening odor and a grease stain extending "several feet beyond the ashes and smoldering mesquite fagots."

For nearly a year, Texas left its heroes where they lay. But in late February 1837, Juan Seguin rode into Béxar at the head of a cavalry company with orders to rectify the situation. Seguin found the ashes of his comrades "in three heaps." In a report to the commander of the Army of Texas, he described the multilocation funeral he had arranged.

"I caused a coffin to be prepared neatly covered with black," he wrote, and to be filled with ashes from two of the three heaps. He had the coffin carried in a solemn procession to San Fernando Church—whose bell had rung a year earlier to warn of the Mexican approach—then back to the places from which ashes had been collected. At each of the two spots, Seguin's men put the coffin down and fired three musket volleys over it. Finally, they carried it to "the principal spot and place of interment" and set it atop the larger heap of ashes there. Seguin said a few words in Spanish; an English-speaking officer added a few more. Coffin and ashes were duly buried, and the men fired three last volleys over the grassy site.

A month later, an official account of the funeral appeared in a Texas newspaper. It noted that "the names of Travis, Bowie and Crockett" had been engraved on the inside of the coffin lid.

It took me two tries to locate the "principal spot" Seguin mentioned, despite having good directions. If you were to fire shots over it today—depending on where you were standing and what direction you aimed—you might hit the Marriott San Antonio River-walk hotel, a red-and-blue Rio San Antonio Cruises boat, a white Hummer trying to squeeze its fat butt into the parking garage at the Rivercenter Mall, or, just possibly, the statue of American Federation of Labor founder Samuel Gompers in front of the Henry B. Gonzalez Convention Center.

You'd be unlikely to hit the pair of historical markers that talk about the funeral pyre, however.

They're far too small—and in the wrong place.

"On this spot bodies of heroes slain at the Alamo were burned," the older marker informed me. "Fragments of the bodies were afterward buried here." A cracked marble plaque affixed to a low stone wall along East Commerce Street, it identified itself as the work of the De Zavala Chapter of the Texas Landmarks Association. Adina De Zavala was a name I knew. An early Alamo addict whose grandfather was the first vice president of the Republic of Texas, she had been hugely influential in preserving the Alamo as a historic site, beginning her campaign in the 1890s, recruiting the wealthy donor who funded its rescue from commercial interests a few years into the twentieth century, and later barricading herself inside what had been the Long Barracks for three days to keep that building from being destroyed.

Even she couldn't save the pyre site, though.

Next to the marble marker, a smaller, shinier one explained why. The original had been placed on a building "near here" in 1917, it said, but the building had been torn down in 1968 as part of a River Walk extension. The owners had kept De Zavala's marker in "protective custody" and, twenty-seven years later, it had been reinstalled "in the vicinity of the original location."

Near here.

In the vicinity.

Rick Range, the man who gave me the new idea about where Crockett might have died, demonstrated what those words really meant. Standing on an East Commerce Street bridge, a few feet from De Zavala's marker, he pointed east across that River Walk extension, which had created a new chunk of river as well. On the far side of the bridge, Range said, "there used to be a street called Rusk," and where Rusk and Commerce intersected "is where the big main pyre was, where Seguin said he buried the coffin.

"Now it's just midair, you know. It's the river. It's just *gone*."

A historian's mission, however, is to bring lost times and places to life as well as give them context, and minutes before, we had heard Stephen Hardin do just that. The *Texian Iliad* author had chosen to end an Alamo walking tour at the pyre site—or sites, really; it's generally believed that a second pyre burned just across East Commerce Street. A big, bearded, silver-haired man who used his walking stick as a pointer, Hardin has a flair for the dramatic that serves him well both in print and in public.

"People have asked: Why would the Mexicans have dragged the bodies all the way from the Alamo and burned them here?" he said. "How many of you saw that old movie *Spartacus*? Okay, remember at the end of that movie—and this is historically accurate—that after the Romans took down that slave rebellion, they crucified the prisoners along the Appian Way for miles? Why? So that people coming into Rome could see, and other slaves could see: this is what happens when you get out of line." It was the same in medieval Europe, he continued, where gallows sprouted on major thoroughfares, and by the way, did anyone remember the scene in *Pirates of the Caribbean* where Captain Jack sees the skeletons and the placard reading "Pirates, ye be warned"?

He jabbed the air with his stick, pointing it in the direction of the noisy traffic on Commerce.

"Why here? That's the road to Gonzales. Anybody going *out* of town, anybody coming *into* town has to pass this pile of charred bones. And I think this location was picked on purpose, because this is the main thoroughfare. People coming into San Antonio can see what happens to rebels."

I tried to calculate the odds, which seemed quite good, that Crockett's bones had been in that pile. Hardin, though, was thinking about Susanna Dickinson, the best known of the battle's surviving noncombatants. Dickinson was around twenty-one, he said, and her daughter under two. As the battle ended, "she's led out of the compound and catches a stray round in the calf—they're still firing." She was taken in by the Musquiz family, with whom she and her husband had lodged, but before long, she was headed out of town, riding toward Gonzales with "two dollars and a blanket" given to her by Santa Anna.

"Here is the thought I want to leave you with," Hardin said. "To get from the Musquiz house to Gonzales, what would Susanna Dickinson have to ride past? What's the last thing she sees? That's a very human moment, Susanna leaving San Antonio and having to ride past these pyres, in which her husband—" His voice had been shaky for a while, and now he began to cry.

"I'm sorry!" he said, almost shouting. "These were *people* here. These are powerful places—if you know where the hell they are!"

I couldn't have agreed more.

But I still didn't know where David's ashes ended up.

By that time, in fact, I wasn't even sure I could list all the places where people had suggested they might be. Bruce Winders had told me there'd been a pyre, probably a small one, near where a fire station now sits behind the Alamo grounds. A lifelong Crockett fan from Philadelphia had told me that when he'd seen some kind of excavation near the palisade, fifteen years before, he "knew it was the ashes of those men" and "knelt down and said a prayer for them." Stephen Harrigan once wrote, without elaborating, that he thought the main pyre site might have been closer to "where the Denny's or the La Quinta Inn now stands" than to the East Commerce Street markers. Meanwhile, more than one Alamo expert, Winders among them, had pointed me toward the strangest Crockett-related site I ever saw: the Odd Fellows Cemetery on Powder House Hill, maybe a mile east of Alamo Plaza, where some defenders' remains were said to have been reinterred with those of two Texas Rangers who had been killed—a decade after the Alamo—while fighting in the Mexican-American War.

Huh?

I made my way to the cemetery one evening at dusk. Sirens

echoed through the neighborhood, and the occasional police car cruised by. Eerie-looking palm trees caught the day's last light. Some of the view to the west was blocked by a decaying factory building on Pine Street, but I could see the Marriott Riverwalk towering over the main pyre site. And sure enough, at the graves of Samuel H. Walker and R. A. Gillespie, I found a marker titled LOST BURIAL PLACE OF THE ALAMO DEFENDERS. It quoted a 1906 newspaper article explaining that a man named August Beisenbach had told a reporter that one day in 1856, when he was eight years old, he had been playing on what's now East Commerce Street, where he had "witnessed the exhuming of bodies or remains consisting of bones and fragments of bones, of victims of the siege of The Alamo" and seen "their transfers from that place to the old cemetery, on Powder House Hill."

That isn't quite as unlikely as it sounds. The story involves Walker's and Gillespie's bodies being brought back from Mexico and buried on the pyre site across from where the markers are now, commercial development commencing in the area, the bodies needing to be dug up and moved, some additional remains being found, and—well, you get the picture.

If you don't, Lee Spencer White can fill you in.

White is the founder and president of the Alamo Defenders' Descendants Association; her Alamo ancestor, Gordon Jennings, was the only defender older than Crockett. She's the woman who got that marker put up on Powder House Hill, which sounds easy enough, but to do it—as I learned when I tagged along with her on another visit there—she first had to stop some folks with a backhoe who had come to move Walker's remains, then persuade the city of San Antonio to take custody of the cemetery. (The place was wildly overgrown at the time, and White had taken to stashing a shotgun in the trunk of her Honda when she drove there.) She'd also been instrumental in getting that marble pyre marker remounted on East Commerce Street.

"I'm a little marker person," she joked, which is true—she's not tall, and she loves historical markers—but also a bit misleading. If I believed in reincarnation, I'd say she was Adina De Zavala, come back to fight the good Alamo fight.

The next time I saw White was on the morning after the dawn ceremony, at yet another place where some of Crockett's ashes might—just possibly—have come to rest. That would be San Fernando Cathedral, where, if you walk through the left-hand door, you will find yourself in an alcove containing a marble sarcophagus and a wall plaque inscribed, unambiguously, HERE LIE THE REMAINS OF TRAVIS, CROCKETT, BOWIE AND OTHER ALAMO HEROES.

Here we go again.

The tale begins, once more, with Juan Seguin. Near the end of his long life, Seguin responded to an inquiry about the defenders' funeral by contradicting his own 1837 account. He now claimed that he had *left* the ashes at San Fernando. "I ordered that the ashes be deposited in an urn and that a grave be opened in the Cathedral of San Antonio, close to the Presbytery, that is, in front of the altar railings, but very near the altar steps," he wrote in 1889. "That is all I can tell you with reference to this affair." In 1936, during a renovation project, some remains were unearthed near that spot and declared by the archbishop to be those of the Alamo heroes. Many have doubted this. Science could resolve the question—it should be easy to determine whether the remains were ever in a fire, and modern DNA testing can work wonders—but so far, White said, the Catholic Church had refused a request that testing be done.

She was still trying, though.

"I'm a very curious person," she said. "I'd *love* for it to be the defenders. I'm not so sure it is. But either way, I want to know."

White had come to San Fernando, as she does each year, to place a wreath in front of the sarcophagus—just in case. Suzie Brooks was there, too, as was Kevin Young, the man who had so presciently told Jim Crisp, "You've really stepped in it now." I had run into Young several times during the weekend and had watched him smoothly field every arcane Texas history question batted his way. Even he didn't know where David's ashes were, though.

Yet by that time, I was starting to be okay with not knowing. After all, the kind of Crockett ghosts I'd set out to look for weren't necessarily attached to grave sites. I'd been seeing them all weekend, in fact—in the streets, in the Menger ballroom, on the grounds of the Alamo, and, yes, floating above the river in the crisp San Antonio air.

Look, here came one now.

White had left her wreath by the sarcophagus in the alcove, and the four of us had retreated to a table in the plaza outside. Sitting there in the twenty-first-century sunlight, talking with people who treated Crockett like one of the family—which in Brooks's case, of course, he was—I looked around and thought: it was *right here* that David climbed onto that packing crate in February 1836 and captivated his final audience with a speech full of tales told "in his own peculiar style."

That morning at San Fernando was the beginning of my last twenty-four hours in San Antonio—and the last travel day, it turned out, of my year of walking where Crockett walked. Sometimes I felt as though I had known him forever, that he was part of my own family, that I could see straight into his head no matter what kind of hat he chose to put on it. But sometimes, even now, I could barely see the outline of the real David.

There were too many ghosts blocking the view.

That moment when I imagined him standing on the packing crate offers a perfect example. I immediately thought of David's first-ever political performance, the one where he got tongue-tied, said there had been "a little bit of a speech in me a while ago" but he "couldn't get it out," then kept his audience roaring with "some other anecdotes, equally amusing to them." Yet I also thought of the Crockettesque character in *The Lion of the West,* the one who says "My name is Nimrod Wildfire—half horse, half alligator and a touch of the airthquake—that's got the prettiest sister, fastest horse, and ugliest dog in the District, and can outrun, outkick, out-jump, knockdown, drag out, and whip any man in all Kaintuck." I thought of how Wildfire's bragging style got picked up in *Sketches and Eccentricities of Col. David Crockett,* reworked in the Crockett almanacs as Davy the screamer's first speech in the House, then cleaned up by a clever Disney screenwriter and plugged into "Davy Crockett Goes to Congress."

And I thought of the Rabbit Ears recording I had come to love during my daughter's personal Crockett craze, the one on which Nicolas Cage's Davy boosts Alamo morale as David Bromberg fid-dles along: "Trying to keep spirits up, I clumb right on top of the ramparts and flapped my arms and crowed like a rooster. 'Cock-a-doodle-doo!' I hollered. 'I am half alligator, half horse and half snappin' turtle with a touch of earthquake thrown in. I have got the closest shootin' rifle, the ugliest coon dog, the roughest racking horse and the prettiest wife in the state of Tennessee. I can whip my weight in wildcats, ride a streak of lightnin' through your crab-apple patch, put a rifle ball between the horns of the moon and outstare all the Frenchmen in New Orleans. I can run faster, squat lower, dive deeper, stay under longer and come out drier than any man this side of the Big Muddy.'" Outside the walls, the Mexican army fell quiet as Crockett bragged outrageously on and on. Inside, men slapped their knees and yelled with delight.

"But mostly, they was less frightened," Davy says. "A good round of brag most always fortifies the heart."

Stop and think about that last phrase for a minute.

To fortify the heart against approaching darkness is a pretty good description of the role we assign to our heroes—and it suggests why we have trouble preventing myths from hijacking the past. We *need* stories that give us hope, stories that give us courage in the face of death, stories that tell us who we are. Even as adults, when we're presumed to know better, we also crave emotional simplicity, uncomplicated heroes, well-defined villains, and clean, dramatic story lines.

In other words, we long for Mythic Davys in our lives, and historians' efforts to teach us the difference between truth and myth will always be an uphill fight.

It's not as if the historians don't know this. As I tagged along on Stephen Hardin's walking tour, for example, I heard him hold forth vociferously on the subject. "Understand and appreciate the mythology, and understand and appreciate the history," Hardin urged, "but for God's sake, place them in different pastures—because where we get into trouble is when we confuse our history with our mythology. There's a difference between understanding, appreciating, and believing."

The point is indisputable—except that the distinctions become exceptionally blurry in Crockett's case.

If there is one thing I learned during my year of stalking ghostly Crocketts, it's that you can go crazy trying to herd the "real" and "mythic" versions into separate pastures. It's hard to do that with anyone's story, but with David's it's close to impossible, because his legend sprang up at a point when there were hardly any facts on the ground. Despite valiant digging by Crockettologists from Shackford on, most of what's on record about Crockett's life has been filtered, in one way or another, through the political persona he deliberately created for himself—a persona promptly magnified and distorted by America's nascent celebrity culture. And as I walked around the

Alamo one final time, I didn't need to be reminded what had happened next.

The Crockett I had come to know—the one whose ghosts I now saw everywhere I looked—was someone with whom the conflation of myth and reality seemed to be the whole point.

Take his famous rifle, universally known (except in his autobiography) as "Old Betsy." The Alamo displays two rifles David is said to have owned, one of which was loudly hyped as Betsy when it was donated in 1947. Well, perhaps. The donor claimed only that a Crockett great-grandson "believes it a strong possibility that it was one of David Crockett's rifles" because it looked like one in a painting "now hanging in the state house in Austin." By that standard, you could argue that the elegant long rifle I saw in the middle of the Long Barrack Museum is an authentic Crockett weapon, too. It was donated by Fess Parker, so at least we're sure what the connection is.

Or take that sacred article of Crockett clothing displayed in the shrine. The beaded vest made me think of the unidentified Indians who supposedly gave it to him and of the way the Cherokees, in particular, still honor David for his vote against Indian Removal. But the vest also reminded me that although every Crockett fan knows about that Indian vote, few can name the issue he *really* cared about.

As we've seen, this is no minor quibble. Myth has completely replaced one narrative with another, erasing the most important political fight of Crockett's life. This was a man—as nothing I saw on display in the Alamo will tell you—who staked his career on the Tennessee land fight; a man who tried to get each of his poor constituents 160 acres of government land; a man who believed that if poor people didn't get such help, the greed of land-grabbing speculators would prevent them from ever "taking a rise."

A few feet in front of the church, I found a subtle monument to another Crockett-shaping myth, maybe the most powerful ever created. It consisted of a narrow strip of bronze, embedded in the flagstones and accompanied by a carefully worded plaque. "Legend states," the text read, "that in 1836 Lt. Col. William Barret Travis unsheathed his sword and drew a line on this ground before his battle-weary men stating: 'Those prepared to give their lives in freedom's cause, come over to me!'" Recalling J. Frank Dobie's comment on the immortality of Travis's line—"Reading the documented historians, you'd think nothing could be so unless it happened"—I thought about how myth dehumanizes the mythologized. The line turned Crockett and the other defenders into godlike superheroes of liberty, but it also foreclosed Mythic Davy's option to be captured, surrender, or, God forbid, try to talk his way out of a martyr's death he never sought.

But enough of the heavy stuff for now. What about Davy's coonskin cap?

I was reminded of this quintessential myth-reality question when I encountered a basket filled with $8.95 Crockett headgear in the Alamo gift shop. "Embarrassing," said an employee when she saw me reading the MADE IN CHINA labels, and that started me thinking about a smart-ass question I had asked on a tour the night before. My guide that time had been not Hardin but a likable man named Martin Leal, whose business card read "Alamo City Paranormal" and who, for a mere ten bucks, produced a hilarious barrage of dubious ghost lore and groan-inducing jokes. He included no Crockett sightings in his spiel, however, so I was forced to inquire whether he knew of any.

Yes, he did—sort of. Years ago, he said, pointing to a flagpole between the Long Barracks and the church, "people were seeing images over in that area, and that's about where Davy Crockett died. So is it Davy? We don't know for sure. But you can speculate."

I couldn't resist.

"Did people see him in a coonskin cap?" I asked.

"Well, is that really true?" Leal shot back. "Did he really wear that kind of cap? A lot of people say it was because somebody portrayed him in a play."

✦

When your ghost tour guide calls you out for perpetuating Crockett myths, it's probably time to head back to Realityland—or at least to the kind of modern reality where you can order some excellent pizza, a food David never tasted; toast him with a glass of watery Chianti, which he would have passed up in favor of whiskey; and watch tour boats motor by on a part of the San Antonio River that he couldn't have seen, because that part wasn't there in 1836. The body of water below my outdoor table at Luciano, which I had chosen because it was close to the East Commerce Street pyre sites, was a man-made inlet ending at the Rivercenter Mall, where it widened out so the boats could turn around.

No matter. My mind was on the Nolichucky, the Obion, the Potomac, and the mighty Mississip, and on the real human being whose story flowed into them all. David Crockett crossed a lot of rivers in his forty-nine years, and as is the case with so many "ordinary" Americans of his time, his life would have been remarkable even if no one remembered his name.

Who might Crockett have been without his legend? There are still a lot of narratives from which to choose.

As twilight fell in San Antonio, I thought about a boy who had likely grown to manhood without once hearing the word "Texas"; a boy with not a single advantage of birth besides his race and, perhaps, his mother's love and faith. I thought about a thirteen-year-old with the gumption to work his way from Morristown to Baltimore and back, and about the sheer chance that had kept him from sailing away to a different future entirely. I thought about a young man who had found a surrogate father in the person of his Quaker employer; who had done his best to give himself the beginnings of an education; and who had won the hand of pretty Polly Finley and headed west to make a new life with her in the wilderness.

I also thought of the self-centered stubbornness with which he had ridden off and left her in that wilderness—perhaps to starve, eventually to die—and I remembered the eerie loneliness of her hillside grave.

I recalled the twinned narratives of Crockett's economic failure and his out-of-nowhere political success; the way Elizabeth Patton had helped make the latter possible; and the rare gift for connecting through humorous gab that David had brought to his campaigns. I wondered if he could have better adapted that gift to the swamp of political Washington and whether it would have been a good thing if he had. I hummed a few bars of "Don't Get Above Your Raisin'" and shook my head, once again, at the thought of the poor man's friend rubbing shoulders with Brahmin factory lords.

And as I thought of the joy his days in "the richest country in the world" had brought him, I considered how his story might have ended if he had hung out in Honey Grove or Clarksville for just a few more weeks, and hadn't gotten to San Antonio in time to die.

We can speculate, but we'll never know.

Then again, if David Crockett *had* lived, we almost certainly wouldn't be telling his story today.

History drives a hard and devious bargain. If you aren't the famous one in the center of the picture, your life will likely be forgotten, no matter how interesting it is. And if you *are* the famous one, as Crockett was in just about everybody's picture of the Alamo, you will never be seen clearly again.

Too many ghosts—be they Fess Parker, John Wayne, or King Leonidas of Sparta—will end up fighting for the starring role.

It was time to say good-bye to the man I had followed from birth to death and beyond. The main pyre site seemed like a good place to do that. I climbed the stairs to East Commerce Street and stood in a cool breeze by the markers, staring into the air above the river.

Then, from somewhere to the west, I heard the faint but unmistakable sound of a bagpipe.

The piper stood alone under the lights at the River Walk Streetcar Station. Thick black hair, pulled together at his neck, fell halfway down the back of his blue shirt. He looked more Hispanic than Scottish to me, but I didn't ask him about that or anything else, because he never stopped playing, just raised a hand in salute as I tucked a dollar under a rock to keep it from blowing away.

I could hear the piping for two blocks as I walked back toward the Crockett Hotel. And for longer than that I could hear David on his fiddle, playing along.

ACKNOWLEDGMENTS

This book could never have been written without the help of dozens of people who know and care about the legacy of David Crockett. I am deeply grateful to them all.

Among those who became part of the narrative, I owe special thanks to Jim Claborn, Bob Jarnagin, and Joe Swann for bringing Crockett's east Tennessee roots to life; to Jerry Limbaugh, Rachel Lee, and Joe Bone for connecting me to Crockett's story as he moved ever westward through the state; and to Woody Austin, Stephen Harrigan, and Bruce Winders for illuminating Crockett's Texas. Susan Rice became "Susan the waitress" in chapter 2 because I didn't learn her last name until long after we met. Without her, this would be a lesser book. Michael Lofaro cheerfully deconstructed the strange career of Almanac Davy. Dolly Leighton and John Lee Welton shared wonderful, unpublished theatrical scripts in which Crockett stars. Joy Bland and Suzie Brooks gave the perspectives of strong-minded descendants. Allen Wiener and Jim Boylston couldn't have been more generous with their research on the political David. Jim Crisp and Bill Groneman patiently refought the Crockett Wars. Bill Chemerka's tireless work with the Alamo Society has connected Crockett researchers for decades. Joan Headley's gracious invitation to her annual Alamo party opened unexpected doors.

The late Kevin Young was an invaluable resource for anyone writing about Texas history. I feel fortunate to have known him.

In addition to the people mentioned in the text, I'd like to thank Sally Baker for her terrific Crockett Tavern tour; James Hanna for his maps of Crockett's west Tennessee lands; Tom Kanon of the Tennessee State Library and Archives for his Creek War expertise; Barbara Duncan of the Museum of the Cherokee Indian for guidance and introductions in Cherokee; Jessica

Wood of the Sterne-Hoya House and Carolyn Spears of the Old Stone Fort Museum for the same in Nacogdoches; Peter Mears of the University of Texas's Harry Ransom Center for a close look at John Gadsby Chapman's Crockett; Caitlin Donnelly and her colleagues at the Daughters of the Republic of Texas Library for superior research assistance; the staff of the Library of Congress, especially Paul Hogroian, for all kinds of essential help; and Alamo author Jim Donovan for, among other things, inviting me to tag along on an unforgettable excursion to the Odd Fellows Cemetery.

I have made my own judgments about Crockett's life and death, of course, and any mistakes of fact or interpretation are mine.

John Nava and Gary Zaboly unhesitatingly gave me permission to use their evocative Crockett artwork. I can't thank them enough. Thanks also to Jim Boylston (again) for getting me a copy of Zaboly's drawing, which he owns, and to Pete Thompson, my nephew, for doing his professional best to make me presentable in the author photo.

Two New Yorkers with Texas roots made *Born on a Mountaintop* possible. My agent, Bob Mecoy, brainstormed historical topics like the smart editor he was in his former life. And my actual editor, Sean Desmond, made the book better at every stage, beginning with our first conversation in 2010. Many thanks as well to Molly Stern and the rest of the hardworking Crown team.

During the twenty-four years I worked at the *Washington Post*, it supported long-form narrative journalism more enthusiastically than any other newspaper in America. I'm grateful to Ben Bradlee, Len Downie, and Mary Hadar for first hiring me in the Style section, then turning me loose to run the *Washington Post Magazine*. Steve Coll, Glenn Frankel, and Deborah Heard encouraged my backward career move from editing to writing. Steve assigned the magazine piece on my family's personal Crockett craze—parts of which are adapted in chapter 1—that eventually led to this book. *Post* friends and colleagues too numerous to list helped me learn the reporter's craft; among them are Henry Allen, Mary Battiata, Katherine Boo, Peter Carlson, John Cotter, David Finkel, T. A. Frail, Joel Garreau, Cynthia Gorney, Walt Harrington, Steve Luxenberg, Liza Mundy, Peter Perl, Paula Span, Linton Weeks, and the much missed Marjorie Williams.

My parents, Helen and Will Thompson, introduced me to books and mountaintops; they would have loved to be around to see the combined result. Mona Thompson and Lizzie Thompson are the best daughters a father could wish for, which would be true even if Lizzie hadn't kicked off this whole Crockett thing in 1994. Their mother, Deborah Johnson, has been my first and most trusted reader ever since I started writing for publication. Not long ago, I told Deborah that I could never thank her properly for her editing skill, supportive criticism, technical assistance, and endless patience.

"That's okay," she said. "All I ask is undying love."

She's got it.

NOTE ON SOURCES

David Crockett had only a few months of formal schooling, and writing never came easily to him. That didn't stop him from producing an auto-biography, however, and A *Narrative of the Life of David Crockett, of the State of Tennessee* is an essential first stop for students of his life and legend. There's a small problem, though. Since it was first published, in 1834, the *Narrative* has been reprinted in any number of editions—many "abridged, bastardized, and plagiarized," as the historian Paul Andrew Hutton once put it—and the advent of e-books and print-on-demand publishing has only added to the confusion.

I ended up using three editions. Two are valuable for their introductions, by Hutton and by Joseph J. Arpad. (Full citations are in the bibliography that follows.) The third is a facsimile edition with detailed annotations by the historian Stanley J. Folmsbee and Crockett biographer James A. Shack-ford. The annotations originated with Shackford's 1948 dissertation, and al-though some have been overtaken by later scholarship, they still make this by far the most useful version of the autobiography.

A year before his own book appeared, Crockett was the subject of a hot-selling celebrity biography published anonymously under two different titles. Though badly written and unreliable, James Strange French's portrait of a wild frontiersman played a huge part in shaping David's image. The version I read carried the more common of the two titles, *Sketches and Eccentricities of Col. David Crockett, of West Tennessee*.

No serious, research-based biography of Crockett appeared until 120 years after the Alamo, when Shackford's *David Crockett: The Man and the Legend* made a valiant attempt to separate fact from myth. Illness prevented Shackford from completing the book himself; his brother had to rework the manuscript before it could be published in 1956. The result was sometimes confusing, occasionally flat wrong, and untrustworthy on the Texas end of the story. Yet it remains central to Crockett scholarship, and its author is rightly credited with rescuing the historical David from the legend that had overwhelmed him.

Of the half-dozen Crockett biographies published since Shackford's, the best, in my view, is not technically a biography of David at all. William C. Davis's *Three Roads to the Alamo* weaves together the lives of the three most famous Alamo defenders (James Bowie and William Barret Travis being the other two). Within its nearly eight hundred pages, however, is an extended, evocative portrait of Crockett that could easily stand alone.

Two other works deserve special mention before I move on to chapter-by-chapter notes.

David Crockett in Congress: The Rise and Fall of the Poor Man's Friend, by James R. Boylston and Allen J. Wiener, deals mainly with Crockett's political career, about which which I'll have more to say below. But Boylston and Wiener also tracked down and included the text of every one of David's letters known to have survived as of 2009, when their book was published, making it a doubly invaluable resource for Crockettologists. Finally, no one setting out to walk where Davy walked should be without a copy of Randell Jones's *In the Footsteps of Davy Crockett,* which offers a state-by-state guide—complete with photographs, good directions, and relevant biographical information—to nearly fifty Crockett sites. I still managed to get lost a couple of times, but for that I had only myself to blame.

CHAPTER 1

One thing that drew me to Davy Crockett as a subject was the extent to which Crockett reality and Crockett myth—despite the best efforts of fact-checking biographers—remain hopelessly intertwined. This point was driven home to me by a children's CD, put together by a company called Rabbit Ears Entertainment, that we encountered at the peak of my elder daughter's Crockett phase. In the *Rabbit Ears Treasury of Tall Tales,* Davy is given voice by Nicolas Cage, and he is delightfully up-front about the mashing together of fact and fiction that made him what he is today.

"My name is Davy Crockett, and I am a legend of American history," he begins. "Young folks ought to *know* their history and how a person gets to be a legend. So these here are the naked green-skinned facts o' my life—and a lot of it is the truth, too."

Robert Quackenbush's *Quit Pulling My Leg! A Story of Davy Crockett* makes a similarly entertaining effort to distinguish facts from tall tales. But to me, Cage's seamless Rabbit Ears performance—which blends stump-speaking bears, outrageous frontier brags, and true Alamo courage—makes his Davy the perfect introduction to the subtle way in which legend creation works.

Chapters 2 and 3

Before heading to Kings Mountain National Military Park (yes, surprisingly, the name lacks an apostrophe), I read up on the battle in J. David Dameron's helpful *King's Mountain: The Defeat of the Loyalists, October 7, 1780.* At the well-stocked park bookstore, I picked up Robert M. Dunkerly's equally helpful *Kings Mountain Walking Tour Guide* and asked about sources that could tell me who had fought on the patriot side. "Oh, you want the 'white book,'" came the immediate reply. "It's in alphabetical order, and there's a list of 'possibles' in the back." *The Patriots at Kings Mountain*, by Bobby Gilmer Moss, turned out to offer the most authoritative list of rebel combatants I would find. It placed "Crockett, John" among those "possibly on the Kings Mountain campaign."

The best evidence that John Crockett fought there, however, is his son's autobiography, which remains the principal source for what we know of David's family and early years. Stanley Folmsbee and Anna Grace Catron, in their 1956 article "The Early Career of David Crockett," added some context and supporting detail from public documents. Still, beyond the basic story in Crockett's *Narrative*, I learned more about his east Tennessee life from conversations with local historians Jim Claborn and Joe Swann than from any published work.

Information on Polly Crockett, unfortunately, is even more scarce—something true of poor Appalachian women in general. Wilma A. Dunaway's *Women, Work, and Family in the Antebellum Mountain South* does an admirably thorough job of pulling together the evidence there is.

Chapter 4

To understand Davy Crockett's place in the pantheon of American frontiersmen, it helps to know that political celebrity and a hero's death, not to mention Walt Disney, helped him dethrone an earlier King of the Wild Frontier.

Michael A. Lofaro's *Daniel Boone: An American Life* tells Boone's astonishing story. As for the Tennessee frontier Crockett inhabited—with its voracious land speculators, opportunity-seeking smallholders, and the Indians they defeated and removed—John R. Finger's *Tennessee Frontiers: Three Regions in Transition* offers a thorough reality check on pioneer myths.

Both Finger's book and Frank Lawrence Owsley, Jr.'s, *Struggle for the Gulf Borderlands: The Creek War and the Battle of New Orleans, 1812–1815* help put Crockett's Indian fighting into its broad historical context. Gregory A. Waselkov's *A Conquering Spirit: Fort Mims and the Redstick War of 1813–1814* examines the fascinating, surprising story behind the specific massacre that spurred Crockett to enlist. Robert V. Remini's *The Life of Andrew Jackson* (a one-volume condensation of Remini's earlier three-volume work) and Sean Wilentz's short biography *Andrew Jackson* were my chief sources on Crockett's political nemesis.

CHAPTER 5

Lawrence County is where Crockett got into politics, which means it's also where sources other than his autobiography begin to assume more importance. That doesn't mean they're all reliable. David's record in the state legislature is generally well covered by Shackford and later biographers, yet there are a number of Crockett stories originating in Lawrenceburg and farther west in Tennessee that could serve as case studies in how legends evolve.

The most notable comes from early in Crockett's first legislative term. The "gentleman from the cane" story, according to Shackford, first appeared in the anonymously published 1833 biography. Shackford repeats that version, supplementing it with a plausible identification of Crockett's unnamed antagonist. Yet I ran across two other versions that make the episode sound quite different. As Judge John Morrison and Col. Bob Hamsley tell the tale in *The Real David Crockett,* a short history published in Lawrenceburg in 1955, David was getting the worst of a "heated debate" on the floor of the legislature when he suddenly "rushed at his antagonist. He grasped his collar, when the entire false front of his shirt came loose. Crockett then seemed satisfied, and carried his token of victory back with him to his seat." Another version—from John C. Spence's *The Annals of Rutherford County,* as quoted in Gert Petersen's *David Crockett, the Public Man and Legislator*—also has Crockett erupting in the midst of the debate, though in this case, having stripped the fancy ruffles from his opponent's shirt, David hurls them to the floor.

Petersen is a story in himself: As a boy growing up in Denmark, he got hooked on Crockett before he learned that David was a real person. He has written two books on his childhood hero—both dense with information, though regrettably hard to find—and he hosts "The Historic David Crockett Homepage" on Facebook, which features a wonderful selection of photographs from Crockett sites.

The tale of the farmer's daughter and David's peg-legged opponent, Adam Huntsman, is traceable to the 1873 *History of the City of Memphis* by James D. Davis. Shackford retells it at length, but not before calling its author "often careless of facts, dates, and sources." Well, yes. Davis has the outraged farmer helping Crockett beat Huntsman (which never happened) during a campaign in which the two men were not running against each other.

Even the most dubious sources, however, can offer helpful information if read carefully. A good example is the untrustworthy Edward S. Ellis (see chapter 9), whose 1884 *The Life of Colonel David Crockett* reprinted the newspaper article in which Elizabeth Crockett is recalled as having done most of the work at the family mills.

Chapter 6

Nothing was more important to Crockett politically than his fight to pass the Tennessee Vacant Land Bill, with which he hoped to secure his poor constituents' rights to the acreage they had pioneered. The story is fiendishly complicated, and some biographers have chosen, essentially, to duck it; others, including Shackford, Mark Derr, and William C. Davis, have done their best to explain David's passionate, failed effort. But no biography has explored the land bill as thoroughly as *David Crockett in Congress*. James R. Boylston and Allen J. Wiener use a detailed history of the bill to bolster their argument that Crockett was far from the political naif that his enemies (and Shackford) made him out to be. You don't have to agree with their conclusion to understand that the land fight is crucial to seeing Crockett whole.

Most people who know anything about Crockett as a politician identify him most strongly with his vote against Jackson's infamous Indian Removal bill. This is misleading. Compared to the land fight, removal was a side issue for David, but Disney's screenwriter made it central to "Davy Crockett Goes to Congress" and thus to the Crockett myth. That said, Crockett *did* give a revealing speech opposing Indian Removal. The full text does not survive, only the paraphrased versions that appeared in a west Tennessee newspaper and in a collection of speeches on the topic. There's no need to track them down, however: *David Crockett in Congress* includes them both.

To my knowledge, James Shackford was the first to report that the words "Be allways sure you are right then Go, ahead" could be found under Crockett's signature on an 1831 bill of sale for a slave girl named Adaline (and on another document executed at the same time). For decades Crockettologists echoed the biographer's assumption that this was "the first positive link" between David and his famous motto. Yet the question remained: Why would a man scrawl a motto on legal documents? In 2003, Jonathan Kennon Thompson Smith's *The Land Holdings of Colonel David Crockett in West Tennessee* provided a possible answer. According to Smith, the deed book containing those words was a *copy* of the worn original—made in 1853, nineteen years after the motto appeared on the title page of Crockett's autobiography—and the copyist, who was known to possess "a keen sense of humor," couldn't resist having his little joke.

CHAPTER 7

James Kirke Paulding's play *The Lion of the West* was reworked many times, but by the twentieth century, all versions of the script appeared to be lost. Then James N. Tidwell found one in the British Museum and published it, with a useful introduction, in 1954.

Sketches and Eccentricities, in which James Strange French borrowed from *Lion,* is discussed above. So is Crockett's own *Narrative,* which David wrote—with help from his friend Thomas Chilton—in response to *Sketches.* There has been a great deal of useful commentary on this autobiography, but I found two works especially insightful: Richard Boyd Hauck's *Crockett: A Bio-Bibliography,* later reprinted as *Crockett: A Handbook,* and Joseph Arpad's doctoral dissertation, "David Crockett, an Original Legendary Eccentricity and Early American Character."

David's contribution to *An Account of Col. Crockett's Tour to the North and Down East* consisted mainly of gathering newspaper clippings for his ghostwriter. I didn't quote much from the anti-Jackson fulminations in the *Tour,* partly because they're tedious and partly because it's not clear how much Crockett had to do with composing them; the book seems more reliable when it simply reports what David saw and did. On the political war over the Second Bank of the United States, Boylston and Wiener—again— have done some heavy lifting on a complex topic. For the context of Crockett's visit to Lowell, I relied on Thomas Dublin's *Women at Work* and William Moran's *The Belles of New England*, as well as the excellent exhibits at Lowell National Historical Park.

Joy Bland reported the discovery of Margaret Catharine Crockett's tragic story in *Go Ahead*, the newsletter of the Direct Descendants and Kin of David Crockett. Tim Massey added considerable detail about the discovery in the *Crockett Chronicle*. I have not seen the family Bible records, though I have no reason to doubt them. It's worth repeating that there is no evidence, one way or the other, as to whether David knew what happened to his sister.

John Gadsby Chapman's word portrait of Crockett first appeared in a Texas newspaper in 1895, but I read it in the *Proceedings of the American Antiquarian Society*, which published it more than six decades later as "A Legend at Full-Length: Mr. Chapman Paints Colonel Crockett—and Tells About It." Curtis Carroll Davis, who discovered, edited, and introduced the manuscript, described it as "a close-up, candid reaction to one of the most myth-muddled figures in American annals." That understates the case: Chapman gives us by far the most nuanced picture we have of David during his living-legend phase.

If history were fair, more would be known about the colorful frontier lawyer who defeated Crockett in 1835; *Adam Huntsman: The Peg Leg Politician*, by Kevin D. McCann, has helped fill this gap. And if all sources were created equal, no Crockettologist could resist the tale of "the last big frolic that grand old Davy Crockett ever had in the land he loved so well," as told by a supposed Crockett acquaintance named Robert Hall. Evidence that Crockett threw himself a going-to-Texas bash can be found in an 1882 newspaper interview—Jonathan Kennon Thompson Smith's book includes a copy—in which David's youngest daughter, Matilda, recalled that her father's guests "had a glorious time." But the most quotable details are from Hall, who described Crockett sawing away on a fiddle, quaffing liquor from a gourd, and rendering himself "blacker than midnight in her zenith" as part of a logrolling competition. Alas, all this appears to have originated with *Life of Robert Hall: Indian Fighter and Veteran of Three Great Wars*, a book put together by an anonymous scribe who called himself "Brazos," who heard Hall tell his story shortly before the elderly pioneer and Texas Ranger died in 1899. The historian Stephen L. Hardin, introducing a reprint edition, felt the need to include a cautionary note: "Hall was part of the breed that folklorist J. Frank Dobie characterized as 'authentic liars'"—a breed, again in Dobie's words, whose "'generous nature revolts at the monotony of everyday facts and over-flows with desire to make his company joyful.'"

CHAPTER 8

Stephen Hardin is best known for a military history whose title compares the Texas Revolution to the Trojan War, and his classic *Texian Iliad* was my introduction to the chaotic, drama-filled rebellion that was destined to end Crockett's life. Paul D. Lack's eye-opening *The Texas Revolutionary Experience: A Political and Social History, 1835–1836* puts the rebellion in non-military context. David J. Weber's *The Mexican Frontier, 1821–1846* pulls the camera back still further, taking the Mexican point of view, and *Tejano Leadership in Mexican and Revolutionary Texas*, edited by Jesús F. de la Teja, zooms in on significant players of Mexican heritage. I could happily have read far more about how the Republic of Texas came to be—it's one of the great narratives of American history—but I had to get back to Crockett's personal Texas odyssey.

With the exception of half a dozen well-documented stops, Crockett's route from west Tennessee to San Antonio de Béxar remains uncertain. Manley F. Cobia, Jr.'s, exhaustively researched *Journey into the Land of Trials: The Story of Davy Crockett's Expedition to the Alamo*, draws on sources both well-known and obscure to address this puzzle, among them Pat B. Clark's *The History of Clarksville and Old Red River County*. A. W. Neville's old "Backward Glances" columns from the *Paris News* revel in local Crockett tradition. W. A. Carter's nineteenth-century *History of Fannin County, Texas* offers an alternative to the tale of how Crockett gave Honey Grove its name.

The unpublished *Statement of the Oldest Native Born Texan, Mr. Charles A. Sterne, Taken Down by Miss Kate Hunter* offers a glimpse of David in Nacogdoches; it's in the Texas State Archives, though the copy I read came courtesy of the Sterne-Hoya House. Daniel Cloud's letter is at the Daughters of the Republic of Texas Library at the Alamo. Whenever I ran into a bit of Texas history not immediately familiar to a nonnative, I knew I could turn to the Texas State Historical Association's *Handbook of Texas Online*.

CHAPTER 9

The fake journal commissioned by David's publisher to exploit his Alamo death is one of the most astonishing Crockett artifacts. Richard Penn Smith threw together *Col. Crockett's Exploits and Adventures in Texas* in a few days in 1836, and the fact that you can now read his work in a 2003 Penguin Classics edition, with excellent commentary by John Seelye, testifies to its lasting impact. That impact was heightened by the repackaging of three Crockett-related works—the genuine *Narrative*, the ghostwritten *Tour*, and the spurious *Exploits*—as *The Life of David Crockett: The Original Humorist and Irrepressible Backwoodsman*. My copy dates from 1902, and decades after that, careless writers were still quoting from its Alamo scenes ("Pop, pop, pop! Bom, bom, bom!") as if David had actually written them.

Davy Crockett: The Man, the Legend, the Legacy, 1786–1986, edited by Michael Lofaro, is a book I returned to again and again. A collection of essays by Seelye, Hauck, Catherine L. Albanese, and Lofaro himself, among others, it adds up to a superb scholarly examination of Crockett's progress from the real to the mythic. *Crockett at Two Hundred*, a later anthology edited by Lofaro and Joe Cummings, provides more of the same. Lofaro's introduction to *The Tall Tales of Davy Crockett: The Second Nashville Series of Crockett Almanacs, 1839–1841* remains the best explanation of how the human David was rebranded as a comic American superman, albeit one who can be "a savage and a bigot." Original Crockett almanacs are rare; I was able to examine a dozen or so at the Library of Congress and the Daughters of the Republic of Texas Library.

Alamo Images: Changing Perceptions of a Texas Experience, edited by Susan Prendergast Schoelwer, provides an extraordinary collection of visual evidence as well as informative essays by Schoelwer, Tom W. Gläser, and Paul Andrew Hutton. Todd Hansen's *The Alamo Reader: A Study in History* includes the most significant texts related to the line William Barret Travis either did or didn't draw in the dirt of the Alamo courtyard. Eric von Schmidt's *Smithsonian* observations on iconic Crockett and Custer paintings are quoted (and expanded on) in James E. Crisp's *Sleuthing the Alamo*. The lyrics to "Pompey Smash" are from Charles K. Wolfe's "Davy Crockett Songs: Minstrels to Disney" in Lofaro's first Crockett anthology.

The pseudonymous Edward Ellis article about the constitutional schooling Crockett supposedly received from a constituent named Horatio Bunce is in the April 1867 *Harper's*. The table of contents lists "J. Bethune" as the author of the first-person piece. The real author could not have gotten the story straight from David, as the article claims, because Ellis was born in 1840; when he published his 1884 biography of Crockett, he recycled the anecdote but distanced himself by attributing it to an unidentified "narrator." Usually titled "Not Yours to Give," the Bunce story has been an Internet staple for years. Jim Boylston debunked it in 2004 in the *Crockett Chronicle* and updated the debunking in a 2009 post on his blog "Jim's Corner."

Hauck's summary of the Murdock-Mayo plot is from "Making It All Up: Davy Crockett in the Theater" in Lofaro's first anthology. Frank Thompson's comments on *The Martyrs of the Alamo* are in his invaluable *Alamo Movies*. The "Santa Anna's Greasers" quote is from J. Walker McSpadden's *Pioneer Heroes*. The quote about Crockett's shocking anonymity in 1939 is from Howard Mumford Jones's foreword to Richard M. Dorson's *Davy Crockett: American Comic Legend*.

CHAPTER 10

As background on the story of how Walt Disney brought Davy Crockett back to life, two biographies were helpful: Neal Gabler's *Walt Disney: The Triumph of the American Imagination* and especially Michael Barrier's *The Animated Man: A Life of Walt Disney*. On Barrier's website, I also found a good interview the author did with Fess Parker.

Parker died in March 2010, and I was not lucky enough to talk with him myself. One rich source is the two-and-a-half-hour interview he recorded in July 2000 for the Archive of American Television; from this I learned, among many other things, about the screenplay Parker wrote in which Crockett and Georgie Russel survive the Alamo. William R. Chemerka's *Fess Parker: TV's Frontier Hero*, a helpful authorized biography, appeared in 2011.

Paul F. Anderson's *The Davy Crockett Craze* is crammed with material on the making of the Disney series and the mania that ensued. John R. Finger's *The Eastern Band of Cherokees, 1819–1900* and *Cherokee Americans: The Eastern Band of Cherokees in the Twentieth Century* give the history of the Indians with whom the Disney crew worked in North Carolina. The quote about "outsiders coming in and attacking our heroes" is from an interview I did with Finger for the *Washington Post*. Parker's story about Richard Crowe and the arrow originated with a 1955 minibiography by Carl Schroeder (*The Real Life Story of Fess Parker*) and was quoted on the website MousePlanet in a March 2009 post by Wade Sampson.

My commentary on watching Disney's Crockett is based on the uncut TV shows reissued in 2001 in the Walt Disney Treasures series. The movies derived from the series are diminished by numerous small cuts and lack the scene-setting introductions by Uncle Walt himself.

Pretty much everyone who writes about the Crockett craze is in debt to Margaret J. King's early work on the subject, and I'm no exception. King's

"The Recycled Hero: Walt Disney's Davy Crockett" is in Lofaro's first Crockett anthology. Her 1976 dissertation, "The Davy Crockett Craze: A Case Study in Popular Culture," explored the phenomenon at greater length.

CHAPTER 11

You can go a long way toward understanding the Crockett Death Wars simply by reading works with the names James E. Crisp or Bill Groneman attached.

For example: Carmen Perry's translation of the de la Peña memoir, which sparked the cultural and historical explosion in 1975, now comes in an expanded edition with an introduction by Crisp as well as some additional material he discovered. Dan Kilgore's incendiary *How Did Davy Die?* recently resurfaced as *How Did Davy Die? And Why Do We Care So Much?*, which features an essay by Crisp that is longer than Kilgore's original text. "Documenting Davy's Death: The Problematic 'Dolson Letter' from Texas, 1836" lays out Crisp's views on what he calls "the second primary source to emerge from the shadows of time" regarding Crockett's possible execution. And Crisp's *Sleuthing the Alamo: Davy Crockett's Last Stand and Other Mysteries of the Texas Revolution* offers a dramatic recap of the Crockett Wars while opening a broader window on how the narrative of Texas history has been shaped and reshaped.

As for Groneman: *Defense of a Legend: Crockett and the de la Peña Diary*, which drew Crisp into the fray in the first place, is best known for its stunning argument that de la Peña's memoir is a forgery. You needn't be persuaded by this, however, to see that the basic question behind the book—what do we actually *know* about the de la Peña documents, and why did historians accept them as a reliable source on Crockett's death?—had not been seriously addressed before Groneman raised it in 1994. Five years later, he reworked and expanded *Defense*, retitling it *Death of a Legend: The Myth and Mystery Surrounding the Death of Davy Crockett*. Meanwhile, Crisp had assaulted Groneman's forgery allegation in the *Southwestern Historical Quarterly* and Groneman had fired back with "The Controversial Alleged Account of José Enrique de la Peña"—the opening salvo of a five-part back-and-forth between the two, in *Military History of the West*, that can fairly be described as hostile.

The *Alamo Journal* exchanges between Crisp and Thomas Ricks Lindley are worth reading in full, both for the obsessive detail in which they debate the Dolson letter and for the passion they display. And speaking of passion: Paul Hutton's "Davy Crockett: An Exposition on Hero Worship," which can be found in the anthology edited by Lofaro and Cummings, is rich with material on what could happen to twentieth-century scholars who expressed a belief that Davy didn't go down fighting.

William C. Davis's "How Davy Probably *Didn't* Die" deserves much wider circulation, though the editors of the now-dormant *Journal of the Alamo Battlefield Association* deserve great credit for publishing it. Gary Zaboly's *An Altar for Their Sons: The Alamo and the Texas Revolution in Contemporary Newspaper Accounts* includes just about every known contemporary journalistic reference to Crockett's Alamo death, and it shows 1830s journalism to be less a first draft of history than first, second, and third drafts of myth.

The columnist with whom John Wayne discussed the politics of *The Alamo* was Louella Parsons; the quote is in Frank Thompson's *Alamo Movies*, along with Thompson's views on the cinematic achievements and historical deficiencies of Wayne's picture. Hauck's endorsement of Wayne's Davy is from *Crockett: A Bio-Bibliography.*

Richard Flores's *Remembering the Alamo: Memory, Modernity, and the Master Symbol* taught me a good deal I didn't know, especially about the way late-nineteenth-century economic and social change in Texas affected portrayals of Crockett and the Alamo. It also introduced me to the remarkable Adina De Zavala and to the story of how the physical Alamo came to be preserved.

CHAPTER 12

Stephen Harrigan, author of *The Gates of the Alamo*, has also written a guide to the landscape of the battle. I got the idea of walking the route of the Texian retreat from his March 2000 *Texas Monthly* piece "My Own Private Alamo." Arriving in Alamo Plaza today, with modern-day San Antonio crowding in from all sides, it's hard to picture the battered, impossibly large mission-fortress that Crockett and the other Texians tried to defend. George Nelson's *The Alamo: An Illustrated History* and Mark Lemon's *The Illustrated Alamo 1836: A Photographic Journey* offer significant help.

When it comes to Alamo prose, of course, there's a lot to choose from. Walter Lord's beautifully written *A Time to Stand* sets a high standard, though the research on which it was based is half a century out of date. *Sacrificed at the Alamo: Tragedy and Triumph in the Texas Revolution*, by Richard Bruce Winders, is an excellent short history that puts the battle in political and military context. *A Line in the Sand: The Alamo in Blood and Memory* by Randy Roberts and James S. Olson combines the facts of the battle itself with the story of its remarkable cultural afterlife. An admirable recent narrative history is James Donovan's *The Blood of Heroes: The 13-Day Struggle for the Alamo—and the Sacrifice That Forged a Nation.*

Writing in the *Southwestern Historical Quarterly* before he published his still indispensable *Texian Iliad,* Stephen Hardin shed some light on the famous story of the heroic, Crockett-like figure who went down fighting. He called the thirdhand 1889 Alamo narrative of "alleged Mexican soldier Felix Nuñez," in which the tale first appeared, "so clearly wrong on so many vital points it would be folly to use any part of it to support an argument."

The 1842 newspaper report that had Crockett leaping from an Alamo wall, only to be pursued and cut down by a Mexican lancer, was examined by Thomas Ricks Lindley in the September 2005 *Alamo Journal.* He took it quite seriously, though others have not. Lindley's *Alamo Traces: New Evidence and New Conclusions* is too dense for ordinary readers but a fascinating read for the Alamo-obsessed; fans of Sam Houston and believers in Travis's line, however, should prepare to have their version of history vigorously revised.

In "Fiddling with History: David Crockett and the 'Devil's Box,'" Bill Groneman addresses the question of whether Crockett ever actually played a fiddle, and his conclusion—"If he did, he remained uncharacteristically quiet about it all of his life"—seems hard to argue with. The donor's quote about the "strong possibility" that the Alamo was getting "one of David Crockett's rifles" is from the September 2, 1947, *San Antonio News.*

Let me end with a few more words about Todd Hansen's *The Alamo Reader.* Early in the Texas phase of my reporting, someone I was interviewing—shocked that I did not yet own a copy—told me I needed to get hold of one *right away.* Hansen's 837-page book, which I kept within arm's reach while writing, is a masterpiece of document collection and intelligent commentary. The paper trails behind the Alamo testimony of John Sutherland, Susanna Dickinson, and Juan Seguin, to take just three important examples, are complex and often contradictory; Hansen presents every scrap of evidence, weighs it carefully, then spells out exactly what he thinks and why.

BIBLIOGRAPHY

Print Sources

Allen, Charles Fletcher. *David Crockett: Scout, Small Boy, Pilgrim, Mountaineer, Soldier, Bear-Hunter and Congressman, Defender of the Alamo.* Philadelphia: J. B. Lippincott, 1911.

Anderson, Paul F. *The Davy Crockett Craze: A Look at the 1950s Phenomenon and Davy Crockett Collectibles.* Hillside, Ill.: R & G Productions, 1996.

Andrist, Ralph K. *Andrew Jackson: Soldier and Statesman.* New York: American Heritage, 1963.

Arpad, Joseph John. "David Crockett, an Original Legendary Eccentricity and Early American Character." Ph.D. dissertation, Duke University, 1970.

———. "John Wesley Jarvis, James Kirke Paulding and Colonel Nimrod Wildfire." *New York Folklore Quarterly* 21 (June 1965): 92–106.

Austin, Moses. "A Memorandum of M. Austin's Journey from the Lead Mines in the County of Wythe in the State of Virginia to the Lead Mines in the Province of Louisiana West of the Mississippi, 1796–1797." *American Historical Review* 5 (1900): 518–542.

Barrier, Michael. *The Animated Man: A Life of Walt Disney.* Berkeley: University of California Press, 2007.

———. "Fess Parker: An Interview." www.michaelbarrier.com/Interviews/Parker/interview_fess_parker.htm, December 20, 2004.

Blair, Walter. *Davy Crockett, Frontier Hero: The Truth as He Told It—The Legend as Friends Built It.* New York: Coward-McCann, 1955.

————. *Horse Sense in American Humor: From Benjamin Franklin to Ogden Nash*. Chicago: University of Chicago Press, 1942.

Bland, Joy. "Genealogical Discovery." *Go Ahead* 25 (August 2008): 3.

Boylston, James R. ("Jim"). "Crockett and Bunce: A Fable Examined." *Crockett Chronicle* 6 (November 2004): 10.

————, and Allen J. Wiener. *David Crockett in Congress: The Rise and Fall of the Poor Man's Friend*. Houston: Bright Sky Press, 2009.

"Brazos." *Life of Robert Hall: Indian Fighter and Veteran of Three Great Wars*. Austin, Tex.: State House Press, 1992.

Brear, Holly Beachley. *Inherit the Alamo: Myth and Ritual at an American Shrine*. Austin: University of Texas Press, 1995.

Carter, W. A. *History of Fannin County, Texas*. Bonham, Tex.: Bonham News, 1885.

Chemerka, William R. *The Davy Crockett Almanac and Book of Lists*. Austin, Tex.: Eakin Press, 2000.

————. *Fess Parker: TV's Frontier Hero*. Albany, Ga.: BearManor Media, 2011.

————, and Allen J. Wiener. *Music of the Alamo*. Houston: Bright Sky Press, 2008.

Clark, Pat B. *The History of Clarksville and Old Red River County*. Dallas: Mathis, Van Nort & Co., 1937.

Cobia, Manley F., Jr. *Journey into the Land of Trials: The Story of Davy Crockett's Expedition to the Alamo*. Franklin, Tenn.: Hillsboro Press, 2003.

Cody, William F. *Story of the Wild West and Camp-Fire Chats, by Buffalo Bill, (Hon. W. F. Cody): A Full and Complete History of the Renowned Pioneer Quartette, Boone, Crockett, Carson and Buffalo Bill*. Philadelphia: Historical Publishing Co., 1888.

Cohen, Caron Lee. *Sally Ann Thunder Ann Whirlwind Crockett*. New York: Greenwillow Books, 1985.

Cooper, Texas Jim. "A Study of Some David Crockett Firearms." *East Tennessee Historical Society's Publications* 38 (1966): 62–69.

Crisp, James E. "Back to Basics: Conspiracies, Common Sense, and Occam's Razor." *Alamo Journal* 100 (March 1996): 15–23.

————. "Davy in Freeze-Frame: Methodology or Madness?" *Alamo Journal* 98 (October 1995): 3–8.

————. "Documenting Davy's Death: The Problematic 'Dolson Letter' from Texas, 1836." *Journal of the West* 46, no. 2 (Spring 2007): 22–28.

————. "The Little Book That Wasn't There: The Myth and Mystery of the de la Peña Diary." *Southwestern Historical Quarterly* 98 (October 1994): 260–296.

———. *Sleuthing the Alamo: Davy Crockett's Last Stand and Other Mysteries of the Texas Revolution.* New York: Oxford University Press, 2005.

———. "Trashing Dolson: The Perils of Tendentious Interpretation." *Alamo Journal* 99 (December 1995): 3–14.

———. "Truth, Confusion, and the de la Peña Controversy: A Final Reply." *Military History of the West* 26 (Spring 1996): 99–104.

———. "When Revision Becomes Obsession: Bill Groneman and the de la Peña Diary." *Military History of the West* 25 (Fall 1995): 143–155.

Crockett, David. *An Account of Col. Crockett's Tour to the North and Down East.* Philadelphia: Carey and Hart, 1835.

———. *The Life of David Crockett: The Original Humorist and Irrepressible Backwoodsman.* New York: A. L. Burt, 1902.

———. *A Narrative of the Life of David Crockett, of the State of Tennessee.* Philadelphia: Carey and Hart, 1834.

———. *A Narrative of the Life of David Crockett of the State of Tennessee.* Edited and with an introduction by Joseph J. Arpad. Albany, N.Y.: New College and University Press, 1972.

———. *A Narrative of the Life of David Crockett of the State of Tennessee.* Facsimile edition edited by James A. Shackford and Stanley J. Folmsbee. Knoxville: University of Tennessee Press, 1973.

———. *A Narrative of the Life of David Crockett of the State of Tennessee.* With an introduction by Paul Andrew Hutton. Lincoln: University of Nebraska Press, 1987.

Dameron, J. David. *King's Mountain: The Defeat of the Loyalists, October 7, 1780.* Cambridge, Mass.: Da Capo Press, 2003.

Davis, Curtis Carroll. "A Legend at Full-Length: Mr. Chapman Paints Colonel Crockett—and Tells About It." *Proceedings of the American Antiquarian Society* 69 (October 1959): 155–174.

Davis, James D. *History of the City of Memphis.* Memphis: Hite, Crumpton & Kelly, 1873.

Davis, William C. "How Davy Probably *Didn't* Die." *Journal of the Alamo Battlefield Association* 2 (Fall 1997): 11–37.

———. *Three Roads to the Alamo: The Lives and Fortunes of David Crockett, James Bowie, and William Barret Travis.* New York: HarperCollins, 1998.

de la Peña, José Enrique. *With Santa Anna in Texas: A Personal Narrative of the Revolution*. Translated and edited by Carmen Perry. College Station: Texas A&M University Press, 1975.

———. *With Santa Anna in Texas: A Personal Narrative of the Revolution*. Translated and edited by Carmen Perry. Expanded ed. Introduction by James E. Crisp. College Station: Texas A&M University Press, 1997.

de la Teja, Jesús F. *Tejano Leadership in Mexican and Revolutionary Texas*. College Station: Texas A&M University Press, 2010.

Derr, Mark. *The Frontiersman: The Real Life and the Many Legends of Davy Crockett*. New York: William Morrow, 1993.

Dewey, Ariane. *The Narrow Escapes of Davy Crockett*. New York: Greenwillow Books, 1990.

Donovan, James. *The Blood of Heroes: The 13-Day Struggle for the Alamo—and the Sacrifice That Forged a Nation*. New York: Little, Brown, 2012.

Dorson, Richard M., ed. *Davy Crockett: American Comic Legend*. New York: Rockland Editions, 1939.

———. *Folklore and Fakelore: Essays Toward a Discipline of Folk Studies*. Cambridge, Mass.: Harvard University Press, 1976.

Dublin, Thomas. *Women at Work: The Transformation of Work and Community in Lowell, Massachusetts, 1826–1860*. New York: Columbia University Press, 1979.

Dunaway, Wilma A. *Women, Work, and Family in the Antebellum Mountain South*. New York: Cambridge University Press, 2008.

Dunkerly, Robert M. *Kings Mountain Walking Tour Guide*. Pittsburgh: Dorrance Publishing, 2003.

Elliott, Michael A. *Custerology: The Enduring Legacy of the Indian Wars and George Armstrong Custer*. Chicago: University of Chicago Press, 2007.

Ellis, Edward S. *The Life of Colonel David Crockett*. Philadelphia: Porter & Coates, 1884.

——— [writing as "J. Bethune"]. "Davy Crockett's Electioneering Tour." *Harper's New Monthly Magazine* 34 (April 1867): 606–611.

Feller, Daniel. *The Public Lands in Jacksonian Politics*. Madison: University of Wisconsin Press, 1984.

Finch, Christopher. *The Art of Walt Disney: From Mickey Mouse to the Magic Kingdoms*. New York: Harry N. Abrams, 1975.

Finger, John R. *Cherokee Americans: The Eastern Band of Cherokees in the Twentieth Century*. Lincoln: University of Nebraska Press, 1991.

———. *The Eastern Band of Cherokees, 1819–1900*. Knoxville: University of Tennessee Press, 1984.

————. *Tennessee Frontiers: Three Regions in Transition.* Bloomington: Indiana University Press, 2001.

Fischer, John. "The Embarrassing Truth about Davy Crockett, the Alamo, Yoknapatawpha County, and Other Dear Myths." *Harper's* 211 (July 1955): 16–18.

Flores, Richard R. *Remembering the Alamo: Memory, Modernity, and the Master Symbol.* Austin: University of Texas Press, 2002.

Folmsbee, Stanley J. "David Crockett and West Tennessee." *West Tennessee Historical Society Papers* 28 (1974): 5–24.

————, and Anna Grace Catron. "David Crockett: Congressman." *East Tennessee Historical Society's Publications* 29 (1957): 40–78.

————. "David Crockett in Texas." *East Tennessee Historical Society's Publications* 30 (1958): 48–74.

————. "The Early Career of David Crockett." *East Tennessee Historical Society's Publications* 28 (1956): 58–85.

Foreman, Gary L. *Crockett: The Gentleman from the Cane.* Dallas: Taylor Publishing, 1986.

French, James Strange. *Sketches and Eccentricities of Col. David Crockett, of West Tennessee.* New York: J. & J. Harper, 1833.

Gabler, Neal. *Walt Disney: The Triumph of the American Imagination.* New York: Alfred A. Knopf, 2006.

Gracy, David B. II. "'Just as I Have Written It': A Study of the Authenticity of the Manuscript of José Enrique de la Peña's Account of the Texas Campaign." *Southwestern Historical Quarterly* 105 (October 2001): 254–291.

Groneman, William ("Bill"). "The Controversial Alleged Account of José Enrique de la Peña." *Military History of the West* 25 (Fall 1995): 129–142.

————. *David Crockett: Hero of the Common Man.* New York: Forge Books, 2005.

————. *Death of a Legend: The Myth and Mystery Surrounding the Death of Davy Crockett.* Plano, Tex.: Republic of Texas Press, 1999.

————. *Defense of a Legend: Crockett and the de la Peña Diary.* Plano, Tex.: Republic of Texas Press, 1994.

————. *Eyewitness to the Alamo.* Rev. ed. Plano, Tex.: Republic of Texas Press, 2001.

————. "Fiddling with History: David Crockett and the 'Devil's Box.'" *True West* 54 (March 2007): 58–61.

————. "A Last Final Reply, Or, How I Learned to Stop Worrying and Love Jim Crisp." *Military History of the West* 26 (Spring 1996): 105–106.

———. "Publish Rather Than Perish—Regardless: Jim Crisp and the de la Peña 'Diary.'" *Military History of the West* 25 (Fall 1995): 157–165.

———. *September 11: A Memoir.* Nashville: Goldminds Publishing, 2011.

Hansen, Todd, ed. *The Alamo Reader: A Study in History.* Mechanicsburg, Pa.: Stackpole Books, 2003.

Hardin, Stephen L. *Texian Iliad: A Military History of the Texas Revolution, 1835–1836.* Austin: University of Texas Press, 1994.

———. "The Felix Nuñez Account and the Siege of the Alamo: A Critical Appraisal." *Southwestern Historical Quarterly* 94 (July 1990): 65–84.

Harrigan, Stephen. *The Gates of the Alamo.* New York: Penguin, 2000.

———. "The Last Days of David Crockett." *American History* 46 (April 2011): 28–35.

———. "My Own Private Alamo." *Texas Monthly* 28 (March 2000): 100–105, 140–144.

Hauck, Richard Boyd. *Crockett: A Bio-Bibliography.* Westport, Conn.: Greenwood Press, 1982.

Heale, M. J. "The Role of the Frontier in Jacksonian Politics: David Crockett and the Myth of the Self-Made Man." *Western Historical Quarterly* 4 (1973): 405–423.

Holmes, Richard. *Footsteps: Adventures of a Romantic Biographer.* New York: Viking, 1985.

Huffines, Alan C. *Blood of Noble Men: The Alamo Siege and Battle: An Illustrated Chronology.* Austin, Tex.: Eakin Press, 1999.

Hutton, Paul Andrew. "The Celluloid Alamo." *Arizona and the West* 28 (Spring 1986): 5–22.

———. "Davy Crockett, Still King of the Wild Frontier." *Texas Monthly* 14 (November 1986): 122–130, 244–248.

Jackson, Dee C., and Joe N. Bone, eds. *Rutherford Revisited.* Rutherford, Tenn.: Rutherford Heritage Committee, 1996.

Jones, Randell. *In the Footsteps of Davy Crockett.* Winston-Salem, N.C.: John F. Blair, 2006.

Kelly, James C., and Frederick S. Voss. *Davy Crockett: Gentleman from the Cane.* Washington, D.C., and Nashville: National Portrait Gallery and Tennessee State Museum, 1986.

Kilgore, Dan. *How Did Davy Die?* College Station: Texas A&M University Press, 1978.

———, and James E. Crisp. *How Did Davy Die? And Why Do We Care So Much?* College Station: Texas A&M University Press, 2010.

King, Margaret Jane. "The Davy Crockett Craze: A Case Study in Popular Culture." Ph.D. dissertation, University of Hawaii, 1976.

Lack, Paul D. *The Texas Revolutionary Experience: A Political and Social History, 1835–1836.* College Station: Texas A&M Press, 1992.

Leighton, Dolly B. *The Gentleman from the Cane: A Two-Act Musical Historical Drama.* Unpublished script, copyright 1976.

Lemon, Mark. *The Illustrated Alamo 1836: A Photographic Journey.* Abilene, Tex.: State House Press, 2008.

Levy, Buddy. *American Legend: The Real-Life Adventures of David Crockett.* New York: G. P. Putnam's Sons, 2005.

Lindley, Thomas Ricks. *Alamo Traces: New Evidence and New Conclusions.* Lanham, Md.: Republic of Texas Press, 2003.

———. "Analysis of the 'Lancer' Account of David Crockett's Death." *Alamo Journal* 138 (September 2005): 3–8.

———. "David Crockett's Road to Texas." Unpublished manuscript, 1991.

———. "Killing Crockett: It's All in the Execution." *Alamo Journal* 96 (May 1995): 3–12.

———. "Killing Crockett (part II): Theory Paraded as Fact." *Alamo Journal* 97 (July 1995): 3–16.

———. "Killing Crockett: Lindley's Opinion." *Alamo Journal* 98 (October 1995): 9–24.

Linenthal, Edward Tabor. *Sacred Ground: Americans and Their Battlefields.* Urbana: University of Illinois Press, 1991.

Lodge, Henry Cabot, and Theodore Roosevelt. *Hero Tales from American History.* New York: Century Co., 1895.

Lofaro, Michael A. *Daniel Boone: An American Life.* Lexington: University Press of Kentucky, 2003.

———. "Davy Crockett, David Crockett, and Me: A Personal Journey through Legend into History." *Tennessee Folklore Society Bulletin* 56 (1994): 96–106.

———, ed. *Davy Crockett: The Man, the Legend, the Legacy, 1786–1986.* Knoxville: University of Tennessee Press, 1985.

———, ed. *Davy Crockett's Riproarious Shemales and Sentimental Sisters: Women's Tall Tales from the Crockett Almanacs 1835–1856.* Mechanicsburg, Pa.: Stackpole Books, 2001.

———, ed. *The Tall Tales of Davy Crockett: The Second Nashville Series of Crockett Almanacs, 1839–1841.* Knoxville: University of Tennessee Press, 1987.

————, and Joe Cummings, eds. *Crockett at Two Hundred: New Perspectives on the Man and the Myth*. Knoxville: University of Tennessee Press, 1989.

Long, Jeff. *Duel of Eagles: The Mexican and U.S. Fight for the Alamo*. New York: William Morrow, 1990.

Lord, Walter. *A Time to Stand*. New York: Harper & Brothers, 1961.

Malone, Bill C. *Don't Get Above Your Raisin': Country Music and the Southern Working Class*. Urbana: University of Illinois Press, 2002.

Marling, Karal Ann. "Thomas Hart Benton's *Boomtown*: Regionalism Redefined." *Prospects* 6 (1981): 73–137.

Massey, Tim. "Crockett Roots: Discovering Davy Crockett's Lost Sister." *Crockett Chronicle* 22 (November 2008): 7–8.

McBride, Robert M. "David Crockett and His Memorials in Tennessee." *Tennessee Historical Quarterly* 26 (1967): 219–239.

McCann, Kevin D. *Adam Huntsman: The Peg Leg Politician*. Dickson, Tenn.: McCann Publishing, 2011.

McNeil, Everett. *In Texas with Davy Crockett: A Story of the Texas War of Independence*. New York: E. P. Dutton, 1908.

McSpadden, J. Walker. *Pioneer Heroes*. New York: Thomas Y. Crowell, 1929.

Mooney, Chase C. "The Political Career of Adam Huntsman." *Tennessee Historical Quarterly* 10 (June 1951): 99–126.

Moran, William. *The Belles of New England: The Women of the Textile Mills and the Families Whose Wealth They Wove*. New York: St. Martin's Press, 2002.

Morrison, Judge John, and Col. Bob Hamsley. *The Real David Crockett*. Lawrenceburg, Tenn.: n.p., 1955.

Moss, Bobby Gilmer. *The Patriots at Kings Mountain*. Blacksburg, S.C.: Scotia-Hibernia, 1990.

Nelson, George. *The Alamo: An Illustrated History*. Dry Frio Canyon, Tex.: Aldine Press, 1998.

Null, Marion Michael. *The Forgotten Pioneer: The Life of Davy Crockett*. New York: Vantage Press, 1954.

Owsley, Frank Lawrence Jr. *Struggle for the Gulf Borderlands: The Creek War and the Battle of New Orleans, 1812–1815*. Gainesville: University Presses of Florida, 1981.

Paulding, James Kirke. *The Lion of the West*. Edited and with an introduction by James N. Tidwell. Stanford, Calif.: Stanford University Press, 1954.

Petersen, Gert. *David Crockett, the Public Man and Legislator: An Account of His Life, While a Resident of Lawrence County, 1817–1822.* Lawrence County, Tenn.: Lawrence County Genealogical Society, 2010.

———. *David Crockett, the Volunteer Rifleman: An Account of His Life, While a Resident of Franklin County, 1812–1817.* Winchester, Tenn.: Franklin County Historical Society, 2008.

Plath, James. "Talking Crockett: A Conversation with Fess Parker." http://moviemet.com/news/talking-crockett-conversation-fess-parker, September 28, 2004.

Poore, Benjamin Perley. *Perley's Reminiscences of Sixty Years in the National Metropolis.* Philadelphia: Hubbard Brothers, 1886.

Quackenbush, Robert. *Quit Pulling My Leg! A Story of Davy Crockett.* New York: Simon & Schuster, 1987.

Remini, Robert V. *The Life of Andrew Jackson.* New York: Harper & Row, 1988.

Roberts, Randy, and James S. Olson. *A Line in the Sand: The Alamo in Blood and Memory.* New York: Free Press, 2001.

Rourke, Constance. *Davy Crockett.* New York: Harcourt Brace Jovanovich, 1934.

Sampson, Wade. "Crockett Memories from Fess Parker." www.mouseplanet.com/8760/Crockett_Memories_from_Fess_Parker, March 25, 2009.

Schoelwer, Susan Prendergast, ed. *Alamo Images: Changing Perceptions of a Texas Experience.* Dallas: DeGolyer Library and Southern Methodist University Press, 1985.

Scruggs, Thomas E. "Davy Crockett and the Thieves of Jericho: An Analysis of the Shackford-Parrington Conspiracy Theory." *Journal of the Early Republic* 19 (Autumn 1999): 481–498.

Shackford, James Atkins: *David Crockett: The Man and the Legend.* Chapel Hill: University of North Carolina Press, 1956.

Shapiro, Irwin. *Yankee Thunder: The Legendary Life of Davy Crockett.* New York: Julian Messner, 1944.

Sibley, Marilyn McAdams. "The Burial Place of the Alamo Heroes." *Southwestern Historical Quarterly* 70 (1966): 272–280.

Smith, Jonathan Kennon Thompson. *The Land Holdings of Colonel David Crockett in West Tennessee.* [Jackson, Tenn.]: J. K. T. Smith, 2003.

Smith, Richard Penn. *Col. Crockett's Exploits and Adventures in Texas.* Philadelphia: T. K. and P. G. Collins, 1836.

———. *On to the Alamo: Col. Crockett's Exploits and Adventures in Texas.*

Edited with an introduction and notes by John Seelye. New York: Penguin, 2003.

Smith-Rosenberg, Carroll. *Disorderly Conduct: Visions of Gender in Victorian America*. New York: Alfred A. Knopf, 1985.

Sterne, Charles A. *Statement of the Oldest Native Born Texan, Mr. Charles A. Sterne, Taken Down by Miss Kate Hunter*. Unpublished manuscript, 1923–1924.

Thompson, Frank. *The Alamo: A Cultural History*. Dallas: Taylor Publishing, 2001.

———. *Alamo Movies*. East Berlin, Pa.: Old Mill Books, 1991.

Timanus, Rod. *On the Crockett Trail*. Union City, Tenn.: Pioneer Press, 1999.

von Schmidt, Eric. "The Alamo Remembered—From a Painter's Point of View." *Smithsonian* 16 (March 1986): 54–67.

Wallis, Michael. *David Crockett: The Lion of the West*. New York: W. W. Norton, 2011.

Waselkov, Gregory A. *A Conquering Spirit: Fort Mims and the Redstick War of 1813–1814*. Tuscaloosa: University of Alabama Press, 2006.

Weber, David J. *The Mexican Frontier, 1821–1846: The American Southwest Under Mexico*. Albuquerque: University of New Mexico Press, 1982.

Welton, John Lee. *A Man Called Davy: An Outdoor Drama Based on the Life of Davy Crockett*. Unpublished script, copyright 2004.

Wilentz, Sean. *Andrew Jackson*. New York: Times Books, 2005.

Winders, Richard Bruce. *Sacrificed at the Alamo: Tragedy and Triumph in the Texas Revolution*. Abilene, Tex.: State House Press, 2004.

Zaboly, Gary S. *An Altar for Their Sons: The Alamo and the Texas Revolution in Contemporary Newspaper Accounts*. Buffalo Gap, Tex.: State House Press, 2011.

Video and Audio

Cabanne, William Christy, director. *The Martyrs of the Alamo, or, The Birth of Texas*. Fine Arts-Triangle, 1915. (With A. D. Sears as Crockett.)

Douglas, Gordon, director. *Them!* Warner Bros., 1954. (With Fess Parker as Alan Crotty.)

Foster, Norman, director. *Walt Disney Treasures: Davy Crockett—The Complete Television Series*. Walt Disney Video, 2001. (With Fess Parker as Crockett.)

Hancock, John Lee, director. *The Alamo*. Touchstone Pictures, 2004. (With Billy Bob Thornton as Crockett.)

Parker, Fess, interview by Don Carleton. Archive of American Television, 2000, www.emmytvlegends.org/interviews/people/fess-parker.

Rabbit Ears Treasury of Tall Tales, Volume 1: *Davy Crockett, Rip Van Winkle, Johnny Appleseed, Paul Bunyan*. Listening Library, 2006. (With Nicolas Cage as Crockett.)

Wayne, John, producer and director. *The Alamo*. United Artists, 1960. (With John Wayne as Crockett.)

INDEX

ABOUT THE AUTHOR

BOB THOMPSON dropped out of graduate school in history after just three weeks and has been trying to make up for it ever since. Turning to journalism after stints as a housepainter and a librarian, he spent twenty-four years writing and editing in-depth feature stories at the *Washington Post*. He edited the *Post*'s Sunday magazine, wrote author profiles for the paper's Style section, and developed a particular interest in bringing complex historical narratives to life. The father of two grown daughters, he lives in Washington, D.C., with his wife, Deborah Johnson, a journalist turned children's bookseller. *Born on a Mountaintop* is his first book.